Lost ...
S...

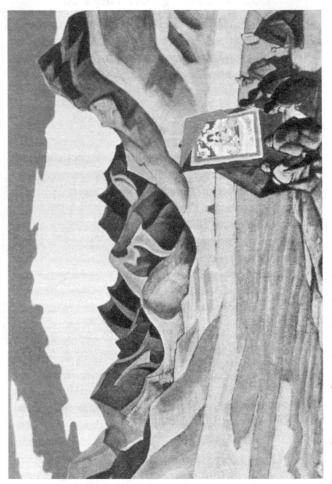

THE COMING ONE *by Nicholas Roerich*

THE LOST TEACHINGS OF JESUS SERIES

Lost Teachings on Keys to Spiritual Progress

Mark L. Prophet
Elizabeth Clare Prophet

SUMMIT UNIVERSITY PRESS®

LOST TEACHINGS ON KEYS TO SPIRITUAL PROGRESS
by Mark L. Prophet and Elizabeth Clare Prophet
Copyright © 2005 Summit Publications, Inc.
All rights reserved. No part of this book may be reproduced,
translated, or electronically stored, posted or transmitted, or used in
any format or medium whatsoever without prior written permission,
except by a reviewer who may quote brief passages in a review.
For information, contact Summit University Press, PO Box 5000,
Corwin Springs, MT 59030-5000. Tel: 1-800-245-5445 or
406-848-9500. www.summituniversitypress.com

This is the third book in the four-volume pocketbook series
The Lost Teachings of Jesus, which contains the complete text of the
two-volume edition of the same name. This book was previously
published as *The Lost Teachings of Jesus 3: Keys to Self-
Transcendence.* Copyright © 1986, 1988, 1994 Summit Publications,
Inc. All rights reserved

Cover illustration: Adapted from Gustave Doré's *Christ in the
Synagogue.* "*And when he was come into his own country, he taught
them in their synagogue, insomuch that they were astonished, and
said, ... Is not this the carpenter's son?*" *(Matthew 13:54, 55)*

For information on the magnificent art of Nicholas Roerich reproduced in this volume, write Nicholas Roerich Museum, 319 West
107th St., New York, NY 10025.

Library of Congress Control Number: 2005921205
ISBN: 0-916766-92-6

SUMMIT UNIVERSITY 🍂 PRESS

09   08   07   06   05   10   9   8   7   6

Contents

Illustrations

PLATES – *Paintings*

Verily, verily I say unto you,
He that believeth on me,
the works that I do shall he do also;
and greater works than these shall he do
. . . because I go unto my Father.

— *Jesus*

*Without you his Lost Teachings
could not have been preached and
published in every nation.*

Foreword

Blessed readers, bear with us as we unfold the mysteries of God. Be patient with our effort as together we walk and talk with Jesus and the servant-sons in heaven whose revelations we bear. For as emissaries of their teaching, we must attempt to make plain according to twentieth-century thinking and beyond and theological modality a vast gnosis of the Lord that does and does not necessarily fit the mind-sets and mind-traps of the very ones for whom his Lost Teaching is sent.

Above all, have patience with yourself, endure to the end of our treatise and pray fervently and without fear to the Holy Spirit to enlighten you—both through and beyond the written word. These pages are a garden path where you meet the Lord Jesus and the masterful beings and intelligences who comprise the "cloud of witnesses" to the Universal Christ, whose point of Light is also in ourselves.

In these four volumes of The Lost Teachings of Jesus series we bring you the most precious instruction we have received for lifetimes from our Good Friend and the Shepherd of our souls. While the words and images may not be those Christ used two thousand years ago, you will find the heart of the message he imparted on the road to Emmaus; at Bethany with Mary, Martha and Lazarus; at meat with sinners and publicans; to the multitudes on the desert, by the sea, and in the mountains; in the synagogue at Nazareth; in the Temple at Jerusalem; and on the Mount of Transfiguration with Peter, James and John—as well as the message he whispered in the ear of Paul.

You won't find two dozen lost parables with a cast of sowers, servants, rich men, virgins and mustard seeds. But you will learn from our cast of Fords, Chevys, homegrown philosophers, our Pierre and our parrot and from the many portraits of life from which Jesus has drawn to teach us the fine points of the Law.

You won't find verbatim the words and phrases expunged from the Gospels, but you will find the essential truths they contained as well as some of the Lord's most precious secrets which we herein transcribe—some plain for all to see, some hidden in enigma for riddle lovers and detectives to sleuth and solve. You may find yourself rereading these volumes as you carefully choose the missing pieces to fill in the mosaic of your inner life as you commune with the Master in the cloisters of your soul.

The chapters we set forth for you in the name of Jesus Christ and in defense of every seeker for his Truth contain the fundamentals of his Lost Teachings which he himself has taught us. Profound in their simplicity, when understood they lead to the complexities of the Law of every man's true nature in God.

The four books in this series consist of fourteen lectures delivered by Mark between 1965 and 1973, illuminated by the lessons Jesus has given us in dictations, sermons and letters over the past thirty years. The message that unfolds as the rose of Sharon is compiled from these as well as private conversations with the Master. It is the Lord's gift to your soul, that you might keep his flame and not lose the way when the darkness of personal and planetary karma covers the land and all else fails of human institutions and nations and their armies and armaments.

As he said to us, "Though heaven and earth pass away, my Word shall live forever—in the hearts of those who are the spiritual survivors of earth's schoolroom. Go and find them and show them the Way!"

Especially do we urge those who have never contacted the heart of Jesus' teachings as we have presented them in our ministry to read with new hope these chapters of the Saviour's wisdom. They are gathered together for the dissolving of schism in the body politic, for the furtherance of the spirit of ecumenism—and for the healing of the diseases of the flesh and the mind, and of the soul's anguish in its aloneness in time of trouble and mourning.

O world, you need this Teaching more than you know for that which is coming upon your soul and the souls of your people in the days ahead. May you take the little book and eat it up, enjoying the sweetness in the mouth, resisting not the bitterness in the belly, but understanding the necessity for the full alchemy of the Word to work his work in you.

We are the two witnesses standing now, one on either bank of Life's great river. We preach his Everlasting Gospel and the hidden wisdom: for the Lamb is come—and the mystery of God which was not to be finished till the days of the voice of the seventh angel.

The prophecy is fulfilled. That which was spoken to the disciples in the upper room is being shouted from the housetops. At last the path of discipleship to which Jesus called his chosen does appear for all to see and know and enter in these end times of the Piscean age—for the Light of Aquarius dawns.

With our life we have given the Saviour's discourses to your hearts' keeping, fully assured by Jesus himself that through these pages and your oneness with his sacred heart, you may seek and find the keys to the kingdom.

The Lord is waiting. Please take his gift, entrusted to us for you, before it is too late.

Faithfully,

Mark L. Prophet

Elizabeth Clare Prophet

Servants of God in Jesus Christ

Behold, I stand at the door, and knock:
if any man hear my voice and open the door,
I will come in to him and will sup with him,
and he with me.

— Jesus

These are the very things that God has revealed to us through the Spirit, for the Spirit reaches the depths of everything, even the depths of God. After all, the depths of a man can only be known by his own spirit, not by any other man, and in the same way the depths of God can only be known by the Spirit of God.

Now instead of the spirit of the world, we have received the Spirit that comes from God, to teach us to understand the gifts that he has given us. Therefore we teach, not in the way in which philosophy is taught, but in the way that the Spirit teaches us: we teach spiritual things spiritually.[1]

—The Apostle Paul

Chapter One

THE LADDER OF LIFE

The Ladder of Life

L ong ago, it was spoken by the Lord, "What went ye out to see? A reed shaken by the wind?" And the word returned, "But what went ye out for to see? A prophet? yea, I say unto you, and more than a prophet."[1]

The Scriptures and the Living Master

We all came into embodiment less than one hundred years ago, less than fifty years ago, less than twenty-five years ago, and some even less than fifteen or sixteen years ago. Yet, although endowed with free will and a clean slate on which to write a new and nobler chapter in our book of life, we have been almost forced into accepting what the ministers have told us is so: that there has been no tampering with the Bible as the word of God, but there has been tampering with everything else in existence.

Now, the indoctrination of the people by the clergy has far-reaching implications. And since we are all affected by it, we ought to say a few words about the hand-me-down religions that have fallen in our laps.

For, if the Bible is the complete and unadulterated word of God—written by him and not by mere mortals (who most assuredly held the pen)—then we should believe every word literally interpreted for us by these well-meaning pastors who desire to save our souls. Yet in the Bible itself are written these words: "The letter killeth but the Spirit giveth life."[2]

Now, if I read this correctly, it means we should not be bound to or by a literal interpretation but liberated by and through the Holy Spirit's *transliteration* of the scriptures—moving from condemnation to the glory of God's righteousness with us.

From time to time we have asked present-day pastors the following questions, and so far there have been no satisfactory answers forthcoming:

If the Bible texts alone could save us, then why did Jesus find it necessary to promise us the enlightenment of the Holy Spirit who would come to us as our Comforter, Friend, and Teacher to bring to our remembrance all those things which Christ has been teaching our souls from the beginning?[3]

If Jesus did not entrust our souls to the written word alone, then why should we?

Nor could the brethren respond meaningfully to our inquiries on the integral relationship of Paul and Jesus:

If the Gospels were the final word and the Gospel writers and apostles had perfect understanding, then to what end was the conversion of Saul of Tarsus?

Clearly, it had to have been for a very special purpose that the Master Jesus personally undertook the tutoring of Paul, whose experiences and writings in Christ dominate the New Testament.

In Truth, his mission was to build Christ's Church upon the Rock of his personal encounter with the Lord—to convert the 'Gentiles', their leaders, and the children of Light and to elucidate Christ's Person and Presence as the living Saviour in sermons and letters delivered throughout Asia Minor and the Mediterranean over a period of thirty years.

But this Paul had still another mission—one to be gleaned from his example and that of the resurrected Christ working with him throughout his life as the Lord's ministering servant. It is their integral relationship that affords insight into the bond of Ascended Master and unascended disciple and through it the fusion of heaven and earth—as when a nova appears in the firmament to beckon us to the higher calling through the I AM THAT I AM.

And so we offer some answers that are not our own but which were given to us from the heart of our brother Jesus, our Mother Mary and the apostle Paul himself, communicated to us through the Holy Spirit.

The mission of Paul, persecutor of Christians, he having consented to the heartless stoning of Saint Stephen,[4] was confirmed through one Ananias to whom the Lord appeared saying, "Go thy way: for he is a chosen vessel unto me, to bear my name before the Gentiles and kings and the children of Israel. For I will shew him how great things he must suffer for my name's sake."

And so Saul, who had been struck to the ground and blinded in his encounter with the Master on his way to Damascus as he was yet "breathing out threatenings and slaughter against the disciples," was now prayerfully waiting for instructions in the house of Judas—and for the one who would restore his sight.

Ananias, following the Lord's directions to the street called Straight, entered the house "and putting his hands on him said, Brother Saul, the Lord, even Jesus, that appeared unto thee in the way as thou camest, hath sent me that thou mightest receive thy sight and be filled with the Holy Ghost."

By the act of this messenger, Paul had the immediate proof that the voice he had heard midst the blinding light was none other than that of Jesus himself:

"Saul, Saul, why persecutest thou me?"

Thus, it is recorded that through the Lord's instrument, Ananias, "immediately there fell from his eyes as it had been scales, and he received sight forthwith and arose and was baptized." And the disciples fed him and he was strengthened and he stayed with them "certain days."

But the more abundant proof of the Master's voice that yet echoed in the chambers of his heart—"I AM Jesus whom thou persecutest: it is hard for

thee to kick against the pricks. . . . Arise, and go into
the city and it shall be told thee what thou must
do"—is that straightway after his conversion and
baptism of the Holy Ghost "he preached Christ in
the synagogues, that he is the Son of God."

After many days of this, even to the con-
founding of the Jews in Damascus, proving to
them that this Master Jesus is the "very Christ," the
Jews took counsel to kill him: "But their laying
await was known of Saul. And they watched the
gates day and night to kill him. Then the disciples
took him by night, and let him down by the wall
in a basket."[5]

As always, the presence of the Holy Spirit in
the power of conversion side by side with persecutions is the greatest proof of our oneness with
Christ—"The servant is not greater than his lord:
if they have persecuted me, they will also persecute you."[6]

Paul's direct and touching relationship with
his Lord shows the intended friendship and personal initiatic path Jesus holds for every one of
us—once we allow ourselves to be fully converted
(the word means "turned around, transformed as
a new creature in Christ") and subject unto the
Universal Christ in life and death and eternity.

What We Have Learned from the Ascended Masters

This is what we have learned from the lineage
of spiritual luminaries who tended the flame of
the Universal Christ in the succession of centuries

preceding the birth of Messiah. Two thousand years ago they taught and initiated the one they called Issa (the Buddhist name for Jesus), who came to the high Himalayas as a youth, the hidden Christ yet to be revealed.[7]

Let those who object to the idea of Jesus' being initiated by the Eastern adepts be reminded of a similar objection voiced by John the Baptist when Jesus came from Galilee to be baptized of him: "I have need to be baptized of thee, and comest thou to me?" This, you will recall, was overcome through Jesus' own words which embodied his recognition of the true Initiator, God the Father, who, as he wills, may employ the worthy instrument to effect his transfer of Light: "Suffer it to be so now: for thus it becometh us to fulfil all righteousness."[8] And John the Baptist, chosen Messenger of the LORD's descent in the incarnate Word, was a worthy instrument indeed for Jesus' baptism by the Holy Ghost.

As Jesus Christ was made a priest forever after the Order of Melchizedek, so did he also descend from the one known to Daniel as the Ancient of Days. And all who preceded him in the lineage of the original Keepers of the Flame of Life on earth both East and West certainly did lay their crowns (attainment) at his feet for the victory of the Piscean Conqueror and the victory of his Universal Christhood in all children of God.

As Jesus was taken by his parents to Egypt for the first seven years of his life that the prophecy might be fulfilled, "Out of Egypt have I called my son,"[9] so we contemplate his journey to the East sowing and reaping seeds of Cosmic Christ consciousness for all nations and peoples — gathering the stones of an ancient pyramid of Teaching upon which he was to place the capstone. And we are reminded of his own timeless prophecy of his return to Palestine after his sojourn in India and Tibet: "As the lightning cometh out of the East and shineth even unto the West, so shall also the coming of the Son of man be."[10] And those who look for his Second Coming today also look to the East. Yet they know not why.

Yet, this Son of man embodied the quintessence of the lights of Eastern antiquity. And by his Life, transfiguring the past into a glorious future, we know the Way; by his voice speaking in us and through us we know his true Universal Doctrine.

The Eastern term for the office Jesus held is *Guru*, meaning God-man, the dispeller of darkness — the incarnation of the Word (Avatar) who is Teacher, Initiator par excellence.* There is no higher office held on the initiatic scale by one in physical embodiment (though the degrees of attainment by the officeholder may vary according to his concentration and endurance on the initiatic path). The Eastern term for the office held by Paul is *chela* — servant of the God-man, devotee of the Light of Christ in the One Sent, the Living Master who wears the mantle of Guru.

Paul's experiences as a direct chela of the

---

*When lowercased, the term *guru* is applied to a leader or teacher in any field, just as we think of the Messiah as the title and office of Christ although it is used lowercased to describe a deliverer of the people.

Ascended Master Jesus Christ show the ardor necessary to withstand the rigors of giving birth in the midst of Jewish law and Roman paganism to the 2,000-year Piscean dispensation of *Christ-I-AM-ity*—and the challenge of every chela following in the apostle's fiery wake to deliver the Everlasting Gospel to those bound by still other cults of orthodoxy and idolatry, East and West.

Now, this term *Christ-I-AM-ity* is used by Jesus to describe his doctrine and the way of deliverance he proclaimed to us as the religion of the Cosmic Christ who overshadowed him. The Piscean Master's religion is the path of the Universal Christ weaving through the hearts of millions of souls tethered to the One through the affirmation of their Being in Christ. *Christ-I-AM-ity:* the way of the Sons of God using the power of the sacred name I AM to affirm their God Identity on earth as it is in heaven.

Jesus further taught us that by the Light of the inner Christ we are not only authorized but surely compelled in the vortex of our fiery destiny to declare the I AM THAT I AM as our eternal nature:

"From the beginning unto the ending, the I AM in me, the Be-ness that I AM, is Christ. This Presence is my original and consummate Reality— a Light to lighten my way, the Knower and the known. Upon this Principle I chart my course. By this fixed Polestar I determine my position day by day, centered, longitude and latitude, in the grid of Christ on the cross of Life."

This Truth of every man's being was crucified with Jesus Christ—not by the Jews, not by the Romans, but by a damnable flesh-and-blood orthodoxy that denied the inherent Godhood of the offspring of God.

Look what it did! It reduced them to mere mortals, consigned them to Death and Hell, sinners without recourse to the divine spark, and then sent them on their way to while away their time/space and life/energy made worthless by a false theology that denies the inherent worth of man by denying the God-worth in him—while officialdom ("ungodly men crept in unawares"[11]) parades with mitre and sword in Church and State, performing deeds of Satan (or themselves) in the name of peace and war, causes of economic good or for the people or perhaps Jesus Christ!

So many diabolical diversions from the central point of personal Christhood! And their name is still Legion.[12]

The Apostolic Mission to Christ's Mystical Body

As Peter was to use the keys Jesus gave him—keys to the kingdom of heaven—to open the door to Christ's consciousness unto the seed of Abraham on Pentecost[13] and to the Gentiles in the house of Cornelius, whereupon all who believed received the Holy Ghost and were baptized[14]—so Paul would set forth the mystery of the indwelling Christ.

He, for whom the LORD unlocked the prison

doors by a great earthquake,[15] would become the liberator of those who were to protest the sensual and superstitious materialism bred by an orthodoxy which was to lock up the mysteries and throw away the keys to the kingdom until the time appointed for the angel to fly in *mid-heaven* (in the plane of Christ the Mediator), having this time not a circumspect man-made gospel but an *everlasting gospel.*[16]

This Everlasting Gospel is given one by one to the disciples of the Ascended Master Jesus the Christ who first receive him in his 'Second Coming' in heart and mind and soul and body as Paul did. The Everlasting Gospel is the direct and living Word which Christ declared would not pass away—though heaven and earth should pass away.[17] This Word is what his *spiritual* apostolic succession was intended to deliver to the little children in Christ—by his Body and his Blood nurtured *in them.* In Divine Reality Jesus anointed *spiritual* shepherds who were to feed his sheep every day until they should put on Christ's consciousness to become fully heirs of individual Sonship.

Advancing on the pure path, John was to bear the torch of Love's revelation, illumining the way of Christian mysticism, leading all of the faithful to the fount of Christ Reality present as potential in each member of the Universal Church, and delivering all from a worldwide orthodoxy grown cold (an ancient/modern "easy way out") in order that finally they might engage the psyche in the Lord's real Work: Christ-centeredness in the Rock.

Paul's preachments—his supreme humility before the inner Christ, born out of his heart-contact with Jesus—laid the spiritual, as opposed to the ecclesiastical, foundations of the early Church for those who could read and run with Christ's Spirit in them.

It should be noted that whereas Jesus gave keys to Peter[18] which must be used in order to be retained—and which Peter indeed retained until he and his successors allowed them to fall into disuse—to Paul and John he gave the gift of Himself.

Into their hearts the Piscean Avatar entered and there he lives forevermore. In them his Word shall not pass away, for today they are Ascended Masters unto his glory. But alas, Jesus has shown us the sad record that the soul of Peter remains treading karma in the valley of decision (and his own indecision) as does the Church which still follows his incomplete example, his unfinished work.

The Universal Church of Jesus Christ composed of the saints in heaven and on earth, functional as Christ's Mystical Body, is built upon the Rock of the unity of the soul with Christ through the I AM Presence.[19] This Body of the LORD—of the I AM THAT I AM who *does embody* in those who keep the Flame of God—is shared in by all who have entered the universality of Christ's triumphant nature and doctrine, regardless of their religious affiliation or race.

Thus, inherent in Paul's writings is our deliverance from the mechanisms of a symbolic but dead

Jewish as well as Christian ritual—handed down as a form devoid of the "Living Flame of Love."* The conceptualization of this Love having been so beautifully captured—as far as anyone can capture the self-transforming vital force of the spiritual fire—by the sixteenth-century saint, John of the Cross.[20]

The body of believers and backsliders and the reprobate to whom Paul preached was the formative community of the called-out ones (Gk. *ekklesia*). They had been called out from the worldly consciousness by the flame within to form the circle of the Corpus Christi—the Body of Christ. They knew they must provide the chalice for "the Light of the world"[21] in order that earth and her evolutions might be rekindled by the Light of the Trinity which their Saviour bore and promised to transmit through his closest initiates to the childlike, the pure in heart, the believers in the Word in him.

Regarding the Revelation of Jesus Christ to his beloved John—the mystic of Love—the Master has told us that he intended it to be the clearest proof that he has the freedom and does exercise it at will to deliver his progressive revelations to whomsoever he may choose. And furthermore that he may "send" and "signify" his mysteries, at any time, by his angels, by the Holy Ghost, or by his own I AM Presence—face to face in the divine encounter with his own.[22]

Our beloved Jesus has told us to tell you that

---

*By no means do we believe that all religious ritual is dead or devoid of the Lord's living Love; sacred ritual is both necessary and beautiful, moving the soul up the spiral staircase to contact God's grace in the interior castle frequented by its chatelaine, Saint Teresa of Avila.

these promises, these divinely intercessary experiences, are for you and for me, beloved. They are our birthright as joint-heirs of the essential Godhood of the Sons of God. And this Word and Work of the Everlasting Gospel, which we present to you herewith, radiant with the Master's presence and the power of his Holy Spirit, is living proof of his witness unto us. You need only try our spirits by the Spirit quickened within your heart to know that our testimony is true.

The Master Jesus Christ Opens Our Understanding

The Master said to the Jews who sought to kill him: "You search the scriptures, believing that through them you will obtain eternal Life, yet you come not to Christ for Life—of whom these very scriptures testify as the One Sent to give you eternal Life."[23]

Once again the unillumined pastors are silent on the question:

If the deeper meaning of the scriptures were self-evident, even to the initiated disciples, then why did it become necessary for the Master Jesus to "open their understanding that they might understand the scriptures"? This took place late in his mission—even after his crucifixion and resurrection, just before "he was parted from them and carried up into heaven," as recorded by Luke.[24]

This necessity for the opening of their understanding bears the implication of the further necessity which Jesus made plain to us—the raising of consciousness to oneness in the Mind of Christ, which is achieved only by the direct intercession of one who has attained that 'Mindfulness', i.e., the Master Jesus Christ.

He is here, now as then, to exalt your heart and mind and soul to that same 'upper room' of consciousness (that altered state that gives access to the etheric planes and the soul's inner memory of God) where the disciples were fed the Word. And to this end he has called us today to publish his Everlasting Gospel.

So that the Truth will not be lost. So that you will have it for your victory, even as the Masters of the Himalayas kept the secrets from the foundation of the world—for the coming of the eternal youth: for the day and the hour of the journey of Jesus, the One Sent, to the retreats of the Great White Brotherhood* to retrieve the lost Word for the seed of the Ancient of Days who had forgotten the Way.

Therefore, inasmuch as it is clear that at every hand the disciples needed Jesus to interpret the inner mysteries of the parables, that they both questioned and doubted him throughout his mission and were still "terrified" and "affrighted" at the end, and that the Master found it necessary to "upbraid them with their unbelief and hardness of heart" just before his final parting,[25] the ardent devotee of Christ ought to consider that perhaps their perception, or want of it, of the Person of

---

*The Great White Brotherhood is a spiritual order of Western saints and Eastern adepts who have reunited with the Spirit of the living God and who comprise the heavenly hosts. The word *white* refers not to race but to the aura (halo) of white light surrounding their forms.

Christ as the Universal Word, and of the man Jesus as the son of man, has clouded Christian theology to the present.

Therefore we do know that the fullness of the mystery of the Incarnation is reserved for the heart-to-heart communion of the Lord with each one of us as we are able to receive it—even as he makes us able. As we do not trust our own five senses to bear accurate witness in mundane matters, how can we trust that of squabbling, rivalrous disciples—who deserted him in his most severe trial—to bear witness in spiritual matters of ultimate consequence to our salvation?

Neither do we trust our own private interpretation of scripture, but only that which the Spirit freely gives us. For no man's flesh and blood can inherit the kingdom (consciousness) of God[26]—but only the soul who is one in the Spirit. Because we have that Spirit we confess that he is LORD[27]—the incarnation of the I AM THAT I AM on earth and in heaven—one in the Universal Christ throughout the Spirit-Matter cosmos.

Thus, the written word, set forth by inspired men, some of clearer understanding than others, is at best the instrument of a direct, divine intervention through God's Word that speaks to our hearts revealing a series of stepping-stones for our soul's trek up the mountain of Divine Selfhood.

While taken by some to be the ultimate, complete, and final revelation on salvation, the Bible actually omits some of the most precious facts concerning the life and teaching of Jesus Christ and the patriarchs and prophets as well, pivotal Truths necessary to the soul's advancement—facts that were known, mind you, at the time that Church councils codified the scriptures which have been handed down to us.

In certain cases these facts have been replaced with an attempted orthodox and very physical, doctrinal interpretation of the events surrounding the birth, life, and death of the founder of Christianity. The result being that for some, salvation is not looked for, hoped for, and worked for through the kingdom (consciousness) of God that he said is *"within you,"*[28] but is rather pursued solely through the God *within Jesus* by means of a vicarious atonement.

The Discovery of the Secret Gospel of Mark

A recent discovery shows that the Gospel writers themselves omitted doctrines they thought should be kept from the profane.

It seems there was a secret Gospel of Mark written for the inner circle of disciples of Christ. It came to light in 1958 when Professor Morton Smith found a copy of a letter written by Clement of Alexandria in Mar Saba monastery in the Judean desert which actually quoted from that Gospel. Here is an excerpt of Clement's letter, who was in a position to know of this Gospel since, as Smith points out, it was a treasured heirloom of his church—and Clement had an interest in secret teachings.

> [As for] Mark, then, during Peter's stay in Rome he wrote [an account of] the Lord's doings, not, however, declaring all [of them], nor yet hinting at the secret [ones], but selecting those he thought most useful for increasing the faith of those who were being instructed. But when Peter died as a martyr... he composed a more spiritual Gospel for the use of those who were being perfected. Nevertheless, he yet did not divulge the things not to be uttered.[29]

The Teachings of Jesus which Mark wrote down have been lost, except for the fragments quoted by Clement. But they are very important fragments. One is a parallel to the Lazarus story, which only appears in the Book of John. It had always seemed strange that only one of the Gospels should record this most important miracle by Jesus—the raising of the dead. The passage from the secret Gospel reads:

> And they come into Bethany, and a certain woman, whose brother had died, was there. And, coming, she prostrated herself before Jesus and says to him, "Son of David, have mercy on me." But the disciples rebuked her. And Jesus, being angered, went off with her into the garden where the tomb was, and straightway a great cry was

heard from the tomb. And going near Jesus rolled away the stone from the door of the tomb. And straightway, going in where the youth was, he stretched forth his hand and raised him, seizing his hand. But the youth, looking upon him, loved him and began to beseech him that he might be with him. And going out of the tomb they came into the house of the youth, for he was rich. And after six days Jesus told him what to do and in the evening the youth comes to him, wearing a linen cloth over [his] naked [body]. And he remained with him that night, for Jesus taught him the mystery of the kingdom of God. And thence, arising, he returned to the other side of the Jordan.[30]

This fragment not only provides reinforcement for the Lazarus miracle but also explains a portion of the Gospel of Mark which has baffled scholars for centuries.

At the point of Jesus' arrest on the Mount of Olives, Mark gives the following verses: "And there followed him a certain young man, having a linen cloth cast about his naked body; and the young men laid hold on him: And he left the linen cloth, and fled from them naked."[31]

Smith reasons that Jesus was baptizing the young man in a rite similar to that which he administered to the Lazarus figure in the secret gospel after he had raised him from the dead. The circumstances are the same, he says—similar attire, nocturnal meeting—and the stream at the foot of the Mount of Olives could have provided the water.[32] This seems the best explanation yet for the presence of the peculiarly attired young man at Jesus' arrest.

Another thing the secret Gospel does is present evidence of a deletion in the Gospel. Are you familiar with Mark 10:46 which reads, "And they came to Jericho: and as he went out of Jericho with his disciples..."?[33] What happened in Jericho? Whatever it was, it was taken out.

Clement's letter apparently quotes the same verse: "And he comes into Jericho and the sister of the youth whom Jesus loved and his mother and Salome were there..." Smith believes that Clement himself added the concluding words to this sentence, "...and Jesus did not receive them," in order to discredit Salome, a woman of ill repute whose name was deleted from Matthew, Luke and John[34] (whether by the Gospel writers or someone else, we do not know).

But we must ask ourselves, Who decided to leave this sentence (and any story which might have ensued about Salome) out of the Gospel of Mark? Did Mark do it because he thought it belonged only in the secret gospel? If so, why would he have made such a clumsy edit on his own work?

Clement says the secret Gospel is an expansion of the Gospel of Mark, but Smith speculates: "What if the secret text had been earlier, and canonical Mark had been cut down from it?"[35]

That would explain the deletion. But this leads us to wonder: How many other accounts of Jesus' words and works were lifted out? How many edits were made?

If Clement edited the sentence about Salome in his letter, as seems likely, from the Church Father's use of a Greek verb virtually unheard of in Mark, Smith points out, we may ask where the editing ended. If Clement, who was a Church Father and saint, had no scruples about editing a sentence of the document he said was the "more spiritual gospel," how can we be sure he or the other fathers did not commit further editing, "for the good of the people," on this and the manuscript that has been handed down to us as *the* Gospel of Mark?

The twentieth century has also brought forth other gospels that are not in the Bible. These were found at Nag Hammadi in Egypt in December 1945 by an Arab peasant who discovered a library of ancient texts in a jar. The esoteric Gospel of Thomas found there opens with these words: "These are the *secret* sayings which the living Jesus spoke . . . "[36]

But this gospel and others like it were denounced as heretical by second-century Church Fathers like Irenaeus, an orthodox bishop who wrote around A.D. 180 in his *Against Heresies*, "[The heretics] boast that they possess more gospels than there really are. . . . They really have no gospel which is not full of blasphemy."[37]

And what was Irenaeus' reasoning for denying the other gospels? Well naturally, there were four corners of the universe, and four primary winds, therefore there could only be four genuine gospels! And secondly, he claimed that only these four gospels were the "true and reliable" work of Jesus' disciples or their followers—calling the others forgeries, "apocryphal and spurious writings" that were "totally unlike those which have been handed down to us from the apostles."[38]

It becomes more and more evident that the Teachings of Jesus have been altered and lost—whether by his own stipulation of secrecy, by the determination of the disciples, by the decay of manuscripts, or by the councils of the Church Fathers and later theologians.

We also know of the Lost Years of Jesus—between the ages of twelve and thirty—and of the ancient texts which say he journeyed to India. But do you know that there are also early writings which say that Jesus did not ascend right after his resurrection, but that he left Palestine and journeyed all over the world preaching the Word, healing and freeing the people from human bondage?

During the subapostolic age and the second century, there was a tradition of a long interval between the resurrection and the ascension. We hear this from the writings of none other than the Church Father Irenaeus. Astoundingly, given his readiness to denounce any other gospels, he tells us that Jesus lived at least ten to twenty years after his crucifixion:

On completing His thirtieth year He suffered, being in fact still a young man, and who had by no means attained to advanced age. Now, that the first stage of early life embraces thirty years, and that this extends onwards to the fortieth year, every one will admit; but from the fortieth and fiftieth year a man begins to decline towards old age, which our Lord possessed while He still fulfilled the office of a Teacher, even as the Gospel and all the elders testify; those who were conversant in Asia with John, the disciple of the Lord, [affirming] that John conveyed to them that information.[39]

And other manuscripts support this view. The third-century Gnostic text Pistis Sophia reads:

It came to pass, when Jesus had risen from the dead, that he passed eleven years discoursing with his disciples and instructing them.[40]

Who knows what other precious facts concerning the life of the Master, what other teachings which might have changed the history of the last two thousand years, remain buried—either in the desert sands or in akasha.*

Because of such omissions and deletions, in many quarters Jesus has become a god too perfect to approach, before whom we can only be helpless, hapless sinners incapable of walking in his footsteps

---

*akasha: primary substance which fills the whole of space. See page 292 n. 60.

and working out our own salvation as he did through the same Christ Self-awareness he had. And the thing which the Master feared most is come to pass—that those who see him do not behold the Universal Christ who sent him.[41]

In fulfillment of our brother Jesus' prophecy, the Bible's missing links and self-contradictions are being overcome by the Comforter, the Teacher, the Holy Ghost overshadowing us and communicating with us through the Ascended Masters and our beloved Christ Self, the LORD's anointed Teacher whom he sent to tutor us heart to heart.

Through the Teachings of the Spirit of the Great White Brotherhood, we follow their words to the living Word who said:

I AM the Way, the Truth, and the Life. No man cometh to the Father but by this I AM THAT I AM, this Christ Presence who I AM.

I AM the Light which lighteth every *manifes*-tation of God that cometh into the world.[42]

Our Role Is to Find Out What Is Real

Thus, having so said, we are not going to say all that could be said. We will say only a part. For all that could be said has so far not been said to this generation. We have heard some Truth. We have heard error mingled with it. And who is really to blame? Our role is neither to fix the blame, nor to criticize or to condemn. But, if possible, our role is to find out what is Real.

All religious traditions that we have received

have reported Truth to us. All religious traditions have reported to us error. This is not necessarily the fault of any one segment of Christianity. Most of us were born into the religion of our parents. And we came into this world not knowing exactly where we came from.

But I would point out to you that we all came from a common source and to that common source our souls will return. We came forth for a purpose and, fulfilled or unfulfilled, our souls will return to that source at the close of this embodiment. Right or wrong, we are going someplace. We are moving through time. Because the sand in the hourglass is falling all the time. And someday our portion will be no more.

Therefore we ask the question: Why are we here? And we all know—if we have any faith at all in the universe—that there must be a purpose.

Naturally, in this funny world where people are manipulating people all the time—and liking it— only *the* Truth can make us free, if we want to be.

But what is the Truth? Christ stood before Pilate, and Pilate asked the question: "What is Truth?"[43] And we ask the same question today. We should understand that here on earth Truth is relative—there are half-truths, there are full truths, there are relative truths—and we have much to learn as a race of Lightbearers running for the Sun.

I say this not from an ivory tower but in the humble acknowledgment that I have from day to day, by God's grace, learned more of the Truth.

But I do not feel that I have it all. I feel that Truth is progressive by nature and cannot be codified into a creed with impunity. When we put it into a creed, it becomes the letter that killeth. We want the Spirit that giveth life, because we came forth from Spirit.

Bilocation and the Illusions of Mere Magic

I believe that the world ought not to be a place of hatred, of darkness or despair where most of us seek a palliative or a series of pleasures as a substitute for the divine experience.

Have you ever read the account of Philip, one of the disciples—how he was in a certain place and the Spirit of the Lord suddenly picked him up and carried him perhaps twenty miles away in an instant?[44] We live in a time where people want instant love, instant oatmeal, instant understanding, instant everything! Well, it happened in those days. The Spirit picked him up and carried him to where *it* wanted him to be.

Thus seek and ye shall find the divine experience!

In our experiences and travels in the Far East, we have learned that it is nothing for the unascended Masters of the Himalayas to pick a person up, to wrap their cloak around him, and then in a fraction of a second to have him 100, 150, 200, 500 miles away—in the time it takes you to snap your fingers.

Jesus Christ practiced bilocation, which is a

little different.[45] You see, in reality, what is bound is our sense of physicality. We think in terms of being fixed in space, of being in only one place at a time. Actually, the soul that is free within us—because it is related to the omnipresence of God that is everywhere—can be everywhere.

And certain holy ones of God both East and West have been seen by their co-servers, *'physically'*, in more than one place at the same time. Bilocation is possible and it is achieved by the agency of the Holy Spirit through the law of replication. More I cannot say.

You will recall that Sri Yukteswar did bilocate for his chela, Paramahansa Yogananda.

One morning, Yogananda sat in his room. He had been expecting Sri Yukteswar to arrive by the nine a.m. train from Calcutta but had received a telepathic message that his guru would not be on time, so he did not go to the station.

Suddenly "the clearly materialized figure of Sri Yukteswar" appeared in place of the window. "Bewildered to the point of shock, I rose from my chair and knelt before him," Yogananda wrote. "With my customary gesture of respectful greeting at my guru's feet, I touched his shoes. These were a pair familiar to me, of orange-dyed canvas, soled with rope. His ocher swami cloth brushed against me; I distinctly felt not only the texture of his robe, but also the gritty surface of the shoes, and the pressure of his toes within them."

"I have now finished my business in Calcutta,

and shall arrive in Serampore by the ten o'clock train," Sri Yukteswar said.

Sure enough, Sri Yukteswar was on that train, wearing the same clothes as when he materialized in the room in Serampore, less than an hour before.[46]

To the adept, these things are not difficult.

But they are difficult to explain.

Consider the conversation in which Padre Pio, the Italian priest who was seen to bilocate many times, was questioned about his gift by Dr. Wm. Sanguinetti, his personal physician:

> Dr.: Padre Pio, when God sends a saint, for instance like St. Anthony to another place by bilocation, is that person aware of it?
>
> Padre Pio: Yes. One moment he is here and the next moment he is where God wants him.
>
> Dr.: But is he really in two places at once?
>
> Padre Pio: Yes.
>
> Dr.: How is this possible?
>
> Padre Pio: By a prolongation of his personality.[47]

For some, this will be a mystery on top of a mystery. For others it will be the key.

Padre Pio, you will remember, had received the stigmata back in 1918. For many years he never left the monastery at San Giovanni Rotondo in Foggia, Italy—nevertheless, people as far away as

Hawaii and Wisconsin and all over Italy reported that he came to them and healed them and blessed them personally. These visitations cannot be explained as mere visions, for many of the things he did could not have been done had he not been there physically.

He actually brought a reliquary to one nun in Rome, at night, and was back in San Giovanni, 160 miles away, at dawn to celebrate Mass. Once he came to a little girl who was an epileptic, cured her, and put his hand on her bed sheet, leaving a cross of blood from his stigmata. They cut a square out of the sheet and framed it, and it is still there today.[48]

Another time, he healed a woman in Genoa, a Mrs. Devoto, who was about to have her leg amputated. As Rev. Carty writes in his book, one of her daughters was praying that her mother would not have to have this operation.

> She also called upon Padre Pio for help. Suddenly she saw Padre Pio standing in her doorway, looking at her. Her desire to obtain the grace for her mother was so great that she did not stop to wonder how Padre Pio could be in Genoa, instead of San Giovanni Rotondo, hundreds of miles away, nor did she have the slightest doubt that he was actually there in person. Throwing herself on her knees she implored him, "Oh, Father, save my dear mother." He looked at her and said, "Wait for nine days." She

wanted to ask him for an explanation, she raised her eyes but saw only the door of her room, no light, no Padre Pio.

The next day she informed the doctors that they must wait. The doctors tried to convince her in vain. Even the other members of her family when they saw that the mother was growing worse each day, could not dissuade her from her decision to wait nine days as Padre Pio instructed her.

On the tenth day when the doctors visited their patient they were surprised to find the leg completely healed and their patient well on the road to recovery.

Mother, father, sons, daughters, in-laws, and grandchildren all came to thank Padre Pio for the grace which had been bestowed upon them, but Padre Pio will never accept thanks and will always say rather gruffly: "Go into the church and thank our Lord and the Mother of Divine Graces."[49]

So you see, he didn't want any credit for it. God was in him and he gave glory to God. And the people knew it. He was genuine.

Another time some devout people came up to him and asked if he had *really* appeared at their prayer meeting the night before. "And who else could it have been?" he replied brusquely. He was actually embarrassed and almost "painfully timid" when questioned about his supernatural abilities.

Still not convinced, they asked him again, "But Padre, were you really present with us at that meeting?" whereupon he chided them as Jesus would have, "Do you still doubt it?"[50]

But, you know, people who are the instrument of God's miracles aren't always as humble or as holy as Padre Pio. Though miracles aren't necessarily a sign of sainthood, we should recognize a saint in the making when we see one, because he may never tell us.

Nor is the possession of mere magical abilities a sure gauge of attainment.

I remember one day when I was in high school, it was announced that there was a man coming to our town by the name of Marcus the Magician. And so, because my first name is Mark— Marcus on my birth certificate—I thought this was very thrilling. And so, just for fun, you know, I would make believe that I was a magician.

And so he came to our high school. And one of the most dramatic presentations he made was to put a horse in a tent on the stage. A horse, mind you! And then he put a young lady—not in hot pants, but in the closest thing to it—in a tent on the other side of the stage.

And then he took out a gun and he fired it into the air, and in the midst of all the smoke and everything suddenly the tent with the horse in it collapsed and was just hanging by the rope. The horse was gone!

And then across the stage, the other tent collapsed. And then he fired the gun again and, lo and behold, this tent filled out with the lines of a horse. And he went over to the tent over here and he unzipped it and out stepped the girl. And the horse came out of the other tent.

I never did figure out just how he did it. So I can't tell you. But it happened. And it should, perhaps, cause us to realize that there are illusions in the world. We see them all the time on television and we see them at magic shows and we read about them. But there is such a thing as true bilocation of identity.

When people come to realize who they are, when they actually learn of the powers that are resident in man's life, they are able to use these powers. But these powers are the very powers that a man ought not to be concerned with at all, because after all the hoopla over psychic phenomena dies down, they're not really that important.

What is important is the reunion, or rejoining of oneself to God, because this world, your world, is intended to be a place of exquisite beauty—and exquisite beauty within—which can only be known through the Divine Union.

The Laws of Vibration

You know, some years ago there was a politician, down in Louisiana I believe, who played the guitar as he stumped. His name was Jimmy Davis.

Among other things, he wrote "You Are My Sunshine," which became his theme song in his campaign for governor. He knew the power of music, and he used it to win the election! You see, harmony as a gift of God is part of God's nature and our own. And people, God bless 'em, are swayed more by music than by high-sounding phrases.

Have any of you ever gone into a home where a terrible happening occurred? It may have been a battle between a husband and wife. It may have been an unpleasant scene between a parent and child—kids fighting. It could have been almost anything. And you came in right after it happened.

And as you walked into the room—I'm sure most of you have had this experience—you suddenly got a very depressed feeling. You didn't know exactly what had gone on in the room until later, but you felt it because, you see, circumstances affect things and negative vibrations can charge the atmosphere with an uncomfortably sharp edge.

I am referring to the vibrations—or "vibes," as they say—which are actually more or less an electronic fluctuation of the atomic structure. Now, in a tape recorder, for example, what actually takes place when we record sound is that magnetically we are inducing a specific fluctuation of vibrations upon our tape, whereupon we can with ease put this tape through the gate—perhaps the flux gate of vibration—to run it through. And what happens? We can reproduce the same sound over again, as many times as we wish.

The same thing takes place in a circular manner on a phonograph record. If you could enlarge the phonograph record—and you can—you would see that you have miniature grooves going around in what look like concentric circles but which actually form a single spiral from start to finish. These grooves are like roadbeds that rise and fall. They undulate. And the undulation records the vibration. So it is no strange thing to us to understand that substance is plastic, records vibration, and has a certain frequency response.

Let us understand this a little better, then. Substance itself—the very molecules—records vibration. The walls of a room, the seat of a bus or an airplane, train or boat, our clothing. If you go into a tavern, for example, where foul language is used and you hang your coat there, it comes out not only with the smell of smoke on it, but also with the vibrations of the place.

Now, vibration has a tendency to lessen. We call it the decay rate. You will find the same thing happening to our tape recordings or to our phonograph records. Our stylus eats up the road, and after a while we discard our records. And the magnetism on our tape does not hold forever this frequency that we have recorded there. Do you see?

And so, there is a lessening response to vibrational patterns. The overcoat that we have carried into a dingy room—where bawdy behavior is going on and certain low vibrations are impinging (or bombarding) themselves upon the actual molecules

of our coat—has less and less of the odor or
negative vibration as time passes. Mama hangs it
out on the clothesline in the sunshine, and the
fresh air comes along—and after a while, it becomes so lessened that we no longer feel the record
of these vibrations.

You see, man does influence man by his
vibrations. Because vibrations are infectious—both
good and bad vibrations. It's easier to throw a
tomato up into the air and watch it come down
than it is to throw a tomato into the air and
make it stay there. We know according to the
law of gravity that everything that goes up has to
come down.

It's the same with vibrations—they rise and
fall. And it is easier for vibrations to fall than it
is for them to rise. In order to make them rise, or
'levitate', we need something to make it happen.

Now, music is the most wonderful thing in
the universe to actually raise our spirits. Let a band
go by and just watch how your heart begins to skip
a beat! And then you get that feeling of exuberance
when they begin to play "The Stars and Stripes
Forever."

Today we get on an elevator or go into a public
place and we hear the kind of music that wants to
pull apart our whole body—our whole atomic
structure. And because perhaps we grew up in that
vibration we are willing to accept it. We think it's
just what we want, because it may affect our spinal
column at certain points (corresponding to our

chakras) in such a manner that it releases the lowest form of energy into our four lower bodies and consciousness.

No, I'm not going to condemn it. I'm just telling you about it. I'm telling you about the laws of vibration, because everyone enters the veil of time through the gate of time and comes into a hostile world or environment that may or may not be of their choosing. Do you see? It may not be the environment that either God or man wants. But it's the situation as it is right now in our world.

The Fountain of Truth

So, we live in a confused world. There are poor people all over the world, hungry people. And this has gone on for centuries. We have spiritually hungry people who go to the fount of human knowledge, hoping to drink of that fount, out of the cup, the chalice—and find nothing there.

We should understand, then, that the fountain we want to drink of is the fountain of Truth whose living waters will change our whole vision of life, until we are able to realize quite suddenly that life not only *can* be beautiful, but it *is* beautiful!

But why? And how? And where?

Why is it beautiful? Because God made it so. Where is it beautiful? In God's consciousness, and in man's consciousness when he attunes with God's consciousness. Where and why is it beautiful? It's beautiful everywhere because the nature of God is beautiful.

Well, a young lady came up to me as I was speaking at the Unitarian church. And she said to me, "Who makes the Masters? Who makes the Masters the Masters?" And I answered her very simply (because the Master gave me the answer). I said to her, "The Masters make the Masters—or *you* do!"

She said, "You mean I can become a Master?"

I said, "Certainly! Because a Master is perfect." And I said, "If you were God, would you create imperfectly?"

And she said, "No."

And I said, "He didn't."

And so God made everything perfect. Why is it not perfect today?

The whole answer is so simple that it almost blows your mind. The reason that it is not perfect today is because of the dichotomy whereby man has inside of himself the Divine Image side by side with the human image. And he has free will. He allows his energy that comes from his Divine Presence through the crystal cord, through his Holy Christ Self, flowing down into his being, to be diverted over to the human image. And he keeps right on building up that "wonderful ego"—which I don't advocate that you destroy, but you should understand how to harness it.

Our ego is a horse we ought to ride, and not be ridden by. As it is now, it's like the old story of the man who was crossing the bridge. He had a donkey and he had a young son. And they were both leading the donkey along, and a man came along and he said, "How very foolish! Why in the world are you both walking when the donkey is well able to carry you?"

Well, the father thought he would try it himself because he was older than the son. So he got on and the son led the donkey. And someone else came along and said, "You ought to be ashamed of yourself, riding that donkey like that. You should let your son get on."

So he put his son on the donkey. Then another man came along and he said, "Why, this is ridiculous! That donkey is able to carry you both."

So the father hopped on the donkey with his son. And the three went across another bridge. As they were approaching the next bridge, a man came along and he said, "You ought to be ashamed of yourselves. Both of you riding that poor donkey! Why don't *you* carry the donkey?"

So they whittled out a pole and made leather thongs, and they laid the donkey on his back and fastened him to the pole and carried him upside down over the stream. And the thongs broke midstream and down he went, kersplash! And that was the end of their donkey foolishness.

Human opinions would drive us half crazy if we let ourselves be moved by them. Yet we never understand the Truth because the Truth is so simple. And that's what's wrong with the world today.

It's a case where everybody recognizes something's wrong with the world, but nobody knows quite what or what to do about it.

You and I recognize it. All of us—we recognize that. We know there's something wrong with ourselves. But there's an awful lot right with ourselves, too. We have a tendency to hang on to personal guilt and national guilt and criticism, condemnation, and judgment of each other.

Christ didn't come into the world to condemn the world. He came into the world to give us the abundant Life[51] and to confer upon man the sense that he is a native of eternity.

In our many Church Universal and Triumphant community teaching centers and Summit Lighthouse study groups throughout the world, chelas of the Ascended Masters are teaching more and more people about the great laws of freedom. With the Lost Teachings of Jesus in hand, they are cutting people free from hidebound tradition that robs man of his sense of worth and makes him feel worthless. He can't accomplish anything as long as he doesn't understand where he came from and where he's going.

Of course, he came from God and he's going back to God, but there's a lot of highway in between and many sidetracks and treacherous turnoffs that go the wrong way.

So the Brotherhood teaches you about what you'll find on the highway of life, philosophies and religious concepts and situation ethics you'll be confronted by. The Brotherhood shows that God did not just bring forth one Son—just one Son sent to embody the Christ Principle.

Now, you say, "Well, I already know that."

But you don't quite understand the mission of Jesus Christ. The man Jesus seems to you to be also the Christ Jesus. And it is so. Jesus *the Christ*. The *man* Jesus internalized the *Christ* who was, before Abraham, the manifestation of the I AM.[52]

And the lesson to be learned, which the Brotherhood will patiently teach you, is that the mission of Jesus in becoming the Christ and internalizing the I AM THAT I AM is also your mission.

You are supposed to be the Son in manifestation all ways. Now do you understand your mission through Jesus' Christ? To be like him and with him in the resurrection you need to put on his Christhood and wear it in Jesus' name and honor as a sacred garment.

Did you ever hear about the young affluent who came to Jesus to acquire the formula for eternal Life, calling him "Good Master"? And the Master took great exception to this. He said, "Why callest thou me good? There is none good but one, and that is God."[53]

When we hear these sayings, we don't quite delve deeply enough into them to realize what the Master was talking about. He was trying to show him that goodness—any goodness that may be manifesting in man—is in the allness of God rather than in the individual person. Although it can be said that it was resident in the individual, and indeed it was, it needed to be brought out and polished and refined and made worthy by conformity to the Divine.

When this is accomplished, man realizes that the good which does appear is God's. And he gives him the glory, as Jesus did. And the Good that is in one can therefore be in all because it's the same God-Good. That's why with God all things that Jesus did are possible unto you. The Master understood that man is a dual being. He is the Divine Monad up here [pointing to the I AM Presence and causal body on the Chart of Your Divine Self.]* But down here [pointing to the figure standing in the violet flame] man has a soul, he has a consciousness, and it's all put together in a physical body.

And what happens? People don't identify with the Divine Monad, so they say, "I'm that body. That's me. Give me a ticket to Las Vegas, please!" You understand? I mean, they think when they carry the physical person that they're carrying everything. And, of course, it seems to be so.

But why is it so? Because of that little tag-along kite that comes behind us so beautifully—the consciousness. Why, we are more consciousness than anything else. We're more energy. And we're electronic in nature, because the nature of God can be discovered in the electron.

---

*See Chart of Your Divine Self, page 329.

And what do we see in this universe but a constant stream of electrons, protons, neutrons, and all kinds of atomic particles everywhere. And they build form. They build the molecules. They are the building blocks of substance. You put it all together, but then if you lay it on the table inert and it is not energized by the Divine Presence— if energy doesn't flow down through the being of man into his creation—you have a stillborn babe.

I remember when Sean Christopher was born. I was present at his birth. And when the child came out—there he was, like a little white marble statue. And he was inert. And then the doctor spanked him—one resounding crack. And as I watched, it looked like the sun was coming up right near his heart—a little roseate dawn of energy pulsing through this white marble form.

And I thrilled as I saw that energy flow over his body, energizing life and limb. And he began to move and cry out. And I saw in that miracle of life the miracle of myself and of yourself and of everyone. This is the physical man.

And then, of course, we later had the view of the placenta. Do you know what that means? Well, esoterically it means the *place* of *entra*—of entry. The place where, you see, there enters a soul.

And what does it look like, the placenta? The placenta is discus-shaped (literally, "flat cake") and it seems to have the rays of the sun coming out in the tracings of the veins upon it. And so it is a most wondrous manifestation. It is a vital part of the chorion, the home of our little child for nine solid months, which is about the size of a basketball and yet filled with a living being. But this physical being—how wondrous it is!—is not the Real Self. It is the place prepared for the soul's journey through the physical plane.

The Doctrine of Reincarnation Denied

Let us understand, then, that man has come into this world for the purposes of gaining soul-growth. For the teachings of reembodiment are most magnificent, and they were taught by Jesus. And Saint Francis of Assisi taught them in the public square.[54]

Today our churches for the most part do not teach these things, although they are presently believed by men and women who have followed the lead of Benjamin Franklin, Louisa May Alcott, Leo Tolstoy, Empress Elisabeth of Austria, Thomas Edison, Henry Ford, Arthur Conan Doyle, Charles Lindbergh, General George Patton and at least a third of the world's population.

The reason for this is that in earlier councils of the Church (when all of Christendom was solidified under one head), many of the priests and bishops and councils denounced the popular belief in reincarnation as heretical. At the instigation of Theodora, who supposedly influenced her husband, the Byzantine emperor Justinian, they eventually anathematized Origen's teachings on fallen angels, the nature of Christ, and the preexistence and evolution of souls[55] — knowledge that provides the essential foundation to a true perception of the spirit's earthly journey through succeeding embodiments.

And so, ever since the Fifth Ecumenical Council convened in Constantinople in 553, the doctrine of reembodiment that was taught by Jesus has been for the most part either ignored or denied by Christians. They do not understand the implications of the law of karma taught by Jesus to the apostles and quoted by Paul to the Galatians — "Whatsoever a man soweth, that shall he also reap"[56] — and the inevitable conclusion that our karma carries over from lifetime to lifetime. Nor do they realize that the mandate to be perfect and to be formed and re-formed in the image of Christ[57] is not necessarily accomplished, nor can it be, in one life.[58]

One of the most vehement deniers of reincarnation is the Reverend Billy Graham, yet he himself took up in this life right where he left off in his last life as a well-known evangelist preacher at the turn of the century. And what he ought to be learning from his last life is that Christian doctrine, as he was taught it and as he preached it in the same inimitable style he uses today, didn't get him to heaven last time and it isn't going to get him to heaven this time either.

And if he and the rest of the preachers who tell us Jesus died for our sins — and all we have to do is respond to the altar call, confess the Lord and we'll be saved — don't wake up, they're going to be mouthing this false doctrine till the cows come home. And no matter how many times and for how many reincarnations they repeat it, all of their preaching does not nullify reembodiment nor does it guarantee salvation to their hearers, who also keep coming back for the old bromide. And one wonders when they're going to wake up and try the true Way of Jesus that'll really get them to heaven so they won't have to come back anymore!

One of the reasons why people continue to carry on the way they do in their cults of pleasure and death is because they have no sense of responsibility for their actions. This is what happens the moment you remove the understanding of karma and reincarnation from daily life. So their pastors don't teach them about their accountability through this Law of Life, this law of cause and effect. They teach them only about Jesus' accountability for *their* sins!

The Son of man came not into the world to condemn the world; but that the world through him might be saved.[59] You see, the law of karma is not a law of condemnation but the very instrument of salvation. It isn't that God wants to keep score on you and then even up with you on the tally. The real purpose of the recordings of akasha (which preserve the record of karma lifetime after lifetime of every soul) and of the record keeping of the recording angels who serve under the Keeper of the Scrolls is so that God can grant you the victory.[60]

As the vibrational patterns in your life become

the same as the vibrational patterns of the saints—and this is one of the best ways I know of making good karma to balance the bad at an accelerated pace—you, too, shall discover that God has already ordained your ascension out of this mortal socket. This will be quite clear to all of us when we shall have "shuffled off this mortal coil"[61] for the last time in the last round of rebirth.

God doesn't even want to punish you when your vibrational patterns are not like those of the saints. In fact, punishment is no part of the Mind of God. It is man who punishes himself by his failure to abide harmoniously within the framework of Cosmic Law. The law of karma embraces both the science and the mathematics of material life. Obey its rules to the letter *and* the spirit and you can literally lead a charmed life.

No, God is not the punisher of mortals; they punish themselves every day by their ignorance of the Great Law and their violations of its golden ratio of Love, the fulcrum of balance in all inter-changes—human and divine. Through the law of karma God wants you to learn by the fruits you harvest from your own Tree of Life just what is the sweet and what is the bitter you have sown. And self-correct.

In reality, you see, a man's life is like the seasons. He plants his thoughts and feelings in the springtime, along with words and deeds, and they return to him in the fall. And winter is for contemplation of last year's effort, a time for planning next year's increase. And summer shows how every sowing is ripening, so that after a while the reaper can himself predict just what kind of a crop will come in.

I read a report recently of a man who had died and then come back to life. The man said that life was so marvelous on the other side that he didn't want to come back! He told of some of his experiences. And he mentioned the fact that all his life he had dreaded death as the most terrifying thing that could happen to him.

So the mercy of the Law granted him the experience of death in order to strip him of his fear, that he might lead a productive life and hopefully fulfill his reason for being without death's fearful shroud upon him. But this, too, is an example of reincarnation the Lord's way. Did his soul not leave the body (which was pronounced dead) for a journey to paradise and back again, whereupon he re-entered, or re-embodied?

This shows that the good Lord can do whatever he wants to with our souls. If he can cause us to come and go in this manner, what's the difference if the body the soul returns to from such an excursion through life and death and back again happens to be that of a newborn babe? And if it can happen once, why, it could happen as many times as the Lord would so choose, couldn't it?

So we ought to study and learn the ramifications that apply to ourselves from such extraordinary experiences of our brothers and sisters on the path of Life. For God would teach us through one another and we should not expect that for every precept desired, the Great Lawgiver is going to come with the fanfare of archangels to our front door. We should be humble before all demonstrations of the science of Being observed by fellow alchemists of the Spirit experimenting in the temples of Matter.

Reincarnation until the Final Judgment

Just as some people are afraid of death, I suppose that souls might also shudder a bit at the idea of birth because they know they're coming into a world of confinement and misery and all kinds of situations in which people in their egotism will work out their ego problems on each other and make it difficult for one another.

You know the old story of poor little Arthur at Rugby, where he kneeled down to pray by his bed as his mother had always taught him to—and some of the boys laughed and sneered at him. And finally one bully threw a slipper at him.[62]

Well, that's the way the world is—because they don't understand that what counts is where we are on the ladder of life. We have a ladder. Jacob dreamed and he saw a ladder reaching up to heaven and the angels of God ascending and descending on it.[63]

So people are born and they create karma. This means we sow our seed. And some of the seeds we sow are good, and some of the seeds are bad.

And whatever we sow, that we'll reap. And if we don't get it back all in one lifetime, it comes back in the next. And this is what determines your position on the ladder of life.

Why, it's just not possible to achieve equality in this world of accidents and problems, is it? We couldn't achieve equality of life experiences if one of us lived to be 10 years old, another to be 30, another to be 50, another to be 75, and some to be 90 or 110, could we now? That isn't equality.

You see, people keep coming back for thousands and thousands of years. They keep embodying until their "time is up," until their cycle of opportunity to choose who and what they will be is fully spent.

Most of you in this room have been on this planet at least twelve thousand years. And this is true. Some of you many more aeons than that. Because, you see, the purpose of our coming to earth is to graduate from the planetary schoolroom and eventually to enter one of the Father's many mansions of dominion. That's where we go when we have taken dominion and power over the elements of our life and are no longer some kind of a puppet on a string—we might say, the monkey of Darwin's evolution dangling on a string.

And we can conceive of the supposition that we are descended from apes! Well, I will admit that sometimes we may act that way, but personally I can't conceive of the good Lord doing it.

And so, we are given the gift of eternal Life—

unless we lose our soul. Oh yes—this can happen. In the "second death" man can lose his soul.

The first death is the death of the ego; and if this take place by free will, the soul is resurrected in Christ. On such an one the second death,[64] the termination of the id-entity, hath no power. But when the soul allows the ego to take it over—body, mind, heart, and consciousness—it devours the soul like a cancer, melding itself to it until it is no longer possible to separate the soul from the dweller of its own creation.[65] It chose and has chosen at the Y on the Path and at steps and stages subsequently (while it still had opportunity to recant its position of idolatry to the almighty self) to glorify that dweller instead of Almighty God.

By the time the soul stands before the judgment seat, it is already self-consumed. It is pronounced spiritually "terminal," for by no means of cosmic surgery can the soul and her freewill election and predilection be reversed: the twain have become one 'flesh' and mentality, one entity whose Light has been turned entirely to Darkness. And the central sun of being that once shone with the glory of First Love is but a self-consuming black hole in space whose time is no more. And the final judgment and the second death are the ratification by heaven's law of that which the soul herself has already decreed for herself by free will.

This, then, is the full and complete canceling out of identity. All that ever was of the individual— cause, effect, record and memory of both the soul and its creations, including the dweller-on-the-threshold—is dissolved in the white fire of Alpha and Omega, self-canceled by its own denial of Being in God.

It is of supreme importance that the individual on the Path understand that he is making daily choices for Life or Death in the ultimate and final sense. For so many are throwing away their Life with abandon and the fool's folly of carelessness or dare-devilishness as though no matter what they did or did not do, somehow they would be preserved in perpetuity.

This happy-ending psychology is as pernicious a lie as you'll ever find spawned by the agents of Death and Hell. And it is hotly defended by metaphysicians and new-age leaders. But I'm sorry to say that all of their protestations will never cancel the law of the final judgment and the second death.

But the real damnation is not the final judgment. The real damnation is the damnable doctrine of the false pastors' denial of karmic accountability and opportunity for the rebirth of the soul daily and through reincarnation—the mercy already provided for the soul to justify herself through the Word and Work of her LORD *before* the Judgment Day—the Day of no return.

Thus, one can see that the final judgment and second death are divine decrees uttered by the Christ by way of upholding the right of choice bestowed on every individual: To be or not to be.

So, then, we come back to the scene, following

our Lord's transfiguration, of Jesus with Peter, James, and John as they came down the mountain. They were talking about John the Baptist because the disciples had just seen the vision of the Ascended Masters Moses and Elias* talking with Jesus, and one of them asked why the scribes were saying that "Elias must first come."

"When's he going to come back again? When's he going to be reborn on this earth?" And Jesus said, "He's already come. He's already been born. But they didn't know who he was and they did to him whatever they wanted to, and they will do the same to me!" And it says, "Then the disciples understood that he spake unto them of John the Baptist."[66]

That is one record they missed when the old priests began tearing out of the Bible some of the references to reincarnation.

Do you remember the time they asked him this question: "Who did sin, this man or his parents, that he was born blind?" Well, don't you see how that very question proves that the knowledge of and belief in reincarnation was common, not only among the people, but with Jesus and his disciples?

"Who did sin, this man or his parents?" Well, how could he have sinned and been born blind as a consequence of his sin unless he had sinned in a previous life? And yet the question the disciples asked of Jesus was a legitimate question: Was his blindness karmic or hereditary? They didn't doubt that he could have sinned in a past life, nor did

---

Elias is the Greek, New Testament version of the Hebrew *Elijah*.

Jesus; they just wanted to know the cause—past sins or a congenital birth defect caused by his parents' genes.

When you come to think of it, if Jesus had wanted to set the record straight for all time on reincarnation, it was an opportune moment to publicly rebuke his disciples for their obvious belief in reembodiment. But the Master did not. He answered them instead with a still more astonishing Truth that defied the laws of cause and effect outplayed in both reincarnation and genetics.

He said, *"It was for the glory of God!"*

The World Teacher said, "Neither hath this man sinned, nor his parents, but he was born blind that the works of God might be made manifest in him."[67]

So, you see, there are many answers to many questions. We do not have a simple, little standpat answer. And you aren't going to get from me—although I'd gladly give it to you if I could—all the answers to your hidden questions. You know why? I'll tell you why.

First of all, some of the answers you wouldn't understand, even if I told you. And that's not an egotistic statement, because it wouldn't matter whether I was here or who was here—you still wouldn't understand. You cannot explain everything in words. Some things can only be experienced—number one. Two, most people have a mess of preconceived notions about everything and they don't let go of all those ideas all at once with the snap of your fingers, even if they want to.

I remember in my own experience when the doctrine of reembodiment was first proposed to me—the *idea* that I had lived before. Why, this was contrary to the Methodist church, and I was born a Methodist. So right away I said to myself, "Poppy-cock! Nonsense!" I said to myself, "Why, this isn't even scriptural." And I didn't understand what the powers that be of this world had done to the Bible.

You've got some preachers here in America today, and do you know what they'll tell you? They'll tell you that God has put a ray on the Bible and that ray is so powerful that nobody can ever change the Bible.

Ridiculous! This is the most ridiculous idea that has ever been postulated! They have changed the Bible in my own lifetime about twenty times, and they're coming out with new editions right now. So they've changed the Bible, and they've changed it over and over again. And in the process, they've left out all kinds of truths from it.

The Law of Self-Transcendence

I remember one time in a talk I had with Jesus, we were discussing this statement: "No man can see God and live."[68] I said, "Jesus, this is a statement that seems to close the door—that if a man gets enough spiritual development where he sees God, then he dies."

Jesus said, "That is not the complete statement." He said, "Shall I give it to you?"

I said, "Please do."

And he went into the akashic records and he brought out from them something that tingled my spine—and I think it'll tingle yours. He said, "No man can see God *and live as man*." And he told me that that is what it originally said.

I'll explain it. No man can see God and live any longer as man because, you see, once you see God you're no longer going to be satisfied with the lesser image. You're not satisfied with your way of life.

And that's exactly what happened to Saul of Tarsus—once he saw Jesus. He could no longer live as the persecutor of Christians; through his vision of the LORD, he became the mightiest apostle. And yet he said, I die daily.[69] With each new perception of Christ, something less Christlike in him died daily. In partnership with God, his Divine Image working alchemically within you, you can never really be satisfied with yesterday's version of yourself. And this is a very healthy state of self-dissatisfaction.

Because the Law of Life involves the law of self-transcendence, and this is one of the greatest mysteries Jesus has taught us. It is the real key to the kingdom. It simply means that by that coiled spring of the creative force within us each day, spiritually speaking and in every way, we all have the innate desire to go beyond the measure of yesterday's awareness and achievements.

The key is that through the sacred fire we can

self-transcend. We can surmount. We can press the outer limits of our human habitation. We can go beyond ourselves and actually live here and now on earth in our higher selves.

Because self-transcendence is the Law of Life: That which ceases to grow—i.e., to self-transcend—ceases to be. As a matter of fact, in order to live and to retain the quickening of the Spirit, we *have to* self-transcend. Life moves on and so must we. (And this gets us to the heart of Jesus' teaching on transcendentalism.)

The problem is people have forgotten how to self-transcend. So they stagnate and they die long before they're pronounced dead. But the instruction of the Ascended Masters, bringing to the fore of our memory the Lost Teachings of Jesus, shows us how to transcend our former state by many spiritual, health and yogic techniques.

Furthermore, you need to know that socio-economic systems which run counter to this law of the Creative/Re-creative Self breed in their people the stench of nonproductivity and decay. For to self-transcend is to create; and that which ceases to create also ceases to be.

Therefore, those nations which afford their citizens the greatest economic and spiritual freedom to be self-governed will be the most dynamic—hence, the most powerful; whereas those nations whose socialistic systems run counter to Life's self-renewing stream fail to tap the limitless flow of the crystal cord as each individual tree of life gives of his lifestream to the expansion of all.

Apart from its early golden ages, earth's history has been bowed down with a stifling economic totalitarianism run by pagan gods. In the founding of the United States of America, Saint Germain and those working with him determined to break that stranglehold.

And they purposed to replace the old order of the gods with true God-government—where the government is squarely upon the shoulders of the Holy Christ Self of every citizen—and with an economy based on the golden rule and the gold standard and the principle of the abundant Life (opportunity for all through the Word and Work of the LORD), and also with the Holy Spirit directing the free creativity of the people in religion and education, science and the arts.

Yes, Saint Germain stands with Mother Liberty to set us free from that idolatrous paganism where the old gods reborn are often the new stars of screen and stage, the nouveau riche or royalty or the old guard on Wall Street, aristocracies and jet sets or the power elite who gather in secret societies like the Order or covens like the Bohemian Grove—one and all ever worshiped by the masses.

Some strands of paganism have their roots in the worship of the gods, the space people, called Nephilim because they fell (landed? in rocket ships?) or were cast out of heaven by Archangel Michael.[70] The records of their religion of pagan sacrifice, with themselves upheld as the idols of the people, are sprinkled throughout the Old Testament.[71] This is what the Hebrew patriarchs like Abraham and the prophets came to cast down. Even John the Baptist wrestled with them. Both he and Jesus told them off.

Why, can any of you really imagine in your heart that God compares to some of the pagan gods and their pagan concepts of absolute tyranny and appeasement (not forgiveness) through human (not divine) sacrifice? Where you have to take a beautiful young maiden and perch her on the edge of a fiery volcano and cast her down to her death in order to appease the wrath of the Nephilim gods?

Do you have a God like this? Why, the original teachings of God did not provide that kind of a concept for the propitiation of tribal sin.

Elizabeth hasn't remembered this yet, but the Master showed me that she was once hurled into a bottomless pit of blackness by pagan priests in Central America. It was a pond as still and deep as night into which virgins were sacrificed to satisfy the Nephilim gods. If it weren't for reincarnation, such a fate would be life's ultimate tragedy.

But in the light of hundreds of thousands of years of soul evolution in and out of many physical embodiments, it becomes the ultimate lesson in the long lesson Jesus and the prophets have been trying to teach us: Don't trust the flying Serpents in their *wit*craft and spacecraft. For the supergods have genetic designs *on you*. And the Brotherhood of the Black Raven returns to roost; and yesterday's enemies are preying in yonder pew, watching you while you pray. (And I pray you'll remember my words when you need them most.)

Atonement and Self-Transcendence by Rebirth

After the fall from grace—the descent from the etheric octave (paradise) through disobedience—the LORD God provided the means for atonement unto those who, by their own willfulness, had subjected themselves to the law of mortality, the law of death.

And do you know what his solution was?

God's solution to the conundrum of sin and mortality was reincarnation! And through it he granted renewed opportunity for souls to demonstrate the law of self-transcendence!

You see, the old law states that the penalty for sin is spiritual death. It is written, "The soul that sinneth, it shall die."[72] When applied to the human condition, this means that the soul that sinneth shall die in her sin—shall pass from the screen of human life still wearing the garment (the aura and the karmic record) of sin and receive the final judgment therefor.

But the Mediator between Perfect God and imperfect man, the Universal Christ, said:

"Not so, LORD. May it be that the soul shall live again, to learn again, to be tutored of me, that I, the Beloved, might turn that one again to Thee. Let there be established, LORD, the median ground between eternal Life and that eternal damnation which is reserved only for the Devil and his fallen angels.[73] Let earth be the place where Thy souls (the Light-emanations of Thy immortal Selfhood) return to meet Thee again, face to face in one another. Let them learn to love again and to extend mercy to Life as Thou doest extend mercy to them."

Thus the Great Law illustrates the supreme mercy of God's grace as well as the advocacy of the eternal Christ.

Indeed, reincarnation is the means to work out a karma that cannot be otherwise balanced—a karmic debt that in order to be "paid in full" requires greater longevity than the bounds of man's habitation and his threescore and ten afford him in a single lifetime—a karmic infraction of the Great Law that decrees the death of the soul on the Judgment Day unless it be erased by the holy angels from the Book of Life.

Surely this royal road to salvation, this opportunity for the soul's *re*incarnation, granted by I AM THAT I AM, is the grace of Christ's own intercessory power—the all-power of heaven and earth which the Father has given him[74]—by which we are saved.

Why, reincarnation was not necessary in paradise when our souls were sinless and without guile and sometimes a single 800-year or a 1,000-year embodiment was sufficient for twin flames to prove the Law of Spirit in the Matter cosmos and ascend to God—thence to go on expanding Spirit's worlds with the immortals, moving in the trackless realms of Infinity.

By disobedience to Nature's law of harmony, mankind have sinfully destroyed their bodies time and time again; they have squandered the sacred fire in discord, deceit, and degenerate living; they have consumed the Light of Elohim* upon their lusts; they have failed to balance their karma, keep their lamps trimmed, or weave their wedding garment (the deathless solar body)[75] — thus aborting their avowed purpose and reason for being: to ascend to God by a conscious and freewill mastery of self and circumstance and a loving submission and submergence in Christ.

And so, by dispensation of the Logos the word went forth: Henceforth the merciful alternative to humanity's self-induced and addictive nihilism shall be the path of re-creation in Christ. This shall be accomplished through the soul's reembodiment, an opportunity (grace) granted in order that she might study and apply the lessons of her karma — the fruit of action — in earth's schoolroom.

The compassionate purpose of reincarnation is to postpone the soul's Day of Karmic Reckoning (Isaiah calls it the Day of Vengeance of Our God[76]) and to prolong the option for responsible choice by the sons and daughters of God — the choice to accept personal accountability for every thought/feeling, word and deed, and for the purification of

---

*Elohim [Heb., plural of Eloah] is one of the names of God, used 2,500 times in the Old Testament. It refers to the twin flames of the Godhead — the "Divine Us" who created male and female in their image and likeness (Gen. 1:26, 27). See also pages 218–19.

the desires of the heart; hence, to accept personal accountability for one's immortality in Christ.

By the intercession of Christ, mankind return to the scene of their desire and their suffering, their sinful sense and their karma where Christ would teach them the way back Home through his all-consuming Love. A Love sufficient for the burning of every sin forsaken, every record brought to divine resolution, every prideful act that now bends the knee in penitent love, every sense of injustice that surrenders to the personal accountability of the Law who is Christ, the Logos evermore.

Saint Paul points to the karmic choices then and now: "to be carnally minded is death; but to be spiritually minded is life and peace."[77] From Jesus he knew the law of reincarnation and karma and the ultimate consequences of the misuse of free will. He saw man moving from cause to effect, from choice to consequence. He himself fulfilled the law of accountability in his next incarnation as Saint Hilarion, who was born near modern-day Gaza over two hundred years after Paul's death.

Hilarion, like Paul, was a convert to Christianity. When he was just fifteen, he gave up youthful pleasures to devote his days to prayer and fasting in a tiny hut in the wilderness, living on fifteen figs a day for six years. During the long life God gave him, he performed many miracles and finished the work (karma) God gave him to do, and at its conclusion he made his ascension from inner levels. Thus, today the apostle Paul is known and loved as the Ascended Master Hilarion.[78]

Let the Mind of Christ Be in You!

So, you see, it is a matter of our minds—what we think. What we think is what we are. And this is what the Masters teach us. And what a marvelous gift this is—both the self-knowledge and the knowledge of man's power not only to create but to re-create, and therefore transcend, himself!

There are many references in the Bible that bring out the teaching of reembodiment. And this brings us to the point of understanding the true greatness (the greatness of God which he made his own) of John the Baptist. I'm going to show you why.

In the annals of the Great White Brotherhood, hardly anyone from this planet has ever taken the ascension, going up to heaven as Jesus did, and then come back down again.* But Elijah did. He ascended to heaven in a whirlwind after the "chariot of fire and horses of fire" had parted him from Elisha.

Eight hundred years later he returned through the womb of Elisabeth, wife of Zacharias, to be the messenger of the LORD's anointed. And the soul of Elisha, who had been the disciple of Elijah, came into embodiment as Jesus, now the Master and Christed One.

And it was meet that the pupil should exceed his teacher through his own attainment multiplied by the power of the mantle—the double portion of

---

*Since the ascension is reunion with God (the soul's 'fusion' with the I AM Presence) and freedom from the wheel of rebirth, the orderly progression of the now-ascended Master would not necessitate reincarnation in the physical octave.

Elijah's Spirit which Elisha asked for and received in the hour of their tender parting.[79] As John said, "He must increase, but I must decrease."[80]

Whereas Jesus must increase his Spirit on earth to set the matrix for the Piscean path of Christic initiation, John knew that as his Spirit decreased on earth, it would increase in heaven in order that he might hold the balance for the Saviour's Work; and he shortly took his leave of this plane, beheaded at the hand of Herod Antipas. And this precious scenario does show us one thing: that "the last shall be first, and the first shall be last."[81]

Sometimes in spiritual matters someone may decide to play tortoise and hare with you — someone you think is way, way ahead of you, advanced spiritually. You say to yourself: "Well, if I could only be as good as that person . . ." Let me tell you something. There's no competition in God. We can all be just as good. How can you get better than perfect?

And it says so right in the Bible: "Let this mind be in you which was also in Christ Jesus, who, being in the form of God [made in his image], thought it not robbery to be equal with God but made himself of no reputation, and took upon himself the form of a servant, and was made in the likeness of men."[82]

You see, Jesus set out to be just as good as God because he was *of him*. Quite simply, the Son wanted to be just like his Father. And so it is the prerogative of every son to follow in his father's footsteps.

But, then, centered in God-Good, Jesus took on the form of a servant to minister to the God flame both in his disciples and in the seed of God scattered in the earth. He ministered unto them and washed their feet (symbolizing the genetic foundations of their understanding which had to be restored) so that they, too, could put on the Mind— countenance and consciousness—of the Universal Christ and aspire to a like equality to the Godly presence and vibration. This is true initiation of the God flame that leads to its crystallization in man.

We have to understand the beautiful ritual that Jesus performed the last night before his betrayal, for this is the example of the great work of the servant-Son ministering to those made in the Divine Image. You remember how he laid aside the garments of his office, girded himself with a towel, and took a basin and washed his disciples' feet in fulfillment of the words of the Teacher who sent him: "He that will be great among you, let him become the servant of all."[83]

He didn't say, "Everybody you meet on the street—show them that your car can go faster. Show them that you know how to buy smarter clothes." (Or you can follow the system of sort of knocking what they have by wearing dingier clothes.) He didn't say, "You should try to bring down your fellowmen or society's cherished institutions or wreck havoc in the world or abuse your body." He didn't talk about any of those things.

He said that you should have respect for the

temple of God. And he said, as Paul taught it, "Know ye not that your body is the temple of God?"[84] We should have respect for ourselves, including the body—because it is a chalice into which the wine of the Holy Spirit is poured. And that is part of the beauty of God.

Young and old alike, I say to you that the Great White Brotherhood and the Ascended Masters and the eternal and living God in whose image we all were made loves us one and all. And his Love is extended to the whole wide world. And there is no need for religious or racial conflict when the Truth is known.

I attended a meeting of ministers out at Fort Carson. The commanding general had invited us for coffee and doughnuts and then luncheon. And we all wore name tags to get acquainted. Now, most of the ministers from Colorado Springs did not know the name of our organization. We were rather new there at the time. And do you know that there had been some conversation about us in the community, nothing based on actuality, nothing which could be proven in a court of law, but what we call hearsay.

And so I was alone at Fort Carson. Individual after individual came up to me and looked at my name tag and then turned away or abruptly left off introducing himself; and one minister even spun on his heels and refused to even speak to me.

Am I moved by such antics of the human consciousness? Of course not! Nor should you be if you ever find yourself in a similar situation. Because they truly knew not what they did.[85] Therefore Jesus said, "Bless them that curse you, do good to them that hate you, and pray for them which despitefully use you and persecute you, that ye may be the children of your Father which is in heaven."[86] And Jesus practiced what he preached—and so did Mohandas Gandhi.[87]

We must not have any harmful feelings about these things whether towards ourselves or others, but we should understand that people are where they are. They're where they are. And this is true of all men. You cannot tell me today—you cannot tell yourself—that everybody does not have a certain place upon the ladder of life. For they do. And no one is an exception. No one.

A man may be president of the United States, and yet he may lack the stature befitting the office. He may be a famous chemist in a laboratory, but he may lack certain knowledge of the elements. A man may be a schoolteacher, a professor—he may be a doctor of law, but he may have areas in his own field that he is not familiar with.

Coequality with God through Christ's Sonship

It is most unfortunate, but I have had people come in to the sanctuary thinking that I would "tell it all" in one night. And afterwards, they would say, "Why, I heard so much that I have never heard before. He must have told me everything!" But we really told very little, because there is so much to learn.

It's unfortunate, not from my standpoint—because we are compelled by God's Law to stand up and teach the Law—but from the standpoint of people's misconception, that they actually believe that the true Teachings of Christ are that simple. And salvation itself has been reduced to a formula that could be told in one night. And with that formula the people believe, because their ministers have told them it is so, not once but many times over, that they could go on their way fully enlightened.

Sometimes when I have traveled to one of the temples of the Great White Brotherhood (out of the body during sleep) where we sit in class and receive instruction in the laws of God, I have marveled at the extent of the wisdom of the Ascended Masters. And I am here to tell you that unless you know these things of the Spirit, you are indeed in a state of meager knowledge.

One of the greatest problems in the world today, as I see it, is the fact that men reach a point of sophistication where they suppose that they know all the answers, when in reality they know only a few. And this is nowhere more prevalent than in matters of religion.

Tell me, in what other branch of human knowledge do you find such smugness, such spiritual conceit and self-satisfaction, as you do among the churchmen of today, who are neither hot nor cold, who say they are increased with spiritual goods and have need of nothing—no Teacher or Teaching? Why, they even shun the progressive revelation of the Holy Ghost (through the dictations of the Ascended Masters) whom Christ promised to send us as our Teacher—because we would need him to lead us unto all Truth.

There is nothing that happened to Jesus Christ that cannot happen to you. You can heal the sick. You can be healed. You can heal your mind. It *can* be healed. You *can* free yourself from boredom. You can free yourself from it by simply finding out that the universe is the most animated place you ever saw! Well, there isn't any other, is there?

You suddenly find out that it's really animated and literally jumping with energy. And you realize that it has a grand purpose. You're going down a grand hall. You're going into a miracle world, but it's got to be because you know the Truth. And if you don't know the Truth, you will never be free. Never! And you will never get it if you suppose that it's a matter of someone else vicariously paying the price for you.

We love Jesus with all our hearts. We know that "all things were made by *him*" refers to the Christ, and without the Christ was not any thing made that was made.[88] And we know that there is a difference between Jesus *the man* and Jesus *the Christ*.

You, the man, the woman, the child, like the child Jesus—you can be a Christ. In fact, your Christhood is your highest destiny. And that attainment on earth as it had always been in heaven had been Jesus' goal during a series of embodiments in which he exercised various aspects of the Law of initiatic Christhood. You can be a Master like Jesus or El Morya or Saint Germain, every one of you, if you *"let this Mind be in you which was also in Christ Jesus,* who, being in the form of God, thought it not robbery to be equal with God..."

Saint Hilarion Performed the Works of Christ

Paul, both as the apostle and in his next incarnation as Saint Hilarion, performed many miracles similar to those of Jesus.

Hilarion spent twenty years in the desert in preparation for his mission and only then wrought his first miracle — he cured a woman of barrenness, enabling her to bring forth a son.

From that moment on, he carried out a healing ministry. He healed children of a fever by invoking the name of Jesus, cured paralysis and cast out many devils. Crowds would gather to be healed of diseases and unclean spirits. They followed him even into the most desolate and remote places. He tried many times to hide, but they always found him, forcing him to follow his true calling.

Once, he sailed away and hid in Sicily, but a devil cried out through a man in St. Peter's Church in Rome, "Hilarion the servant of Christ is hiding in Sicily. I will go and betray him." So the man got on a boat, still possessed by the demon, and went directly to Hilarion, threw himself down in front of his hut, and was cured. So he couldn't hide from the people and he couldn't hide from the devils! As Jerome said of him, "A city set on an hill cannot be hid." Hilarion had become that city by his devotion to Christ.

So, Jerome, whose biography of the saint provides most of the information we know about him, goes on, "The frequency of his signs in Sicily drew to him sick people and religious men in multitudes; and one of the chief men was cured of dropsy the same day that he came, and offered Hilarion boundless gifts; but he obeyed the Saviour's saying, 'Freely ye have received; freely give.'"

And then Hilarion did something really amazing. It was on the occasion of a great earthquake, and the sea was threatening to destroy the town, as Jerome reports: "The sea broke its bounds; and, as if God was threatening another flood, or all was returning to primeval chaos, ships were carried up steep rocks and hung there."

So the townsfolk, seeing these mountains of water coming towards the shore, ran and got Hilarion, and, "as if they were leading him out to battle, stationed him on the shore.

"And when he had marked three signs of the Cross upon the sand, and stretched out his hands against the waves, it is past belief to what a height the sea swelled, and stood up before him, and then, raging long, as if indignant at the barrier, fell back, little by little, into itself."[89]

You can imagine how the crowds flocked to

him more than ever after that alchemical feat—
Christ's alchemy through him, you see: "and even
the wind and the sea obeyed him."[90] So, the most
popular living saint retreated to a spot in Cyprus
that was so remote that he didn't think anyone
would find him. It was even haunted, and he
thought that certainly people would be afraid to
so much as approach the spot. But a paralyzed man
managed to drag himself there, found Hilarion,
was cured, and told others.

And so the saint ended his days in that valley,
with many people coming to see him. After he
died his followers buried him there, as was his
desire, but after several months his closest disciple,
Hesychius, secretly dug up his grave and carried
his body off to Palestine!

Just think what they would have done to the
body of Jesus if he'd have left it behind. They deify
the miracle worker instead of internalizing his example and teaching on the crystallization of the
God flame.

The greatest scientists who have ever lived,
Jesus and the saints of East and West, stand before
the people, and they just take the miracles and
the healings but never ask how or why or, "Can
I do it, too, Lord?" They want to know who
amongst them will be greatest in the kingdom
while Christ is looking to bestow his mantle for
world regeneration upon anyone who will apprentice himself to him and Saint Germain to learn
the science of healing and longevity with good

health and the art of the miraculous abounding like roses falling from Nada's chair!

People just can't get beyond the miracles!

So don't you be like the rest and get all excited about miracles and forget about your own souls and the sacred fire of God that is within *you*. People don't realize that the Holy Spirit can empower them to perform miracles for the glory of God if they emulate Jesus and the saints. But you do. You know better. And because you know better you'll do better.

It's because people haven't been taught it. And no matter how many times you tell them, they still won't believe you, or they'll accuse you of some terrible crime—the crime of just trying to be like Jesus, of establishing a sense of mission through co-measurement with the World Saviour.

One of the biggest problems we have in the world today is the accusing finger. Somebody came along and the finger was pointed at me. The finger said, "Well, do you think you're equal with God?"

Well, I sure hope I can be. I want to be. But it's not a matter of self-righteousness. It's not a matter of saying that I did it. It's a matter of accepting what he did. And you accept it for yourself.

I want to be equal to the image of Christ—in whose image I am most fearfully and wonderfully made.[91] I want to be equal to the task of glorifying God in my body and in my soul. I want to be of the same mind Jesus was when he thought it not robbery to be equal with God. No robbery because God had so ordained it when he gave him Sonship. So gave he yours and mine. It is our Sonship that makes us one with the Father, and it is upon this oneness that our equality is based.

If you don't believe it, you try it. You take the idea of equality through Sonship home with you, and you see what happens when you start thinking of what would Jesus do, what would God do, and what would you do if you had all-power.

You couldn't be bored. You couldn't feel inadequate. How can you feel inadequate if you have the power of the universe within you? Why, you can't! You've got it right there. And what the all-power of God does for the whole world when you use it wisely is so wonderful.

It's the harmony of the spheres, the interplanetary radiance that flows between the planetary bodies. It's the interconnecting link between man and God. You have it! It's the Divine Image. You aren't hopeless! You aren't helpless. You can know your oneness with God—and therein lies your co-equality!

Sure, we'll all die physically. And some will make their ascension from inner planes (the soul in the etheric sheath rising in Christ to the plane of the I AM Presence) and some will reembody to finish the Lord's Work who sent them. But remember, if you do reembody—if you have started to sow your seeds in the right way, righteously, God's way—when you make the transition to another octave in another body (your etheric body), you're going to be given the opportunity to come back to the physical plane in an environment where you can pick up where you left off.

You say, Why? I'll tell you why. Because there is a giant computer in heaven. No—IBM, the "itty-bitty machine" company, didn't make it. They didn't make it, but God did. And it's a computer that's inherent within nature. It's in the whole structuring of life. And if God sees, and the All-Seeing Eye sees— not in the sense that God is a venerable old man sitting on his throne in a corner of the universe, but in the sense that God is in you and he can change you—you don't have to worry. He can do such marvelous things with you, including create the perfect environment for your development here and now and in the future—if you'll only realize that.

Really, you're kind of Play-Doh[92] for God. You know how a child sits on the floor and plays with his Play-Doh and molds different images? Well, this is very easy. God can mold you, but he gave you free will. And he's not about to do it if you don't say something to him. That's one of the laws—you have to ask for what you want. You have to ask him to form and re-form you in Christ.

And if you don't believe that this can be done for you, if you think that there isn't any hope for you or you're going to run around to this church and that church and you're going to find out what God and Christ and salvation are all about—well, you won't. Because they're going to tell you that somebody paid the price for you. And you're going to say, "Now, because he paid the price, it's all done. And it really doesn't matter too much what I do."

And yet somehow you're a bit uneasy. You don't think it's a very good insurance policy, and you say to yourself, "Maybe I'd just better live a little better." And you suppose that you are going to live and be good. And you try for a while but it's hard to be constantly good—especially when the weekend rolls around.

And Jesus is saying, "Why callest thou me good? There is none good but one, that is, God." Well, you can't do it if he couldn't do it! You see, the human can't do it without God. So the answer to living right has to be found in the emanation of the First Cause, or the Divine Logos, pouring forth the divine energy into time and space.

From the beginning, with the beauty of the first photon, all substance is endowed with the substance of God. "All things were made by him, and without him was not any thing made that was made." It's still true. And it's true of all of us. And that is the wonderful thing. That's the wonderful gift of God. We were made by him and everything we do, if it's going to last and be good, has to include him. Do you see that?

We may have a little more Light—you know, some people have a little more Light than others. Like Saint Paul said, one star differs from another star in glory.[93] But it doesn't say that you can't get more Light, does it?—that is, if you want it.

But, of course, in this day of easy lessons and instant life and instant victory and instant achievement, people do not want to expend the effort of themselves. They would rather believe that somebody else did it for them.

Mantra/Meditation: The Soul Omnipresent in God

And what do the Masters teach? They teach the science of meditation—of meditating upon the principle of who you are and what you are. So, why don't you join me in a little experiment in the science of realizing your True Self. Why don't you just believe that there is a perfect image of you and that this is part of the Godhead and that you are actually a "sky" being rather than an "earth" being.

Do you know what the great Magi said when they came from afar on their camels? "We have seen his star in the East and are come to worship him."[94] You've got a star there, too. There's a star in the heaven-world that is your own. It's the star that shone when you were born. And it can grow and grow in magnitude until it's so beautiful. And it signifies that you are a growing divine being, entering into your divine inheritance.

You see, the Masters' Teaching is so wonderful because it's all true. There are so many things that are based on cosmic law, that I'm sure your eager young minds and hearts, regardless of your physical age, will want to reach out for higher Truth. You'll want to find it. And so, how can you find it a little more? Why, through the mantra, and meditation upon God!

Now, according to orthodox tradition, when the Master Jesus was here on earth he lived thirty-three years before his ascension. We can account for his early days in Nazareth until the age of twelve. But what was he doing in those interim years between the ages of twelve and thirty? And where was he?

There is a legend concerning Issa that we came upon in India, near Kulu. And through this legend we found out a great deal about Jesus' travels in the East. One of the things that Jesus did during the so-called lost years was to make a pilgrimage to many temples of the Great White Brotherhood—some physical and some on the etheric plane. He traveled to Egypt, India, Tibet, Nepal and even to the Americas. He came here in a manner that would amaze you.

But I want to point out to you that Jesus had many experiences in the course of his travels. And one of these experiences, of course, was his familiarization with the mantra of the Far East.

The mantra is a vibrational pattern. And when it is spoken, because it has been recited by thousands and perhaps millions of people—certainly millions and billions of times—each one a living soul saying it as an act of devotion, we realize that the stylus of life has cut a deep vibrational pattern in the ethers. And so the mantra becomes endowed with terrific spiritual power.

I am going to invite you to have a little experience with the mantra, because your loving recitation of the mantra will have a beneficial effect upon your whole being. It is a momentary act of regeneration. It can charge your physical body. It can free your mind from some of the comic strips that you may have watched on Saturday morning, which vibrationally are patterns of destruction.

Did you know that there are war patterns and destructive patterns in many of the cartoons that are shown to our children on television? We see them as innocent little pastimes, but in reality they're not because in many cases there are forces not so benign that influence the people (albeit unbeknownst to them) who create them. And, you see, this is all part of the vibrational pattern that I was talking about earlier.

So, we use these mantras to consume any and all patterns of destructivity—even negative astrological patterns—that may be impinging upon our conscious or subconscious minds. You can start right now wherever you are with a very simple mantra which will give you tremendous benefit if you pour into it your heart's devotion to God.

Just separate your hands and your feet so they do not touch. And sit up straight in your chair or in the lotus or half lotus, as you please. Rest your hands, cupped, on your knees, the thumb and index finger touching in the *jnana* mudra. You're going to use a powerful Indian mantra which we learned in Rishikesh. This is the *Om namo Nārāyanāya.* It means "Obeisance to the Sacred Name (vibration/identity) of the Creator within the creation."

And *Narayana*, we find, as the ancient writings

have been deciphered by James Churchward in his books on the lost continent of Mu, gives to us the concept of the seven-headed serpent, the symbol of the Creator and creation. He says that *Nara* means "Divine One," and *Yana,* the "Creator of all things."[95]

The concept of the cosmic serpent swallowing his tail (which is an allegory based upon Narayana, who is the embodiment of the living God) shows that all of us are involved with that pattern of Spirit. The seven heads are the seven rays of the Godhead, illustrating God's mind permeating cosmos as seven planes of consciousness.

Thus, the Creator enters the creation through the seven rays. And the tail, symbolizing the Omega, the ending—Matter—returns to the beginning, to Alpha-Spirit, in the successive rounds of the Great Inbreath following the alternating cycles of the Great Outbreath. And it's up to us to grow in grace (spiritual attainment) by our own devotion and acts of love in drawing forth that divine energy.

Om namo Nārāyanāya.

Now, when you chant the *Om,* remember that it is the soundless sound which is a subtle pulsation of the union of the Divine Father and Divine Mother. And that cosmic sound, and the soundless sound beyond all sound, which has entered into our being is Narayana. Thus, the meaning of the mantra, again, is: "I surrender, I prostrate to the Sacred Name of that divine one Narayana, who is present in all being as the pulsation of Life and of the soundless sound."

Now, I will be singing it alone first to transmit the pattern, then with you to accelerate your own giving of it.

> *Om namo Nārāyanāya*
> (Om nah-mo Nah-rye-uh-nye-uh)
> *Om namo Nārāyanāya*
> *Om namo Nārāyanāya*
> *Om namo Nārāyanāya*

The more you concentrate on the Light in your heart, visualizing the threefold flame* of the Godhead burning there, and still your thoughts and feelings, the more you are going to feel the tremendous power of your I AM Presence that is generated for your use in the physical plane. This we attain by the singing of this very ancient mantra. Its momentum goes back thousands of years to devotees who have been chanting in Hindu, Buddhist, and even Jain caves and other holy places.

By giving the mantra we express our profound love for the Person of God in his many attributes and principles. The creative sound, charged with the sacred breath and our love, is the means of magnetizing God's qualities into our lives.

This is a very deep spiritual science, and its benefits are genuine. So be sure that you maintain the proper respect for the mantra, because if you do, it will become a transforming power in your life. Let's give it again:

> *Om namo Nārāyanāya*   (33x)

─────────────
*See page 329.

In the temple of Rishikesh we sat on straw mats and chanted these mantras with the sages of India. And I want to tell you that they maintained their chants for as long as a half an hour with just one chant. And your first impression, as an American who has been taught that our religious tradition is all there is, is to just get it over with. But you find at the end of a half an hour of this chanting that your body is so charged with spiritual energy that you are able to reach out in consciousness, if you experiment with it—and you can see sometimes for a mile or sometimes ten miles, sometimes for hundreds of miles.

Your eyes are actually imbued with a spiritual vision and you begin to sense your existence less subject to the confinements of time and space. All this through the power of the spoken Word—and it's the same Word flowing through you now by which the worlds were framed and God made you a living soul.

You know, one time an interesting thing occurred in my life. I was in the Blackstone Hotel in Chicago, and during the night I traveled from the hotel to Paris in my spiritual body. And as I was on the way to Paris, I came to the Empire State Building. And I was very much a novice—I had had very little experience at all in consciously traveling outside the body. And so, I saw that large dome on top, where the aerial for the early television was placed. And so, I actually stepped on it. And then, as I was standing on it, I got the silly idea

that I was in the physical—and it was a very foggy
night—and I fell off of it and toppled into the fog,
expecting to be dashed into pieces. And then I said
to myself, "This is ridiculous! This is nothing but
a dream."

So, the next morning, I went down to have my
breakfast in the Blackstone Hotel. And I was sitting
there having my Kadota figs and my coffee, and suddenly I looked across the table about ten feet away,
and there was a little old lady in a white dress and
she had the funniest little smile on her face. And
I thought, "What in the world is she doing? Why is
she looking at me like that?" And she kept grinning
this sort of a Mona Lisa smile, you know. And so,
suddenly she turned to me and she said, "I saw your
foot slip last night on the Empire State Building."

And this really happened. And I'm telling you,
I had chills going up and down my spine. That
which I thought was a dream wasn't a dream at all.
And you know, it's kind of silly really, I mean, we
get into all these stereotypes where we say to ourselves, "Well, this isn't real. This can't happen." But
it can and it does, because man is a spiritual being.

So, now I'm going to give you one more mantra and then I'm going to give you a brief meditation. This one is a bit more complex. It's a very
important mantra and if you can't figure it out, you
can have a cassette of it to learn with.* So here's
how it goes:

---

*If you would like to give these mantras with Mark and Elizabeth Prophet,
available on CD, order your copy of *Mantras with Mark and Elizabeth
Prophet* at www.tsl.org/bookstore or call 1-800-245-5445.

> *Om Trayambakam yajāmahe*
> *Sugandhim pushti vardhanam*
> *Uruva rukamiva bandhanāt*
> *Mrityormukshiya ma'mritat*

The literal translation of the *"Trayambakam"* mantra is "We worship the three-eyed one, Lord Shiva, the Holy Spirit, or Third Person of the Trinity, who is fragrant and who nourishes well all being. May he liberate us from death and attachment for the sake of Immortality, even as the cucumber is severed from its bondage to the vine."

Trayambaka is another name for Shiva. This is a *bija* (seed) mantra. As he consumes all darkness and negative energy, Shiva gives the nectar of life. He transports your soul to the eternal, changeless existence. This mantra takes you completely away from confusion and divisive forces within and without the self. Shiva separates us from all illusions about ourselves and our world. He also kills death.

Let's give it together. Wherever you are, know that I AM giving it with you now:

> *Om Trayambakam yajāmahe*
> *Sugandhim pushti vardhanam*
> *Uruva rukamiva bandhanāt*
> *Mrityormukshiya ma'mritat*   (4x)

The longer you chant it, the more power you draw down from the Word, who is the origin of all mantras.

Now let's meditate together.

Do not feel that you are a body, but recognize that you are a soul and that your soul is of the divine nature and thus omnipresent with God. You are everywhere—*everywhere* in the universe. The consciousness of God is with you. You are not confined to a physical body. You are a free spirit, born free, free still.

And as you realize this, try to feel the Light/ Energy that interpenetrates cosmos. Try to realize the power of single-eye vision focused in your third eye in the center of your forehead just above the brow.

O Our Father who art in heaven, we open our consciousness to the great continents of the Mind of God, the power of thy omnipresence.

We are one with thee.

Long involved in ourselves as a human snarl, an entangled skein of ego and identity, we ask that we may receive the Light in order that our individual souls may flow as the eternal Tao out into the spiritual universe where thou art everywhere, omnipresent.

Our Father, let us contact through thy consciousness those benign beings of Light who are aware of their oneness with thee.

In the beginning, we came forth with a perfect sense of the vision of thyself being everywhere as one Being. We were not separate but one in thy Consciousness.

Let this our meditation on thy Love, then, be our return gift to thy heart. Let us journey in consciousness to the place where the Lord lay, where Christ is.

Everywhere thou art, and there is no place that thou art not.

We are aware, then, of the rings of Saturn. We are aware of Mars, Jupiter, of Neptune, of the hosts of suns that compose our system. We are aware of the spatial galaxies and of the permeation of thy omnipresence there.

No longer glamorized by the manifestation of our outer self, we seek thee as bliss and joy and peace and the abundant consciousness. For forever is forever. And we shall always be thy children. For we will it so. Consciously we ask that all desire that we have ever had to glamorize or to glorify or to serve the outer self be removed from our hearts and be replaced by the desire to serve the inner man, the hidden man of the heart[96]—even Christ, the Lord.

Let us grow in grace, in the knowledge of thyself and the ascended hosts. Keep us ever in the hollow of thy eternal hand. For thou guidest the sparrow through the air. Thou receivest our winged prayer.

Thou art God, the essence of true Being. As we speak thy name, I AM, as thou

appeared long ago to Moses, saying, I AM
THAT I AM—OM TAT SAT OM—so let
it be, Eternal Father strong to save, unto the
love of the Cosmic Christ. Let thy name be
given by each heart, the accompaniment of
the continuing search for thee until in all
of thy children the grail of consciousness,
filled with the Holy Spirit, is become the
complement of thy eternal grace.

In the name of Jesus the Christ, Amen.

TORCHBEARERS
OF THE HIMALAYAS
by Nicholas Roerich

Saint Panteleimon the Healer

DAUGHTER OF ZION

COMPASSION

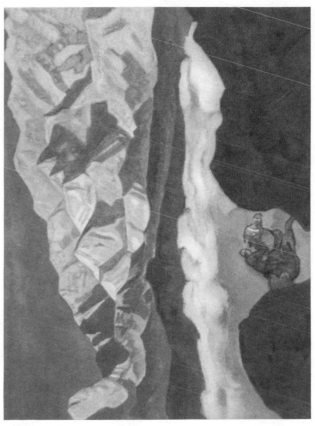

He Who Hastens

STRONGHOLD OF THE SPIRIT

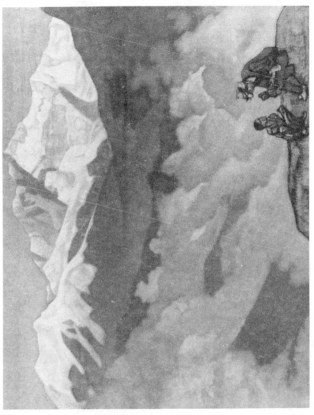

PEARL OF SEARCHING

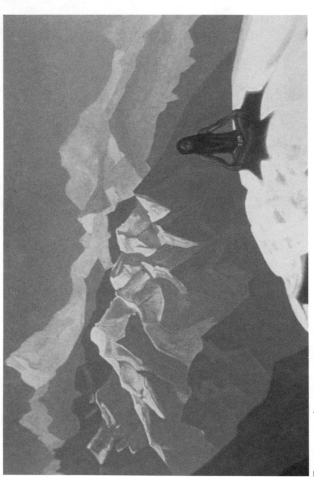

Peaks of Attainment

WAYFARER OF THE NIGHT

PATH TO KAILAS

YEN-NO-GUYO-DJA *Friend of Travelers*

Aura of Sainthood

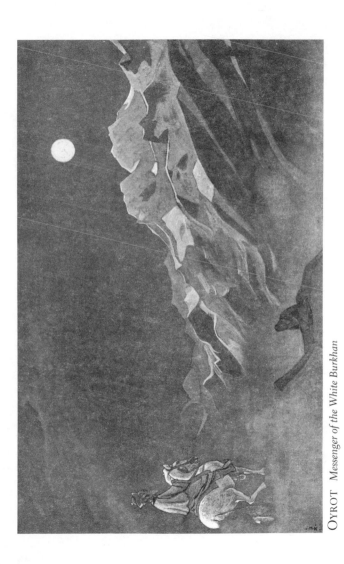

OYROT *Messenger of the White Burkhan*

FIRE BLOSSOM

TREASURE OF THE WORLD

MIRACLE

Chapter Two

THE MIRROR
OF CONSCIOUSNESS

The Mirror of Consciousness

The whirling of the mind must be stilled. The thoughts that arrange the molecules of the mirror of consciousness need the calmness of a still pool—that we may be able to see clearly.

For centuries mankind have had dangled before them the baubles and trinkets of life. Swinging before our gaze, their hypnotic effect has confused and diffused our sense of direction so that the meaning of Love is lost in the strange phantasmagoria of the world whirl.

Let us, then, still our minds, the mirror in which God is reflected.

Though we had never seen before—if this were our first day on earth and we had come in with the full-blown consciousness of our present moment—in order to see the face of God, we would still require a clear mirror. For it is we, the individual, who must perceive God.

It is not enough that his Spirit is omnipresent in the world. He is everywhere. But we do not necessarily perceive him in the wind that blows nor in the temperature changes that affect the weather. Nor do we see God in the faces of those whom we meet, for our attention goes to the outer appearance, the overlay of error that requires transmutation.

Come, let us still the mind for a more perfect vision.

Mediators of the Word and Work of the LORD

There are many hearts hungering and thirsting after righteousness. And it is the will of Christ that they should be filled.[1] Who will fill them? Where are the shepherds who will feed the sheep? — shepherds who see themselves as the LORD's instruments, through whom he will answer the soul longings of his children.

Yes, the command "Feed my sheep"[2] tells us that God expects us to do that which he, by the divine Law and the divine Will, has reserved for his servant-Sons and their disciples.

"Feed my sheep." The very words and the imploring of the Master tell us we are needed by the LORD above to care for his own here below. Because we are so loved, we are sparked with the desire to serve as mediators of the Word, to be positioned in an orderly hierarchy of offices ordained for the performance of specific duties and responsibilities within the Body of God that are vital to the Holy Spirit's intercession.

Listen, now, to the apostle Paul as he recounts Jesus' teaching to him on the mystery of Christ's Body:

For as the body is one and hath many members and all the members of that one body, being many, are one body: so also is Christ.

For by one Spirit are we all baptized into one body, whether we be Jews or Gentiles, whether we be bond or free, and have been all made to drink into one Spirit....

And whether one member suffer, all the members suffer with it; or one member be honoured, all the members rejoice with it.

Now ye are the Body of Christ, and members in particular.

And God hath set some in the church, first apostles, secondarily prophets, thirdly teachers, after that miracles, then gifts of healings, helps, governments, diversities of tongues.

Are all apostles? are all prophets? are all teachers? are all workers of miracles?

Have all the gifts of healing? do all speak with tongues? do all interpret?

But covet earnestly the best gifts: and yet shew I unto you a more excellent way.[3]

And that "more excellent way" is Charity[4]— the Self-givingness of Love itself. Therefore in Charity's flame we see the disciples as intermediaries between Christ and the sweet children of the Light who hunger and thirst after righteousness and must be filled day by day by the co-workers and co-servants of the Brotherhood.

And Charity herself, the beloved complement

of Archangel Chamuel, is the heavenly handmaid of our labor of Love. Through her compassionate, all-knowing eyes we perceive that as man hungers for his daily bread, so his soul thirsts for the one thing that can quench his thirst: the spiritual graces that are here and everywhere reflected in and beyond the world order.

We see them hiding in the sunbeams and just behind the rainbow in the sky. In the play of light and shadow in the clouds. In the dancing of wind and wave upon the sea and in the rolling of the waters undulating with the earth currents. Through the golden wheat and the blue-green grasses, as they bow to the dominion of the hierarchs of the elements.

We also glimpse the spiritual graces through the alternate manifestations of sickness and health and the ups and downs of the economy that so affect our world—and sadly. For here, man—by reason of his artificiality, his fickleness, his shams and hypocrisies (all masks of his pseudo-self)—has created the illusions of life that make him think that God plays hide-and-seek with him. And we ourselves have set up the obstacles to the crystal mirror and the clear seeing of the Divine Image all around us.

"For now we see through a glass darkly..."

Let us invoke the Dispeller of Obstacles! Let us seek and find the true Teacher of our path and our spirit's calling!

For we would see him face to face. We would know him even as we are known of him.[5]

The Maha Chohan and the Seven Chohans of the Rays: The Nine Gifts of the Holy Spirit

The manifestations of God in Nature are woven in and through the Spirit-Matter cosmos by the Holy Spirit, whose Sons—known as the Seven Chohans of the Rays and the Maha Chohan, their hierarch—tutor our souls for receptivity midst the all-pervasive spiritual graces. To these servant-Sons in heaven, graduates of earth's schoolroom, Jesus introduced us many years ago.

The Master pointed to this teaching on Christ's universal Body which he gave to Paul to explain to us that in heaven the same Body which we all share with Lightbearers* on earth consists of angels and masterful beings, great spirits akin to our own, ensouling and directing the cosmic forces, all of whom 'embody'[6] some special office and function of the universal activity of the Mind of God.

The Lord showed us his emissaries who teach the godly on earth the path of individual Christhood on the seven rays and the seven chakras[7]—each ray being a Light-emanation of the Universal Christ concentrating particular gifts and graces and principles of self-awareness in the Logos that can be developed by the disciple through his life's calling.

He explained with perfect logic that the work of the Great White Brotherhood and all heavenly

---

*Lightbearer: The word means Christbearer, one who bears the Light which is Christ, one who bears the responsibility for Christhood in himself and others by defending the Truth and Honor of God; one who is anointed with the Christ consciousness and bears this enlightenment to all. The Lightbearer is the Keeper of the Flame whose motto must be "I AM my brother's keeper—I AM the keeper of the Light who is Christ in my brother."

hosts associated with it, including those whom they sponsor on earth, was and is to nurture the nascent divinity of every child of God while teaching him self-discipline and love for his sacred labor—which love kindles the soul to be in love with her Lord and to desire to glorify the full complement of his Light (Christ consciousness) in all her members.

He showed us that in this cycle of our cosmic history, earth's evolutions transiting from the Piscean age to the Aquarian age are scheduled to balance the threefold flame of the heart and to expand the attributes of the Trinity—Power, Wisdom and Love—through each of the seven rays as these rays are consciously focused in the seven chakras.

This work of the soul—and it is indeed *our* work, even as we are His handiwork—is the preparation that is necessary prior to receiving the very special spiritual and physical assignment with one's twin flame*—a mission drawn from the higher spheres of their divine plan (causal bodies) which must be fulfilled ere they are allowed to graduate (i.e., ascend) from earth's schoolroom.

Yes, we can learn, and we would do well to take the opportunity, from the Seven Chohans of the Rays, our mentors of the Spirit who lead us on the paths of righteousness for His name's sake[8]— I AM THAT I AM—toward our soul's receptivity to the gifts of the Holy Spirit.

In divine order, they are:

---

*the soul's masculine or feminine counterpart conceived out of the same white fire body, the fiery ovoid of the I AM Presence

I. El Morya, Chief of the Darjeeling Council of the Great White Brotherhood, statesman, poet, economist and saint, founder of The Summit Lighthouse and beloved Guru of the Messengers and chelas:
"Not my will but thine be done!"

II. Lord Lanto, sponsor of the Royal Teton Retreat and Council overseeing all systems of education and institutions of higher learning, exponent of the ancient wisdom made practical for the Western mind, facilitator of the new age path to Eastern traditionalists:
"Wisdom is the principal thing; therefore get wisdom and with all thy getting, get understanding!"

III. Paul the Venetian, divine artist conferring by the excellence of works the image of Christ unique to every soul, preparing lifestreams by Love's disciplines for the initiations of the Sacred Heart and the Tree of Life:
"Learn to love to do well and you shall!"

IV. Serapis Bey, hierarch of Luxor, initiator of the ascending ones in the applications of the sacred fire, architect of holy orders, the inner life, and golden-age cities, military disciplinarian of the forces of Light, Peace, and Cosmic Freedom:
"I AM the Guard!"

V. Hilarion, teacher of immortal Truth, Divine Science, all physical and metaphysical branches of science and the healing arts; the eternal empiricist who brings the seeker to the initiatic path of the apostle Paul:

"And ye shall know the Truth, and the Truth shall make you free!"

VI. Lady Master Nada, the soul's advocate before the bar of divine justice, unifier of families and twin flames, qualifier of Love as ministration and service to every part of Life—a path of deeds prerequisite to self-mastery on the Ruby Ray:

"The servant is not greater than his Lord."

VII. Saint Germain, sponsor of the United States of America, Lord of the Seventh Ray and Age, alchemist of the sacred fire who comes bearing the gift of the violet flame of freedom for world transmutation:

"The Light of God never fails, and the Beloved Mighty I AM Presence is that Light!"

Tutoring the souls of humanity in the internalization of the Word and the Work of the LORD on each of the seven rays, these Ascended Masters are selected to hold their offices in the spiritual hierarchy of the planet by the Maha Chohan (his name means "Great Lord"), whose official title is Representative of the Holy Spirit. Also involved in the selection proceedings are the World Teachers Jesus Christ and Kuthumi; Lord Maitreya, representative of the Cosmic Christ; and the eight-member Karmic Board.* The Lord of the World, Gautama Buddha, seals their appointments with

---

*In 1993, Vairochana joined the Karmic Board as the eighth member.

the blessing of the Seven Holy Kumaras, who ensoul the seven rays of the seven spheres.

Each Chohan teaches the balance of the three-fold flame, the harmony of the four lower bodies* and the transmutation of personal and planetary karma through the qualities of his ray. Their function includes meeting the needs of humanity's ascent to God by means of the rainbow rays (the seven rays), which culminate in the white light and the Law of the One.

Thus, through the Seven Chohans and the entire Spirit of the Great White Brotherhood we find fulfilled the prophecy of the LORD through his scribe Mary Baker Eddy: "Divine Love always has met and always will meet every human need." Truly the heavenly hosts are the hands of God in action gaining Victory for human life every day.

For the seeker following in the footsteps of these representatives of Christ Truth, each step of self-mastery secured on one ray is gain on the other six rays, for the shaft of white light in the center of each ray is the unifier of them all. This shaft *is* the Law of the One in manifestation, even as the white-fire core of the seven flames and seven spheres corresponding to the seven rays is also their sun center—the unifying Holy Spirit of these Light-emanations of Cosmos itself.

The title *Chohan* means "Lord." The Chohan is therefore one who embodies the consciousness of the LORD—the I AM THAT I AM—who is the Lawgiver of the ray. The Word and Work of the

---

*the etheric, mental, emotional and physical bodies

Chohan (i.e., his 'Path') are the expressions of the authority he holds in the interpretation of the Law of the ray.

Thus we know this 'YAHWEH' of the ray, this individualization of the God flame, by his outpicturing of the ray in the outplaying of events. And when we ask the beloved Chohan, "Who art thou? What is thy name?" the answer comes back— "I WILL BE WHO I WILL BE: Know the LORD, and you will know me as I AM one in Him in the stream of history and in the cosmic cycles: WHAT I HAVE SPOKEN, I HAVE SPOKEN. I Will Be Who I Will Be."

The Chohan, or Lord, of the Ray is also the authority of the path of Christic initiation leading the children of the Light who are joint-heirs with Christ[9] to their full Sonship through the incarnation of God's Word "on" (in the frequency of) the ray. In this role the Chohan bears the veneration "Guru" to the chelas advancing on his Path; he is fully the Dispeller of Darkness on behalf of his chelas by his Light-incarnation of the ray. Always he is the glorifier of the Divine Mother and the Trinity through the ray, even as he is the God flame of the ray personified in his service as Judge and Advocate before, and on behalf of, the people.

Truly, the authority of the Lord of the Ray vested in his mantle derives from his attainment of the Cosmic Christ consciousness in the Light frequency of his ray of service *and* from the grace of God who is "a rewarder of them that diligently seek him."[10]

As the Representative of the Holy Spirit, the Maha Chohan embodies the white light of all the rays. He teaches the sevenfold balance of the rays of the Seven Mighty Elohim, which in turn manifest upon the brow of the initiate as a crown of crystal light when that God-mastery of the seven rays is reached.

The Maha Chohan is a very present help to all who call to him. Because of his pledge to all mankind "I am keeping the flame for you until you are able," the Maha Chohan is called the Keeper of the Flame. He is the endower of Christ-mastery through the disciplines of right choice and right action—patterned after the eightfold path of Lord Gautama Buddha, which parallels the path taught and demonstrated by Jesus Christ.

These disciplines are accomplished through the mastery of free will, of the desires and the desire body, and of the path of the Sacred Heart and the Ruby Ray* as the initiate balances the threefold flame and attains equilibrium in the white light of the seven rays in his chakras. Engaging in service to Community—the world body of Lightbearers—by the engagement of one's forces, body, mind and soul, is the means to accomplish this goal.

---

*The path of the Ruby Ray is the path of perfecting the soul through the initiations of love. It includes the initiations of sacrifice, surrender, selflessness, and service.

Finally, the Maha Chohan prepares the Christed one for the empowerment by the LORD, the Mighty I AM Presence, of "the all power in heaven and in earth." Conferred through Maitreya, this initiation was acclaimed by our Lord and Saviour when he gave the great commission to his disciples:

All power is given unto me in heaven and in earth.

Go ye therefore, and teach all nations, baptizing them in the name of the Father, and of the Son, and of the Holy Ghost:

Teaching them to observe all things whatsoever I have commanded you: and, lo, I AM with you alway, even unto the end of the world.[11]

Truly, the key to Christhood through loving obedience to Father and Son is fulfilled in the disciple's acceptance of Jesus' calling to be a mediator of the Word and Work of the LORD. Mirroring His consciousness that all might see His reflected image, the disciple is readying himself to receive the chakra initiations of the Holy Spirit given by the hand of the Maha Chohan through the Seven Chohans according to the degrees of the seven rays.

These initiations are the measured steps and stages of the soul's preparation to receive and put on the graces of the nine gifts—first as a bridal veil, her pure conception of the quality, virtue, and vibration of each gift; and then as the wedding garment, the full awareness and infilling of the flame of the gift and its application in her ministrations to life.

The Seven Chohans acquaint her with the powers, principalities and angelic hosts of the nine gifts of the Holy Spirit as she diligently applies herself to the putting on of the graces, even as each gift bestowed is beautified by her special qualification of the rays.

While this training is taking place, the Maha Chohan strengthens the fibers of the spirit in his role as counselor, comforter and enlightener, laying firm foundations for the rainbow spheres to descend in concentric rings of Light, coalescing the aura of the causal body around the central sun of the heart chakra here below, as Above. Tenderly the Great Lord shows each bride of Christ how to fill in the rough places and make them plain[12] for the mirroring of the Holy Spirit's healing presence to all life.

And for those who have the understanding of the Inner Light (to use a Quaker term), we will say that the bestowal of the nine gifts is, by definition, the transfer of the initial matrix of *the power of the three-times-three* which the disciple must learn to wield, enhancing it through the balanced threefold flame and the Science of the Spoken Word.*

As Paul would not have his converts to Christ ignorant of the spiritual gifts *(pneumatika)* conferred by the Holy Ghost, so we would not have you who would study the Lost Teachings of Jesus

---

*i.e., using the power of the spoken Word through decrees, affirmations, prayers and mantras to invoke God's light for constructive change

that are being brought to the fore by all the Ascended Masters remain in ignorance of the law involving the conveyance of spiritual gifts. Listen again to the Christ-anointed apostle:

Now concerning spiritual gifts, brethren, I would not have you ignorant.

Ye know that ye were Gentiles [aliens to the Spirit of Christ], carried away unto these dumb idols [Nephilim gods and their mechanization (robotic) man], even as ye were led.

Wherefore I give you to understand that no man speaking by the Spirit of God calleth Jesus accursed: and that no man can say that Jesus is the Lord, but by the Holy Ghost.

Now there are diversities of gifts, but the same Spirit. And there are differences of administrations, but the same Lord. And there are diversities of operations, but it is the same God which worketh all in all.

But the manifestation of the Spirit is given to every man to profit withal.

For to one is given by the Spirit the *word of wisdom*; to another the *word of knowledge* by the same Spirit; to another *faith* by the same Spirit; to another the gifts of *healing* by the same Spirit;

To another the *working of miracles*; to another *prophecy*; to another *discerning of spirits*; to another *divers kinds of tongues*; to another the *interpretation of tongues*:

But all these worketh that one and the selfsame Spirit, dividing to every man severally as he will.[13]

And so, we come to the Chohans, who are also mirrors reflecting to us from the ascended state, as well as from their past lives, the image of Christ made clear through their accomplishments on each of the seven rays, or paths, to God. For theirs are the gifts of the Holy Spirit. Heart to heart we would learn of them and their transfer of the spiritual graces by which our souls should also be adorned. For the Beloved said: "My grace is sufficient for thee..."[14]

Let us embark, then, upon a journey of discovery through the causal bodies of the Seven Chohans. As our vessel ventures forth upon the stream of their consciousness, we will pull the charts of their missions, examining their karmic circumstance in the recurrent cycles where they have been the lights of history.

We will enter into vignettes of their lives taken from forgotten ages on legendary continents and civilizations buried in the sands of time or beneath the seas. For we would understand the making of a Chohan, why they were chosen to administer the gifts and graces of the LORD's Spirit, and learn of them the path of our soul's preparation to be the bride of Christ.

From this introduction to the heart and spirit of the Noble Seven we move on to an inner

THE MAHA CHOHAN AND THE SEVEN CHOHANS AND THE GIFTS OF THE HOLY SPIRIT

Ray	Master	Retreat	Gift
I	El Morya	Darjeeling, India	Faith in God's Will Word of Wisdom
II	Lord Lanto	Grand Teton, Wyoming	Word of Wisdom Word of Knowledge
III	Paul the Venetian	Southern France Temple of the Sun, New York	Discerning of Spirits
IV	Serapis Bey	Luxor, Egypt	Working of Miracles
V	Hilarion	Crete, Greece	Healing
VI	Nada	Saudi Arabia	Diverse Kinds of Tongues Interpretation of Tongues
VII	Saint Germain	Transylvania, Romania Table Mountain, Rocky Mts.	Prophecy Working of Miracles
IX All Rays Law of the One	Maha Chohan	Ceylon (Sri Lanka)	Free Will, Threefold Flame Initiation of the Chakras All Power in Heaven and in Earth

To facilitate the student's progressive perception of the rays, the Chohans, their retreats, and their initiatic path in the acquiring and mastery of the gifts of the Holy Spirit, we offer this chart for easy reference.

knowing and love of the best of Friends earth's experience has allowed us.

Eastward ho! The Mahatma of the Himavat awaits.

El Morya, Chohan of the First Ray
Gifts of Faith in God's Will
and of the Word of Wisdom

El Morya has served in numerous embodiments as a ruler of men, monarchs and nations, becoming thereby an expert in economics and the affairs of state, in the psychology of power in the human psyche, hence in its outworking in the politics of personal and international relations.

Through the initiations of his individual path of Christhood, this beloved Master of the Himalayas has acquired a quintessential devotion to the will of God—a virtue for which he is supremely adored and trusted by his chelas and for which he was twice canonized by the Roman Church. All of this and more has qualified him preeminently to hold the office of Chohan of the First Ray.

Come! Let us trace the image of this soul in his life as Akbar, greatest of the Mogul* emperors. This will provide us with a study in the correct use and mastery of the blue ray of power as it was focused through the blueprint of his life.

Akbar established an empire that spanned a large part of India, Afghanistan, and modern Pakistan and made him the richest and most powerful

*An Indian Muslim of or descended from one of several conquering groups of Mongol, Turkish, and Persian origin; especially the sovereign of the empire founded in India by the Moguls in the sixteenth century.

monarch on earth. Born in 1542 in Sind, he ruled wisely for fifty years, exercising a tolerance and an enlightenment astounding in one descended from the line of Tamerlane and Genghis Khan. (But then we already know that more than human genes make up our true self—indeed more than human genes could ever convey.) Distinctly apart from his ancestors, Akbar has been described by a leading historian as "one of the few successful examples of Plato's philosopher-king."[15]

His genius was apparent in military, religious, and social affairs as well as in his ability to rule once he had established his empire—a quality lacking in his forebears. Instead of crushing the conquered Hindus, he brought them into positions of government; he even took two Hindu princesses as wives. He abolished the practice of enslaving prisoners of war and of prejudicial acts against Hindus and set up an efficient and fair system of administration, tax collection, and justice.

All of this Akbar did because he believed he was the divinely appointed ruler of all the peoples of his realm and that he must deal with them equitably, regardless of their religion or race. Thus he is known as the father of religious tolerance in India and his legacy persists to this day.

However, to bring to his people peace and prosperity was not enough: Akbar would bring them to a higher spirituality. Accordingly, he took upon himself a seven-year study of the world's religions, whereupon he concluded that all of them contained limitations, prejudice, and superstition. So, true to temperament and the zeal of his calling, he set about establishing his own universal religion with himself at its head! For tenets he drew upon whatever good he had found in the belief systems of his day and he called it Din-i-Ilahi, "divine faith," or Tauhid-i-Ilahi, "divine monotheism."

But as for his doctrine-bound subjects, Akbar's innovation placed his person too close to the divinity—too close for comfort. Members of Din-i-Ilahi would greet one another with the words *"Allāhu Akbar,"* meaning "God is great," and the reply was *"Jalla Jalāluhu,"* meaning "resplendent is his splendor." But *Allāhu Akbar* could also mean "Akbar is God," and the response would then apply to Akbar himself. This was insupportable!

Since the Mogul emperor did not force adherence to his new religion, few joined it. And, although the nation basked in the glory of his reign, after his passing the empire declined. The Light of Akbar was no longer the Light of India, for neither his sons nor his followers nor his people had captured the spark of God's will that burned in the heart of their leader.

Tracing his footsteps back through the desert sands and oases to the advanced civilization of Sumer c. 2100 B.C., we discover the keystone in the arch of El Morya's past lives: Abraham, great 'prince' of the Chaldees[16] and father of the Hebrew nation to whom the LORD said, "I AM the Almighty God; walk before me, and be thou perfect.

And I will make my covenant between me and thee, and will multiply thee exceedingly.... And thou shalt be a father of many nations."[17]

And so the seed of the Lightbearers—descended through him and the twelve tribes, now Christed ones reborn—are his spiritual progeny, a lineage continuous by the Guru-chela relationship they share with the God Presence of Abraham, Isaac and Jacob—for flesh and blood alone could not contain it.

As Melchior, this Master Morya, who pens his initial "M" with three dots, came with the wise men of the East, Balthazar and Caspar (known today as the Masters Kuthumi and Djwal Kul), following the signs of the stars and the inner calling of the Christ all the way (historically speaking) from Ur of the Chaldees to Bethlehem.

Reappearing in the fifth century as Arthur, King of the Britons, warrior and guru of the mystery school at Camelot, he guarded the flame of the inner teachings, instilling the quest for the Holy Grail by triumph over tyrants and the greatest tyrant of them all: that idolatrous carnal mind. His lessons in "might for right" were an exercise in the qualified use of the power of the will of God by the standard-bearers of Christ's mission, for and on behalf of the people—always.

Thus, under King Arthur the chivalry of knighthood, side by side with fair maidenhood to Motherhood, portrayed the ideals of twin flames united in Love for the defense of Truth. Endued with piety and a genuine concern for those of lowly estate, these keepers of the flame of Camelot endured tasks and tests which included exorcising dragons, giants and demons and battling wicked kings, bastards and female enchantresses.

Throughout their quest these initiates were balancing karma on a path foreknown—of individual excellence in Christhood leading to the inner unfoldment of the mysteries of the Holy Grail and true self-knowledge: "I AM the Grail."

In the end as the shadows fell upon the once and future mystery school, the wounded Arthur, having fought his last, was heard (as recalled by Tennyson) to breathe these words to Sir Bedivere from the barge where he lay dying:

The old order changeth, yielding place to new,
And God fulfils himself in many ways,
Lest one good custom should corrupt the world.
Comfort thyself; what comfort is in me?
I have lived my life, and that which I have done
May He within himself make pure! but thou,
If thou shouldst never see my face again,
Pray for my soul. More things are wrought by prayer
Than this world dreams of. Wherefore, let thy voice
Rise like a fountain for me night and day.
For what are men better than sheep or goats
That nourish a blind life within the brain,
If, knowing God, they lift not hands of prayer
Both for themselves and those who call them friend?
For so the whole round earth is every way

Bound by gold chains about the feet of God.
But now farewell. I am going a long way
With these thou seest—if indeed I go—
For all my mind is clouded with a doubt—
To the island-valley of Avilion;
Where falls not hail, or rain, or any snow,
Nor ever wind blows loudly; but it lies
Deep-meadow'd, happy, fair with orchard lawns
And bowery hollows crown'd with summer sea,
Where I will heal me of my grievous wound.[18]

Sic transit gloria mundi. Thus passes the glory of this world. Enter the glory of the next.

Reentering the familiar lists in the twelfth and sixteenth centuries, the soul of Arthur, who with tender words and gifts of love so touched the heart of a world forever, served as chief advisor and conscience of English kings Henry II and Henry VIII in the persons of Thomas Becket and Thomas More. The twice-born Henry twice elevated him to the role of Lord Chancellor and twice martyred him for obstructing his ambitions.

Lastly, Morya was poet and prince—poet laureate of Ireland Thomas Moore and Rajput prince of India in the nineteenth century. He seems also to have once occupied time and space as Prince Mori Wong of Koko Nor, having alluded to this unknown Chinese figure without a hint of a historical context.

In these and other lives he qualified himself for his future role as Lord of the First Ray. And all who

anticipate his return as the once and future king—
Jew and Christian, Moslem, Hindu and Buddhist
alike, calling Abraham! Arthur! Akbar!—have today
the opportunity to know him as the Master Teacher
of chelas on the path of God's will.

Enfired by his ever-present goodwill, these
devotees know that they must rise to emulate his
example in assuming responsibility for leadership
roles in all fields. In Morya's presence they are
able once again to capture the vision and make the
sacrifices crucial to the survival of a viable existence
on planet earth.

If this world has a dearth of knights, heroes,
statesmen, saints and poets, it does not have a
dearth of Teachers. Among them standing tall is
the chiefest of them all, whose title is Chief of the
Darjeeling Council of the Great White Brotherhood: El Morya Khan, our most beloved Guru
who faithfully brought us to the diamond heart of
God's will in Christ, in Buddha, in the Mother and
in all the luminaries of history.

Devoted friend of Lightbearers in every religion, race and creed, formidable enemy of serpents
who have inveigled themselves into the govern-
ments, economies, and religious orders of East and
West, champion of the people, inspiration and
verve of kings, rulers, advocates and presidents, he
is indisputably the chela's "man for all seasons."

Without Morya's godly person and presence the
universe would suffer a cruel vacancy, our hearts
a void unspeakable, and the earth should have missed

the sparkle of one so initiated by the sapphire star of God's holy will: *"Allāhu Akbar... Jalla Jalāluhu!"*

Appropriately and to the great blessing of devotees of all faiths, El Morya initiates souls in the stepping stones of the path that leads to the Holy Spirit's bestowal of the gifts of *faith in God's will* and the *word of wisdom.* He is ever the instrument of the Father and the fearsome Comforter. Sharper than a two-edged sword, his word is the extension of the Lawgiver who sent forth His First Ray in the beginning as His will to be in manifest form—the crystallization of the God flame—by faith...

> And by faith Abraham, when he was called to go out into a place which he should after receive for an inheritance, obeyed; and he went out, not knowing whither he went.
>
> By faith he sojourned in the land of promise, as in a strange country, dwelling in tabernacles with Isaac and Jacob, the heirs with him of the same promise:
>
> For he looked for a city which hath foundations, whose builder and maker is God.
>
> Through faith also Sara herself received strength to conceive seed, and was delivered of a child when she was past age, because she judged him faithful who had promised.
>
> Therefore sprang there even of one, and him as good as dead, so many as the stars of the sky in multitude, and as the sand which is by the sea shore innumerable.[19]

As Akbar, this original model of First Ray achievers was convinced that the course he set for his nation was the will of God. With single one-pointedness, he acquired the penetrating wisdom to strip the layers of misinterpretation from the ecclesiasticism of the times and to bring forth the wisdom of the Word as God—he was certain—had intended it to be. He was thorough and exacting both of himself and others as he endeavored to deal wisely and judiciously in the affairs of state.

And so it was in each of his embodiments: increasing in the power of these gifts as he exercised them, he grew in grace and evolved to a masterful understanding of the dynamics of the First Ray.

Morya's sensitivity to the individual, his respect, honor and deference to the God flame of the One within the one, was and is the key to his love for the will of God expressed individually in all of His handiwork. His profound understanding of the soul on the path of God-realization drawn from many a round in earth's schoolroom is brought out in his dictations and fond notes to his chelas which extol the word of wisdom perceived through faith in God's will.

These have been published in *The Sacred Adventure, The Chela and the Path, Morya: The Darjeeling Master speaks to his chelas on the Quest for the Holy Grail,* and bound volumes of *Pearls of Wisdom,* weekly letters from the Ascended Masters to their chelas dictated to the Messengers and published by The Summit Lighthouse since 1958.

Morya is the singular Friend for whom everyone he has befriended (excepting evildoers) has felt a special loyalty and commitment. As Abraham he was counted the Friend of God, who placed such stock in his chelaship and the purity of his heart that the LORD did not impute his sins to him.[20] He was the best friend Henry II and VIII ever had and lost, and to this day he is the friend of every Briton and of generations who have continued to benefit from his policies on the Indian subcontinent.

And his enemies? They too were bound to respect him—even to admire if not himself, then his sense of justice and fair play.

Above all, he is the staunchest of friends at court a chela could ever have. No one loves us more. As a brother he has picked us up in our soul's nakedness and properly clothed us in robes of disciplined whiteness, presentable and acceptable to meet our God and our Saviour Jesus Christ.

By 1898, Morya had fulfilled the requirements for his ascension and then some. As an unascended Master, known as the Master M. of the Himalayas, he had sponsored the Theosophical Society—H. P. Blavatsky, Col. H. S. Olcott and early heralds of the new age—with Koot Hoomi, Serapis Bey, the Master R., Saint Germain and others of the mahatmas.

In his etheric retreat over Darjeeling, India, called the Temple of Good Will, situated among the pines on the slopes of the Himalayas, he holds classes in God-government and the path of personal Christhood through the soul's blueprint in the will of God. Let us go, then, to El Morya's retreat and sit in on one of his famous fireside chats...

Traveling in our etheric bodies, we enter the library and take our seats in cushioned chairs before a crackling pine-log fire. We look up and the Master is seated in his favorite chair before us.

He begins to weave the story of the Brotherhood's work on earth, of battles fought for the sake of nations—or of one single soul. Of the triumphs and failures of our lifestreams and earth's evolutions.

He tells of the aims of the Brotherhood at Darjeeling whose credo is "I will," their desire only to see men free from self-limitation, narrow-mindedness, and the ego-centered consciousness of the synthetic self. And he challenges us to become chelas of the will of God.

"Here at Darjeeling we offer a crash program in chelaship and initiation on the Path for those who are willing to follow implicitly the demands of their own Christ Self and to respond with a flame that leaps and with eyes that sparkle with the kindling fires of soul discernment."[21]

Many have passed through the doors of Darjeeling. "We have entertained the world's statesmen in our retreat and we have received the humble chela. We have received all whose love for the will of God has been greater than the love for the will of the lesser self."[22] He speaks of those who come to the retreat for counsel—souls "who serve in the govern-ments of the nations, who serve as teachers and scientists and musicians, and those who control the flow of the will of God that is power, that is the abundance of supply."

Now we hear the sound of an ancient bell intoning, and the Master explains, "It is a call to the humble the world around, to the servants of the will of God, and to the avant-garde who would carry civilization forward into a new age. Morya sum-mons chelas of the sacred fire who would become adepts, followers who would become friends of Christ, exponents of the word of living Truth, imitators of the Master, and finally the heart, head, and hand of our cosmic retinue....

"The path that offers much requires much. As you say in the world, you get what you pay for. The price is high, but then you are purchasing the ultimate reality."[23]

He pauses, then begins to speak more force-fully, cautioning: "Let it be made clear at the beginning that all who read the words of the Ascended Masters and all who hear our word are not necessarily counted as chelas of our will. Let it be quite clear that there are requirements. As the chips of wood fly when the pines in the forest are cleared, so the winds of Darjeeling blow. Let the unworthy chela be cleared from our path. We clear for a noble purpose—the ennoblement of a cause and a race. Hierarchy has also said, 'Let the chips fall where they may.'"[24]

He speaks of the problems burdening the world, and of the dire need for dedicated hearts to assist it. "The weight of world karma has never been greater. The Divine Mother intercedes before the Court of the Sacred Fire on behalf of the children of God that the descent of their own karma might not destroy the very platform of their evolution. As Thoreau said, 'What is the use of a house if you haven't got a tolerable planet to put it on?' So we say, what is the use of the path of initiation if the planetary platform can no longer sustain its evolutions?"[25]

With this unsettling thought, Morya bids us farewell.

"I thank you for your attention, I thank you for your love for the Light, I thank you for your presence here, and I ask you to remember that I am a cosmic being, that I am an Ascended Master, that I am your friend so long as you adore that will. For there is no other power in the universe that can act except the will of God, which goodness surrounds you now. . . .

"May the angelic hosts and the ascended hosts surround you always and keep your goings and comings until you enter that state of consciousness equal to my own. And I care not if you surpass it; for in adoration to my own divinity, I give all that I am to the service of the Light—to the service that raises, that lifts, that transmutes, and makes hearts reverent, happy, and God-free.

"Thank you, and good night."[26]

El Morya reminds us in parting that he waits for the knock of the chela upon his door. Angelic hosts now arrive to escort us back to our physical bodies after our sojourn in the etheric realm. And we are left with grateful hearts: What a privilege to know such a one as this!

To become worthy of him as the Guru of our soul, to extol his virtues, to serve his mission, to combine our forces with his own for a planetary revolution in Higher Consciousness — to this, to all of this his presence has inspired us. Our spirits need no other ennobling than to know him as he is.

In the strength of his vision of the future we discover the will to be Godlike.

Lord Lanto, Chohan of the Second Ray
Gifts of the Word of Wisdom
and of the Word of Knowledge

Lord Lanto, great light of ancient China, now serves as one of America's foremost savants. The devotion to the *word of wisdom* and the *word of knowledge* of this quietly wise sage and fiery-eyed bodhisattva has truly qualified him to initiate the evolutions of earth in both gifts of the Holy Spirit.

Chohan of the Second Ray, he is an Ascended Master in whose presence the sublimity of the Mind of God can be touched and known, by portion, as he teaches the path of Americans — Yes! a Chinese master teaching Americans the ancient way of universal Christhood that made the golden age of China great, that comes down from Maitreya, the

Coming Buddha who has come,[27] and is brought to the fore by the hierarch of the Royal Teton Retreat— another master from China, more famous than his Guru, the Ascended Master Lord Confucius himself!

Lanto conducts classes at the Royal Teton Retreat, congruent with the Grand Teton range in Wyoming, where the paths of all the Seven Chohans are taught. It is an ancient focus of great Light where the seven rays of the Elohim and Archangels are enshrined. The Lords of Karma, Gautama Buddha, and all members of the Great White Brotherhood frequent this gathering place of the Ascended Masters and their disciples while also maintaining the specialized functions of their own private retreats.

A master of sages and philosophers, Lord Lanto teaches us the path of attainment through enlightenment, definition, and dominion in the crown chakra. He gained his mastery while studying under Lord Himalaya, Manu of the Fourth Root Race, whose Retreat of the Blue Lotus is hidden in the mountains that bear his name.

Electing to use the yellow plume to enfold the hearts of all mankind, Lanto dedicated himself to the perfectionment of the evolutions of this planet through Cosmic Christ illumination. The golden flame he bears is charged with his momentum of God-victory for the youth of the world.

In his basic lectures, he invites to the Royal Teton Retreat "all who pursue Wisdom, though Her veils and garb be varied as She passes through all levels of learning—all who seek Her knowledge as that true knowledge which comes forth from the fertile Mind of the Creator."

"Come to Wisdom's fount," he says, recalling the cry of Isaiah—"Ho, every one that thirsteth, come ye to the waters..."[28]—"and make ready while there is yet time for you to become all that Wisdom has held in store for you throughout the ages."[29]

In the splendor of the Royal Teton, conclaves attended by tens of thousands of lifestreams from every continent who journey there in their finer bodies are held. In addition there are smaller classes and tutorials. It is the initial retreat of the Great White Brotherhood to which the neophyte may ask to be taken.

Through our experiences with Jesus and Saint Germain in this retreat in the heart of America's Rocky Mountains, we can see that the ties that bind the seed of Light from the Far East to the Far West run deep. And what with the Lady Kuan Yin, Goddess of Mercy, serving on the Karmic Board (which convenes here at the solstices) and the annual New Year's Eve and Wesak addresses of the Lord of the World, Gautama Buddha, broadcast from the great council hall (as from Shamballa and a valley in the Himalayas), complementing the service of Jesus and Saint Germain—what with the golden flame of illumination and the Chinese-green flame for the precipitation of the abundant Life focused here—the souls of all nations and planetary systems are at One and at Home.

Let us go there!

It is now New Year's Eve, when Masters from around the world come for a great convocation and solemn council. We arrive early—just as the sun is setting, tinting the snowy peaks of the Grand Teton a golden pink.

Lord Lanto greets us warmly as we bow to him and welcomes us to this ancient palace of spiritual splendor.

While we await the New Year's Eve address of beloved Gautama Buddha, we go to a massive etheric amphitheater where tens of thousands of unascended souls are gathered. Lanto leads us out of the great council hall, down the corridor to a door which opens into the starry night where tier upon tier of seats rise from a central stage. The amphitheater was recently constructed, he says, for the "Lightbearers who, on earth and in America today, are a part of the body of believers who are seeking the LORD God in churches and not finding him in doctrine or dogma."[30]

He takes the lectern at the center of the platform and begins to teach these Truth-starved souls:

"... Let us understand that illumination and its flame must not be snuffed out in this land—as youth are in delirium and their senses dulled by drugs and rock, and think of no other thing but lyrics that take them down and down again to a lower level and therefore deprive them of the blossoming of the yellow fire of the crown! Let us realize that there is a movement, a force—and

I must say, it is the tremendous force of 'hell' itself moving across the land to take a stand against the Light—against the wisdom of the heart!

"Who shall pursue the fount of wisdom? Who shall be able to rise and mount the ladder of the chakras when these drugs and the downward-spiraling beat does take the youth even beneath their feet to subterranean levels of hellish fires of fallen ones—who themselves long lost their wings, blackened now with other things, and therefore dwell in places of insects' origins and biting and stinging things that ought to be no more but are—fed as they are by mass ignorance?

"I come to pierce the veil of ignorance!... If I had my say, I would tell you that unless the flame of illumination be understood as the apex and culmination of all of life and the key to immortality, unless it be revered, all else must go down.

"Think upon it, blessed hearts. One may tell you the law; but without the understanding, did you always obey it? Nay. It requires a teaching, a reasoning of the heart, a motive that comes through understanding and understanding alone. You may know the truth, but the truth that sets you free is the truth that is understood by illumination's flame....

"I am your teacher, friend, and mentor of old; and I have come to claim you once again. At any hour of the day or night when you would be free of the bondage of mortality, call to me and I will send forth that golden ray to quicken, to awaken, to hallow the sacred ground beneath your feet made holy by your endeavor to be the fullness of the God flame."[31]

To grateful applause, Lord Lanto exits the platform and excited whispers fill the audience. It is now nearly midnight and Gautama Buddha is seated on a golden throne, the Lords of Karma standing beside him. The Lord of the World is ready to address the members of the Brotherhood gathered in the great council hall as well as invited guests who fill the amphitheater. These see clearly through the now-transparent mountain wall directly into the hall where we have been ushered to our seats for the event.

A hush descends over the starlit amphitheater as he begins to speak. Soon the Seven Chohans rise, step forward, and bow, acknowledging their obeisance to the God flame. They present a scroll to Lord Gautama and the Lords of Karma.

These presiding Masters open the scroll and read it; in a moment the Buddha looks up and explains that this is a request made by the Chohans to open universities of the Spirit in their respective retreats where thousands and tens of thousands of students may be summoned to attend courses in Ascended Master law.

He outlines the plan for those "who will diligently pursue the path of self-mastery on the seven rays systematically, mastering most especially the First and the Seventh Rays whereby they might establish the Alpha and the Omega of their identity—the will of God, the divine blueprint, the inner plan for twin flames—and immediately begin an action of personal and world transmutation" through the violet flame.[32]

Studies are to begin with El Morya at Darjeeling for a fourteen-day cycle, then a fortnight with Saint Germain at the Royal Teton Retreat. The student will alternate these periods between the two centers until he successfully passes certain levels and receives an opportunity to study with the other Chohans.

The Lord of the World announces that he and the Lords of Karma have approved this petition and that "in this hour it is formally granted."

The crowds in the amphitheater leap to their feet, cheering the dispensation as the mountains resound with the shouts of the people's acclamation. So great is the desire of their souls to attend the Mystery Schools of the Brotherhood!

This is a most opportune dispensation for the unification and enlightenment of the Lightbearers of the world. The Royal Teton Retreat thus becomes a launching pad for thousands of souls to reach the star of their own God Presence through the Teachings of the Ascended Masters. Here the I AM Race of all nations and kindreds and tongues are welcomed and they do gather nightly, for the Grand Teton is the sign of the rising SUN—the Spiritual Unity of Nations—to all Lightbearers whom Saint Germain has called, making himself heard like the town crier in every city, town, hamlet and home:

"Lightbearers of the world, unite!"

May they respond with the scientific statement of their universal religion taught by the Lords of the Seven Rays—and may it be Wisdom's smile that turns on the universal age.

Paul the Venetian, Chohan of the Third Ray Gift of the Discerning of Spirits

One problem which we can solve through the Holy Spirit—which we find to be one of the greatest problems of all—is our failure to penetrate the facades of friend and foe alike and thereby to determine what is real and what is unreal. This we can turn around through the exercise of the spiritual gift of *discerning of spirits.*

Oh no, we don't want you to get involved in looking at people with a view to deciphering just what makes them tick. We think this is a great error. Besides, what makes them tick in a worldly sense is not what makes them tick in a divine sense with the tick-tick-tick of infinity, which is a contact with the cosmic heartbeat.

The little outer signs that we find so similar in all people—these are not the things that we are interested in, for they are only the effects of larger causes that must engage our search for the science of Being. This which we're about is the removing of the mask by the Holy Spirit so that people can be healed by Love of their predilection for the doings of the pseudo-self.

It is Paul the Venetian, Chohan of the Third

Ray, who will tutor your soul in discerning the foul spirits of demons below and the fiery spirits of angels above, both of which may work through people according to their up-and-down moods and vibrations.

He will also teach you to "try the spirits, whether they are of God," as John admonished us to do, "because," as the apostle said, "many false prophets are gone out into the world."[33] And by the Holy Spirit he will show you how to exorcise those spirits if they are not of God and how to harness their forces if they are. This training, which prepares you for self-mastery through God's love, involves the initiations of the Ruby Ray under the Maha Chohan and Lord Maitreya and the ritual of exorcism taught by the Ancient of Days.[34]

In order to bind evil spirits in the name I AM THAT I AM, in the name Jesus Christ, you must establish a strong heart-tie to the Sacred Heart of beloved Jesus and to the Immaculate Heart of his Mother, Mary. It is essential that you develop a close working relationship with Archangel Michael and his legions of blue-flame angels as well as with the cosmic Mother-figure called Astrea, as you learn to wield the *sword* of the sacred *word* in giving dynamic decrees.*

Yet this you can learn. And this we do, for Jesus has taken us to Paul the Venetian's retreat on the etheric plane in southern France to study the spiritual skills involved, although currently the

_____
*a dynamic form of spoken prayer used by students of the Ascended Masters to direct God's light into individual and world conditions

Lord of the Third Ray is holding classes in the Temple of the Sun over Manhattan, the retreat of his spiritual Mother, the Goddess of Liberty. It is to this university of the Spirit that you may call to be taken for the development of the heart chakra on the Third Ray. Truly, this training awaits you, as do your Teachers—when you are ready.

"Paolo Veronese," as he was known in his last life as the Italian Renaissance painter (1528–1588), has taught us about sharpening the tools of the spiritual senses:

"What tremendous import there is in the development of the spiritual senses. The old senses must pass away to give place to the new. Transmutation, transcendence, and transfer all speak of translucence, even of transparency; for the idea of seeing through a glass darkly but then face to face is always the miracle of a moment when opacity yields to translucency and translucency to transparency. The thinning of the veil and the clarification of nebulous concepts together with their reduction to orderly simile will provide mankind a golden rule by which he may measure his doings—his goings and his comings—and his progress in a universal sense."[35]

The Master has promised an important initiation to those who come knocking at the door of his retreat, the Château de Liberté, ready for a greater increment of the love flame:

"I will take you by the hand and show you my castle. I will show you the works of art that have been brought forth by chelas unascended and ascended. And we will go through many rooms, and lastly I will take you to the room where there is that frame that hangs. In some cases it will be an empty frame, in some cases it will have a canvas in it. It will be your frame, the frame of your identity waiting for you to bring forth the genius of your soul. And when you see that frame, if it is empty, you will want to fill it.

"And so I will take you to that place, the *atelier* where you can work with other artisans who are learning the art of living Love by the discipline of the hand and the discipline of expression so that you can draw the image of your own Christ-perfection. And when it is the best that you have to offer, it will be placed in your frame."[36]

This is the essence of the path of the Lords of the Seven Rays—teaching us how to unfold the image of the Christ in all that we do. And you can make the call each night to go to their retreats in your finer bodies while you sleep to learn how to do just that. El Morya explains that you can adapt the following prayer as you call to be taken to one of the retreats of the Seven Chohans each night:

In the name of the Christ, my own Real Self, I call to the heart of the I AM Presence and to the angel of the Presence, to Archangel Michael and Beloved Kuan Yin, to take me in my soul and in my soul consciousness to the retreat of Paul the Venetian

in southern France (or to the Goddess of
Liberty's Temple of the Sun) according to
the direction of my Holy Christ Self and the
Maha Chohan.

I ask to receive the instruction of the
Law of Love and to be given the formula for
the victory of the Love flame within my
heart—especially as it pertains to the gift of
the discerning of spirits. And I ask that all
information necessary to the fulfillment of
my divine plan and that of my beloved twin
flame be released to my outer waking consciousness as it is required. I thank thee and
I accept this done in the full power of the
risen Christ. Amen.[37]

Serapis Bey, Chohan of the Fourth Ray
Gift of the Working of Miracles

Serapis Bey, Chohan of the Fourth Ray, was
a high priest in the ascension temple on Atlantis.
While other Masters with their circles of devotees
transported the various flames they guarded on the
continent to focuses across the earth, establishing
both etheric retreats and mystery schools adjacent
to temples built to the Divine Mother (wherein the
flames were still enshrined in the physical octave),
Serapis and his band, leaving Atlantis well before
the final cataclysm, bore the ascension flame to
Luxor, Egypt.

The hierophant tells us why, out of the seven,
he originally chose to serve on the white ray of the

Divine Mother: "When I was a chela determining on what ray I would serve, what ray I would preserve in the office of preserver of Life, I contemplated all, but I came to the light of purity, and I said—master of geometry that I was—'The shortest distance between two points, point A and B, is purity. Purity I shall be.'"[38]

To the students who make it to Luxor, Serapis introduces himself with characteristic directness: "I am the hierophant of Luxor, Retreat of the Ascension Flame. I am known among the Brotherhood as the disciplinarian, and among my disciples as the fiery Master, and among those who have rejected the disciplines of our retreat by various and sundry names."[39]

El Morya describes Serapis as "a Spartan if I ever saw one—whose fiery determination has saved many a soul from the mush of self-indulgence. His chelas reflect the fierceness of their Master as they are immovable in their dedication to purity focused as the Mother light in the base-of-the-spine chakra."[40]

The raising up of the sacred fire is accomplished through various techniques of mantra and Kundalini meditation. Serapis teaches that dynamic decrees as well as meditation combined with the visualization and acceleration of the white light and the violet flame in all of the chakras are very important keys to the integration of the soul faculties as well as the nine gifts of the Spirit within one's being.

And so we are told that after bearing the flame to Egypt, Serapis continued to reincarnate there for the perfecting of the Work, foregoing his own ascension until about 400 B.C. As Amenhotep III (reigned 1417–1379 B.C.), he constructed the physical temple that is at Luxor.

The temple is actually built to correspond to the outline of the human skeletal framework, traced according to anthropometrical methods and precisely proportioned. Its courtyards and rooms closely correspond to the body. As R. A. Schwaller de Lubicz, who spent over fifteen years studying its architecture, has said, "The Temple of Luxor is indisputably devoted to the Human Microcosm. This consecration is not merely a simple attribution: the entire temple becomes a book explaining the secret functions of the organs and nerve centers."[41]

In truth this temple displays the idea of the rebirth of the divine man based on his transformation through the universal Mother Principle. And to those who have eyes to see and ears to hear, the mysteries are unveiled. The Principle and Presence of the Mother in the matter body is taught by the Lord of the Fourth Ray as in metaphor he raises our consciousness to the plane of causation:

"Out of the Word is Mother and the Word is Mother and in this Word was the soundless sound that passing through her lips became the AUM of the creation. Thus the science of sound and the science of the Word are known in the white-fire core of the Fourth Ray. And Alpha stepped forth and Omega was the One and through her the beginning became the ending."

"For the sake of her children's restoration to the House of Spirit," he explains, "Omega entered the Matter universes. And our Dear Mother became one with the Matter cycles below even as She is in — for her Blessed Being constitutes — the Matter cycles Above. And now in the last days the Mother, even the Great Kali, strips from her own all violations of Her Matter Body by the dark ones.

"Therefore I give you this prayer to sustain you through the rigorous initiations of the Fourth Ray: 'Even so, come quickly, Dearest Mother, to liberate our souls forever from the bondage of the senses, the illusion of time and space and the violators of thy Word incarnate in our souls! Come, Blessed Mother, Come.'"

Thus we learn at our nightly class at Luxor that the Fourth Ray of Alpha and Omega embodies the quintessence of every other ray. It is the white on white which outlines Mother's many faces in all her sons and daughters.

In this bas-relief of white fire, Purity — and this is one of the many-virtued names of our Divine Mother — reveals a higher beauty and a truer harmony of Love in music and art, and a technology beyond any achieved through the applied sciences of today. This purity, Serapis says, is the fierce innocence of the Mother that reaches the "stars" (i.e., the fallen angels[42]) and with the laser beam of the Ruby Ray annihilates their star wars.

Immersed in the beauty and power of the Divine Mother, we are left in silent meditation to contemplate his closing words:

"And She is the All, and the sacred fire of the creation is both her servant and her Lord."

In addition to purity and the rituals of soul-purification, the qualities of the Fourth Ray of God's heart are the desire for the perfection of the inner patterns to be outpictured in the matter matrix and the desire for self-discipline under one's spiritual hierarch in order that one might attain the pristine goal.

Devotees of the Fourth Ray take delight in the architecture of the Matter cosmos, the music of the spheres, the science of sound and the precipitation of the Word, which also come under the guardian-ship of the mentors of the Fifth and Seventh Rays. These studious ones meditate upon the blueprint of the soul and its tracings upon the molecules of the four lower bodies. Out of mathematics, geometry, astronomy, astro- and nuclear physics, biochemis-try and the wonders of Divine Science mirrored in the physical sciences, they derive an inner satisfac-tion equal to none of communing with the Law of the One and the alchemy of the Word "made flesh."

Beloved Serapis, great initiate of the Mother flame, administers the gift of the *working of mir-acles*—Mother's miracles—to the Lightbearers of earth. This gift, in order to be received, requires utmost Love; for only Love begets self-discipline in the sacred fire that is neither brittle nor fanatical nor self-demeaning. The abundance of every good and perfect, miraculous gift of God is derived from the white light of the Mother, whose sacred fire breath is at the heart of every atom and sun center.

Intense devotion to the Presence of God will result in the natural bestowal of the gift of miracles. As Serapis has said, "In the past, many of the saints who levitated into the atmosphere did so by reason of the intensity of their magnetization of the energy of the God flame above. The floating into the air of these saints was an attest to their devout and intimate relationship with the God Presence."[43]

Serapis cautions against becoming enamored of the gifts that result from attainment on the Path. The ascension and the abilities attendant on the raising of the Kundalini fire must be desired ordinately, he says. Some desire them inordinately and resort to a haphazard use of various forms of yoga, when they could achieve the *siddhis*, i.e., powers, naturally by fulfilling the Seventh Ray requirements for the ascension.

For the daily application of the violet flame in dynamic decrees is the joyful noise made unto the LORD that purifies the aura and chakras, transmutes the records of karma—when combined with Community service—and facilitates the balancing of the threefold flame as the requirements of the path of personal Christhood are adhered to. Truly, the violet ray—as the highest light of the physical spectrum, bursting forth as the transmutative fires of the Holy Spirit—clears the way for the restoration of the white light of the Fourth Ray and its sacred fire in the soul and all her members.

Thus, ask to be taken to the violet flame room at Luxor as you set for yourself goals of acceleration on your Homeward path. Can't make a decision? Don't know which way to go? Or what to do with your life? Take up your copy of *The Science of the Spoken Word* and give daily "Ten for Transmutation." The ten decrees to the violet flame in this chapter may be said by you in multiples of nine times each as mantras of the Holy Spirit.

Establishing your violet flame session nightly before retiring and concluding with a call to Archangel Michael, Kuan Yin and the mighty Seraphim to take you to the heart of Luxor and the violet flame room will do much to focus your heart and mind one-pointedly to achieve the goals of your life which were set before you by Jesus or one of the servant-Sons in heaven prior to your soul's descent into embodiment.

The reason that such Seventh Ray rituals work is that the violet flame transmutes the records of karma and misqualified energies—the very substance of which blocks your vision and your decision-making. According to the law of cycles, only so much substance can be taken from you each day. And each day your decree momentum builds, and as it builds, your capacity to sustain the action of the violet fire in your four lower bodies increases by geometric proportion.

From his Ascension Temple, the beloved hierarch of Luxor initiates candidates for the ascension, assigning tutors to walk with their charges every missed step on the paths of the seven rays. This he does, stickler that he is, in cooperation with the other Chohans. And the line is drawn: the chela may not pass until he fulfills that neglected, long-forgotten or suppressed missed step. This process can be tedious and trying—more for the chela than the Master, I am certain!

Serapis Bey's methods of discipline are tailor-made for each candidate for the ascension. After an initial interview by himself or one of Twelve Adepts presiding in his mystery school, devotees who come to his retreat are assigned in groups of five or more to carry out projects with other initiates whose karmic patterns (graphically illustrated in their astrology) forecast the maximum friction between their lifestreams. This test must be given in order that they may choose to be or not to be centered in God. Soon it is clear that *all* idols of the tyrant self or karmic past must be surrendered if one is to merge with the confluent stream of the Law of the One.

Each group must serve together until they become harmonious—individually and as a cohesive unit of hierarchy—learning all the while that those character traits that are most offensive in

others are the polar opposite of their own worst
faults and that what one criticizes in another is apt
to be the root of his own misery.

Aside from this type of group dynamics, individuals are placed in situations (both in the retreat
and in their day-to-day activities) that provide them
with the greatest challenges, according to their
changing karmic patterns. In this course of Serapis
one cannot simply up and leave a crisis, a circumstance, or an individual that is not to his liking. He
must stand, face and conquer his own carnal mind
and misqualified energy by disciplining his consciousness in the art of nonreaction to the human
creation of others, even as he learns how not to be
dominated or influenced by his own human
creation.

When souls who have been placed in close
proximity precisely because they have rubbed each
other the wrong way for lifetimes have succeeded in
smoothening their rough places, finally preferring
God Harmony to all lesser gods of gosh awful tears
and tirades, they proceed to chambers of advanced
learning. Here in the presence of Serapis the alchemical secrets of the Tree of Life may at last be
made known to those who, weary of the world of
desire, have subdued the passions and polariza-
tions, conceding only to "be still and know that
I AM God."[44]

These, then, are ready to undergo the rigors
of initiation that will eventuate first in the soul's

alchemical marriage to the Holy Christ Self and then in the reunion with her God Presence and causal body through the ritual of the ascension.

Serapis has explained to us how important it is, especially in this Dark Cycle of the descent of earth's karma, that we the Lightbearers come to his etheric retreat at Luxor and strive to win our ascension both from inner levels and conscientiously on the outer, applying what we have learned "out of the body" in the performance of the daily tasks at hand: "For we count not one, but a number of ascensions each year as absolutely indispensable to the holding of the balance of Life upon earth."[45]

Before God, you may declare the ascension to be your goal at the conclusion of this life, and call to your Mighty I AM Presence that your divine plan might unfold and that you might indeed be found worthy to receive the initiations of the sacred fire and the Mother flame under Serapis Bey. Most assuredly, this call will compel an answer.

Hilarion, Chohan of the Fifth Ray
Gifts of Healing

The Ascended Master Hilarion, whether in the historical limelight as Jesus' apostle Paul or in his not so well-known final incarnation as Saint Hilarion, did not think it robbery to take upon himself the mantle of his Lord.[46] Overshadowed by Christ, he could do naught but perform healings in the manner of his Teacher.

Indeed, we know that Paul was privately tutored by the resurrected Son of God in preparation for his role as his apostle. He was personally sent as the Lord's ambassador to deliver his message to the world with a form and content that would go beyond that of the Gospelers. This message he set forth in epistles to the churches and in hundreds of sermons to the early Christians that have not been preserved as scripture.

Think of it! Paul not only took to himself the mantle of the Holy Spirit but he received the divine approbation of the Lord to wear it in his name. Paul had to have had the sense of his self-worth in Christ, which could only have been imparted to him by Jesus, in order to take on so mighty a mission—and succeed.

Because of Paul's all-consuming passion for the Lord's mission, Christianity has survived in a form that has prepared Christ's followers to receive the Lost Years, the Lost Teachings and the Lost Word as they are being restored today. Paul, by his example in putting on Christ Jesus, almost more than by his words, prefaces and anticipates John's vision of the Everlasting Gospel and the new heaven and the new earth.[47]

As we noted in Chapter 1, the fiery spirit of Hilarion performed, the Lord working through him, those works which equaled those of Jesus Christ. This testimony of his Sonship, had he proclaimed it in words rather than deeds, would have been considered blasphemous in his day even as it would in ours.

As a false theology denies the present potential of Sonship to every child of God, so too the works of a "Christed one," i.e., one anointed by the LORD, are frowned upon, lest by the very empiricism of the saints that false doctrine—stemming from Antichrist's deliberate misinterpretation of the "Only Begotten of the Father, full of Grace and Truth"—should be rendered of no use.

The soul of Paul was the recipient fully of the gifts of the Holy Spirit. In him were fulfilled the promises of our Lord: "He that believeth on me, the works that I do shall he do also; and greater works than these shall he do; because I go unto my Father..."[48]

Because none dare say it and none dare tell it, we say it and we tell it: You too can do the works of Jesus Christ, you too can become the fullness of that Christ which he became—if you submit yourselves unto his Law and his Love.

We read in Paul's letter to the Galatians how he did not receive his knowledge of Christ's message from the other Christians of the day:

The fact is, brothers, and I want you to realize this, the Good News I preached is not a human message that I was given by men, it is something I learned only through a revelation of Jesus Christ. You must have heard of my career as a practicing Jew, how merciless I was in persecuting the Church of God, how much damage I did to it, how I stood out among other Jews of my generation, and how enthusiastic I was for the traditions of my ancestors.

Then God, who had specially chosen me while I was still in my mother's womb, called me through his grace and chose to reveal his Son in me, so that I might preach the Good News about him to the pagans. I did not stop to discuss this with any human being, nor did I go up to Jerusalem to see those who were already apostles before me, but I went off to Arabia at once and later went straight back from there to Damascus.

Even when after three years I went up to Jerusalem to visit Cephas and stayed with him for fifteen days, I did not see any of the other apostles; I only saw James, the brother of the Lord, and I swear before God that what I have just written is the literal truth.

After that I went to Syria and Cilicia, and was still not known by sight to the churches of Christ in Judaea, who had heard nothing except that their onetime persecutor was now preaching the faith he had previously tried to destroy; and they gave glory to God for me.[49]

Whence cometh the Lord with his message? We know that Paul was called by Jesus and taken up in the spirit to the Master's etheric retreat in Arabia. Here, night after night and throughout the days of his sojourn his soul was tutored for his assignment to lay the foundation of the Church for the two-thousand-year Piscean dispensation.

As the Psalmist described this divine interchange that comes to the one who is called of the LORD—"The heavens declare the glory of God. . . . Day unto day uttereth speech, and night unto night sheweth knowledge"—so it was with Paul as he tarried with Jesus until he, too, could say:

> The law of the LORD is perfect, converting the soul: the testimony of the LORD is sure, making wise the simple.
> The statutes of the LORD are right, rejoicing the heart: the commandment of the LORD is pure, enlightening the eyes.
> The fear of the LORD is clean, enduring for ever: the judgments of the LORD are true and righteous altogether.[50]

Thus, by stages Paul put on the mantle of his Lord and accomplished his works as his instrument in healings, miracles, prophecies and fiery conversions. This was the true path Christ meant his apostles to walk—as Hilarion once told us:

> If the light that is in thee be filled with the momentum of God and if the gears of the chakras be oiled with the holy oil of Gilead, then by the very vibration of your life you can intensify the currents of God,

you can be one with God, you can be God incarnate as Jesus Christ was.

This is what I learned from him as he became my inner and outer Guru. This is what I understood: that I, too, could become the Christ as the instrument of the Saviour— that where I walked he would walk, that where I stood he would heal, that where I spoke he would speak. This I learned, and yet I understood yet the unworthiness of the lesser self in the state of sin that is made worthy by grace, by transmutation, by fiery baptism and by the balancing of karma in service to Life.[51]

The gifts of the Holy Spirit that Hilarion brings today as Chohan of the Fifth Ray are the *gifts of healing.* "The lost chord of religion," Hilarion says, "is the science of healing. Rebellion upon earth in the hearts of men has kept them from receiving the gift of this divine art. How well I know it, for I was a rebel myself—a rebel against the Christ, a rebel against his cause."[52]

In addition to the light of healing he bears, Hilarion organizes legions of the LORD's hosts for the protection of the Logos, the logic of the Divine Mind in man, by the flame of Truth. And he invites all who espouse the cause of Truth to come in their finer bodies to attend temple training and classes in his Temple of Truth at the isle of Crete.

This retreat of the Great White Brotherhood

is located on the etheric plane at the site of the original Temple of Truth where vestal virgins once kept the flame of Truth as oracles of the Divine Mother beloved Vesta and the Muses. There, along with Pallas Athena, Goddess of Truth and member of the Karmic Board, the Lord of the Fifth Ray teaches the path of mastery through science, truth, healing and the immaculate conception of God.

Hilarion is also concerned with helping atheists, agnostics, skeptics and others empirically centered who, often through no fault of their own but thanks to the blind leaders of the blind in Church and State, have become disillusioned with life and religion.

"The agnostics cry out today against the trivia of this age and quite frequently they take a stand for principles of the Light," Hilarion says. "The atheists deny while the agnostics struggle to see. In our temple at Crete, we have determined to bring new meaning to life through the avenues of science and to stop the perpetual harassment of those forward-moving individuals who seek to assuage some measure of human grief"[53] — even though they may not conform to some people's version of Truth or science or religion.

For all are mounting toward the goal. Until the summit is reached, no man's perspective is complete. Some aiming for the top do not have the goal in sight — other mountains of conflicting desire obscuring the One.

Let us help one another to know Truth in true compassion for the lame, the halt and the blind— which we all are or have at one time been.

The Lady Master Nada, Chohan of the Sixth Ray Gifts of Diverse Kinds of Tongues and of the Interpretation of Tongues

Assisting Saint Germain in his "great gathering of the elect" who will serve with him in the cause of world freedom is beloved Nada, Chohan of the Sixth Ray. This Ascended Lady Master also serves on the Karmic Board as the representative of the Third Ray.[54] Through both offices she teaches Jesus' path of personal Christhood through ministration and service to life.

On Atlantis Nada served as a priestess in the Temple of Love. The etheric counterpart of this temple, which is designed after the pattern of a rose, is centered above New Bedford, Massachusetts. Each petal is a room, and in the center there burns the flame of Divine Love—tended by brothers and sisters of the Third Ray for the healing of earth's evolutions by Love, which Jesus says is the fulfilling of the law of karma.[55]

In other embodiments, Nada took up the avocation of law and became an expert in the defense of souls oppressed by the spoilers[56] in the earth. During her meditations upon the Law of God and in the course of her ministrations in the temple, she perceived the Law "as the certain defense which the Mother must use to protect her children from the wiles of this world, from the fallen ones who seek also to use the Law to their unjust purposes."[57]

In her final incarnation 2,700 years ago, Nada was the youngest of a large family of exceptionally gifted children. The beloved angel Charity appeared to her at a very early age and taught her how to draw God's love from the flame in her heart and to radiate it into the Nature kingdom for the blessing of life. The Archeia of the Third Ray also taught Nada to expand her threefold flame for the quickening of the chakras of her brothers and sisters, that by a heightened inner awareness they might bless the people and uplift the culture of the Divine Mother on earth through the arts.

In a dictation given August 28, 1982, Nada told her story:

> As I was embodied in a large family of many brothers and sisters of great talent, I saw how each one in pursuing his career needed love and ministration and the keeping of the flame of the sacred fire in order to be successful.
>
> And thus, although the choice was given to me to pursue my own career, unbeknownst to my brothers and sisters I quietly kept the flame in deep meditation and prayer as well as outer helpfulness, in [by way of] contacting the great spheres [causal body] of their

divine plan, and in accelerating through the mighty archangels Chamuel and Charity in the understanding that the adversaries of Love are many, and that Love is the full power of creativity, and that the success of the career son or daughter of God depends upon the defeat of Love's adversary, point counterpoint.

And therefore, in the course of defending the Christhood of my brothers and sisters, I had to advance in my own self-mastery to confront the fallen ones who attempted to thwart them in their most magnificent lifestreams and their offering to the world. Thus I understood Love as the consuming fire of the Holy Spirit that does indeed challenge and bind the wicked in the way! . . .

I can assure you that at the conclusion of my incarnation when I saw the victory of each one of my brothers and sisters, the fullness of my joy was in a heart of Love expanded, keeping the flame — keeping the flame and knowing that I was needed, that I was essential to their victory. . . .

It seemed to the world, and perhaps even to my own, that I had not accomplished much. But I took my leave into the higher octaves thoroughly understanding the meaning of the self-mastery of the pink flame. Thus it was from the point of the

Third Ray that I entered into the heart of Christ and saw the application [on the Sixth Ray] as ministration and service.[58]

As Lord of the Sixth Ray of Ministration and Service, the Ascended Lady Master Nada assists ministers, missionaries, healers, teachers, psychologists, counselors at law, professional people, public servants in government as well as those devoted to serving the needs of God's children in every branch of human and health services. You will also find her at the side of businessmen and -women, blue-collar, skilled and unskilled workers, farmers, ranchers, defenders of Freedom and revolutionaries of Love in every field.

Of course, Nada loves them all because she teaches the principle and practice of the sacred labor as the effective means to achieve the goal of the ascension. Fittingly, the mottos of her disciples are "I serve," "The servant is not greater than his Lord," and "I am my brother's keeper."

The gifts of the Holy Spirit which Nada administers are those of *diverse kinds of tongues* and the *interpretation of tongues.* These gifts involve the mastery of nuances of vibration in the five secret rays and their almost infinite combinations with the elements of the seven rays as the qualities of the Word are released through the petals of the chakras.

As pertains to human, divine, and angelic tongues, these gifts involve the mastery of speech, communication and the delivery of the Word. They range from the mastery of earth's languages for the transmission of the Word universally to all to proficiency in the tongues of angels as spoken by angelic messengers through the empowerment of the Holy Spirit.

Such releases given from an enraptured, exalted, or altered state are dictations (sometimes ex cathedra) for the initiation of souls and the transfer of the sacred fires from the altars of heaven. These fires, grounded through the anointed, are surely for the blessing of the saints who labor in Love under the weight of planetary karma they bear, or for the binding, surely, of the embodied seed of the fallen angels whose hour for the final judgment has come.

The gifts of tongues also facilitate understanding between peoples and figure in the art of diplomacy and just plain getting along with your neighbor—the soft answer that turneth away wrath,[59] the bridling of the tongue that James admonished[60]—comforting a child or the wounded soul or dealing in the power of the LORD's Spirit with the Devil's railings and possessing demons.

Thus the Science of the Spoken Word in all of its very human and divine ramifications is Nada's forte, which she conveys with the gifts of tongues and the interpretation thereof. So, too, it must be borne in mind that once the Word is spoken, instantaneously it becomes the manifest Work of the LORD through His mediators on earth.

Following in Jesus' footsteps, beloved Nada had assumed the Chohanship of the Sixth Ray by December 31, 1959. Nada serves in Jesus' retreat in the etheric octave over Saudi Arabia, where many disciples of the Lord have received their training directly from his Sacred Heart, face to face, during the Saviour's two-thousand-year occupancy of that office.

Here in the home of the Prince of Peace Nada instructs and gives exercises in the God-mastery of the emotions and the quieting of the inordinate passions of the desire body. Using Jesus' mantra "Peace be still!" she demonstrates the use of the solar plexus for the release of the power of peace through the seven sacred centers. Here, too, she unveils the mystery of Jesus' saying "He that believeth on me, out of his belly shall flow rivers of living water."[61]

As Nada directs disciples in the application of the radiant purple-and-gold flame of the Sixth Ray—a key step in the nine steps of precipitation taught by the Master Alchemist Saint Germain and the priesthood of the Order of Melchizedek (as well as by the Seven Mighty Elohim and the elemental builders of form)—she stresses the path of devotion (*bhakti* yoga) through the reestablishment of a personal heart-tie to Jesus. This Love-tie, she says, is *the* key to "believing on him." And in this case, believing *is* seeing—seeing just how to put on his consciousness, to assimilate his Body and his Blood, and to internalize his Word.

Oneness with the Christ of Jesus, chakra by chakra, reinforced through the individual Christ Self, is the open door to the disciple's instrumentation of that flow of Light from the Great Central Sun by which sons and daughters of God hold the balance for earth and her evolutions. The flow of Light out of "the belly," which means through the solar plexus, or place of the Sun, is of spiritual significance:

Here the belly refers to the womb as the matrix, or place prepared, for the soul's alchemy of bringing forth the Divine Manchild—the Christ consciousness of the universal age. This realization of the self as the instrument of the Greater Self with its attendant putting on of the Light of the Great Central Sun (the Son of God) leads to the God Self-realization of the Mother seen as the soul who is Woman, "clothed with the 'Sun.'"[62]

By this Sixth Ray alchemy of Christ's Love combined with the Ruby Ray action of the Third Ray—present in the Manchild who has the gifts of the Holy Ghost while he is yet in his mother's womb—Nada, assisted by her angels and devotees, contributes to the mitigation of world tension and the astral weight of the mass consciousness. Thus, this path of practicing the presence of the Lord—pursued by his own who abide in his heart as he abides in theirs—is the Sixth Ray aspect and action of the transmutation of personal and planetary karma.

In an age of Aquarian freedom the demands upon those who would tame its soul fires are great.

True Love for the brethren in Christ engenders a desire for self-mastery and self-control in the timing and teamwork of the Lord's Word and Work— in order that the achievements of Community might reflect the Christhood of initiates who have translated the nine gifts of the Holy Spirit into the nine steps of alchemy for the building of the temple of God and man.

Our beloved Nada is especially concerned that incoming souls receive the necessary spiritual, practical and academic education and that parents understand the need to give their children loving but firm and creative discipline as a prelude to their discipleship under the Cosmic Christ.

Consequently, Nada is very much involved in the initiation and sponsorship of twin flames and the Aquarian-age family. And she draws her circle of Love around homes of Light where father and mother set the example of the Path and children are tutored in the Law from birth by right standard and right action.

Regarding the problems of crime and the burdens of drugs upon our children, Nada has said: "The Love that must be instilled, beginning with yourself, is a Love so tangible for God in the person of one another, for God in the person of his saints, his angels, the Masters, Nature, and the simplicity of life itself, that in the presence of such Love the abrogation of the laws of God is altogether unthinkable."[63]

Her sponsorship of the brothers and sisters

of the Order of Saint Francis and Saint Clare is uniquely toward self-mastery of the sacred fire on the path of the Divine Mother that their service might suffice unto the calling of "kings and priests unto God."[64] Such attainment may also be the lot of householders during and after the childbearing years, if they so choose to consecrate their marriage. For great is our God and great are his dispensations to those who espouse the highest path of the initiates: Christhood through the Son of God.

In a recent dictation with Mighty Victory, Nada spoke of her sponsorship of twin flames:

> I come in the person of the Mother flame, as Chohan and member of the Karmic Board, to teach you and to walk with you. I come as the initiator of twin flames and soul mates and community members of the sangha of the Buddha and the community of Christ. For, beloved, the initiations of the Ruby Ray are tough. Therefore, we have recommended partnership, two by two, as Jesus sent his disciples, who also received some of these tests.
>
> Whenever there is the action of going forth two by two, one is the bearer of the Alpha flame and the other of the Omega, forming a circle of Light that cannot be penetrated, like an impregnable fortress....
>
> Realize, then, that the conferring by

the Lords of Karma of opportunity and initiation for twin flames is to that end that the twin flames together [might] enter the path of initiation of the Ruby Ray. Thus, with or without companion (known or unknown to you), it is well to call upon the Lords of Flame, Holy Kumaras, for those initiations [to be given] to yourself and your beloved.[65]

Since the sinking of Lemuria and subsequently Atlantis, circles of Masters and disciples sponsored by the Great White Brotherhood have held the balance of Light for earth's evolutions. Nada was one of those who kept the flame for the earth during the period of great darkness that covered the land. For, as we have pointed out, the priests and priestesses who tended the flames in the temples of Atlantis and on Lemuria (principally those who came to earth with Sanat Kumara) did carry those flames to other locations.

These keepers of the flame have continued to reembody as initiates of the sacred fire serving on the ray and in the temple of their calling. Whether in physical embodiment or from the ascended state, they maintain the balance of Alpha and Omega in the Spirit-Matter cosmos through the Guru-chela relationship.

Let us now enter their course and run with the torchbearers of the seventh age and its hierarch, the Ascended Master Saint Germain.

Saint Germain, Chohan of the Seventh Ray
Gifts of Prophecy and of the Working of Miracles

Enter Saint Germain May 1, 1684,
God of Freedom to the earth.
Draped with a cloak of stars,
He stands with his twin flame,
The Goddess of Justice,
Against the backdrop of Cosmos.
He is come to ignite the fires of world transmutation
In hearts attuned to the cosmic cyphers
And to avert personal and planetary cataclysm.
He pleads the cause of God-Freedom
Before the councils of men
And presents his case before
The world body of Lightbearers.
He offers a ransom for the oppressed—
Gift of his heart—and of his mind,
Rarest jewel of all our earthly souvenirs—
And of his causal body:
Sphere upon sphere of the richness of himself
Harvested from the divine, and the human,
    experience.

All this he offers.
Like a beggar with his bowl piled high,
He plies the streets of the world
Eyeing passersby
Hopeful that even one in every million
Might take the proffered gift
And hold it to his heart in recognition
Of the Source, of the Sun,

And of the alchemy of the age so close.
Yes, as close as free will and the divine spark
Is our extrication from the dilemma
Of doubt and deleterious concepts and death.
And as far, as far as the toiler's envy
Of our Love tryst is from grace,
So, without him, is the morning of our deliverance
From tangled entanglements of karmic crisscrosses
Of our doodling and dabbling for centuries'
   boredom
With personalities far less, oh yes, than his.

Enter Saint Germain
Into our hearts forever, if we will only let him.

———————

He lived to make men free.

That, in a phrase, sums up Saint Germain's many embodiments. Although he has played many parts, in each life he has brought the Christ/Light in prophecy and the alchemy of freedom to liberate the people of earth.

Enter Saint Germain January 1, 1987.

He comes to the fore as the Lord of the Seventh Ray and Age. He comes to initiate us in the gift of *prophecy* and the gift of the *working of miracles*—that we might foresee by the Spirit of the prophets what is coming upon us and turn the tide by the miracle violet flame.

More than fifty thousand years ago, a golden-age civilization thrived in a fertile country with a semitropical climate where the Sahara Desert now is. It was filled with great peace, happiness and prosperity and ruled with supreme justice and wisdom by this very Saint Germain.

The majority of his subjects retained full, conscious use of the wisdom and power of God. They possessed abilities that today would seem superhuman or miraculous. They knew they were extensions of the Central Sun—Life-streams issuing from the Great Hub of the Spirit-Matter cosmos.

For their wise ruler had charted for them on a great mural in the center of the capital city, "the City of the Sun," their cosmic history—that they should not forget the Source whence they had come nor their reason for being: To become sun-centers in this distant galaxy they now called home, extensions of the Law of the One. For they were part of an expanding universe. And their sense of co-measurement with the One sustained an ever-present cognition of the I AM THAT I AM.

Saint Germain was a master of the ancient wisdom and of the knowledge of the Matter spheres. He ruled by Light every area of life; his empire reached a height of beauty, symmetry and perfection unexceeded in the physical octave. Truly the heavenly patterns were outpictured in the crystal chalice of the earth. And elemental life served to maintain the purity of the Matter quadrants.

The people regarded their hierarch as the highest expression of God whom they desired to emulate, and great was their love for his presence. He was the embodiment of the archetype of universal Christhood for that dispensation—to whom they could look as the standard for their own emerging Godhood.

Guy W. Ballard, under the pen name of Godfré Ray King, recounted in *Unveiled Mysteries* a soul journey in which Saint Germain conducted him through the akashic record of this civilization and its decline.[66]

Saint Germain explained to him that "as in all ages past, there was a portion of the people who became more interested in the temporary pleasures of the senses than in the larger creative plan of the Great God Self. This caused them to lose consciousness of the God-Power throughout the land until it remained active in little more than the [capital] city itself. Those governing realized they must withdraw and let the people learn through hard experience that all their happiness and good came from the adoration to the God within, and they must come back into the Light if they were to be happy."

Thus, the ruler (the embodied representative of the spiritual hierarchy of the earth under Sanat Kumara) was instructed by a cosmic council that he must withdraw from his empire and his beloved people; henceforth their karma would be their Guru and Lawgiver, and free will would determine what, if any, of his legacy of Light they would retain.

According to plan, the king held a great banquet in the Jeweled Room of his palace, with his councillors and public servants in attendance. Following the dinner, which had been entirely precipitated, a crystal goblet filled with "pure elec-tronic essence" appeared to the right of each of the 576 guests. It was the communion cup of Saint Germain, who, with the mantle and sceptre of the ancient priest/kings, gave of his own Light-essence to those who had faithfully served the realm to the glory of God.

As they drank to the "Flame of the most High Living One," they knew they could never com-pletely forget the divine spark of the inner God Self. This soul-protection, afforded them through the ever-grateful heart of Saint Germain, would be sustained throughout the centuries until once again they should find themselves in a civilization where the cosmic cycles had turned and they would be given the full knowledge to pursue the Divine Union—this time nevermore to go out from the Golden City of the Sun.

Now a Cosmic Master from out the Great Silence spoke. His message was broadcast from the banquet hall throughout the realm. The resplen-dent being, who identified himself solely by the word *Victory* written upon his brow, brought warn-ing of crisis to come, rebuked the people for their ingratitude to and neglect of their Great God Source, and reminded them of the ancient com-mand to obey the Law of the One—Love. Then he gave them the following prophecy of their karma:

"A visiting prince approaches your borders. He will enter this city seeking the daughter of your king. You will come under the rule of this prince but the recognition of your mistake will be futile. Nothing can avail, for the royal family will be drawn into the protection and care of those whose power and authority are of God, and against whom no human desire can ever prevail. These are the great Ascended Masters of Light from the golden etheric city over this land. Here your ruler and his beloved children will abide for a cycle of time."

The king and his children withdrew seven days later. The prince arrived the next day and took over without opposition.

As we study the history of Saint Germain's lifestream we shall see that time and time again the Master and his way of God-mastery have been rejected by the very ones he sought to help; notwithstanding the fact that his gifts of Light, Life and Love—fruits of his adeptship freely given—his alchemical feats, elixir of youth, inventions and prognostications have been readily received.

The goal of his embodiments extending from the golden-age civilization of the Sahara to the final hour of his life as Francis Bacon was always to liberate the children of the Light, especially those who in their carelessness in handling fiery principles of the Law had been left to their own karmic devices—in whose vices they were often bound. His aim was to see the fulfillment of his prayer offered at the final banquet of his reign:

If they must have the experience that consumes and burns away the dross and clouds of the outer self, then do Thou sustain and at last bring them forth in Thy Eternal Perfection. I call unto Thee, Thou Creator of the Universe—Thou Supreme Omnipotent God.

As the High Priest of the Violet Flame Temple on the mainland of Atlantis thirteen thousand years ago, Saint Germain sustained by his invocations and his causal body a pillar of fire, a fountain of violet singing flame, which magnetized people from near and far to be set free from every binding condition of body, mind and soul. This they achieved by self-effort through the offering of invocations and the practice of Seventh Ray rituals to the sacred fire.

An intricately carved marble circular railing enclosed the shrine where supplicants knelt in adoration of the God flame—visible to some as a physical violet flame, to others as an 'ultraviolet' light and to others not at all, though the powerful healing vibrations were undeniable.

The temple was built of magnificent marble ranging in hue from brilliant white, shot through with violet and purple veins, to deeper shades of the Seventh Ray spectrum. The central core of the temple was a large circular hall lined in ice-violet marble set upon a rich purpled marble floor. Three stories in height, it was situated midst a complex of adjacent areas for worship and the various functions of priests and priestesses who ministered unto the Flame and mediated its voice of Light and Prophecy unto the people. Those who officiated at this altar were schooled in the universal priesthood of the Order of Melchizedek at Lord Zadkiel's retreat, the Temple of Purification, in the locale of the West Indies.

Through the heights and depths of the ages that have ensued, Saint Germain has ingeniously used the Seventh Ray momentum of his causal body to secure freedom for keepers of the flame who have kept alive 'coals' from the violet flame altar of his Atlantean temple. He has extolled and exemplified freedom of the mind and spirit. Endowing the four sacred freedoms with an identity of their own, he has championed our freedom from state interference, kangaroo courts, or popular ridicule in matters ranging from scientific investigation to the healing arts to the spiritual quest.

Standing on a platform of basic human rights for a responsible, reasoning public educated in the principles of liberty and equal opportunity for all, he has ever taught us to espouse our inalienable divine right to live life according to our highest conception of God. For the Master has said that no right, however simple or basic, can long be secure without the underpinning of the spiritual graces and the Divine Law that instills a compassionate righteousness in the exercise thereof.

Returning to the scene of the karma of his people as Samuel, prophet of the LORD and judge of the twelve tribes of Israel (c. 1050 B.C.), Saint Germain was the messenger of God's liberation of the seed of Abraham from bondage to the corrupt priests, the sons of Eli, and from the Philistines by whom they had been defeated. Bearing in his heart the special sign of the blue rose of Sirius, Samuel delivered to the recalcitrant Israelites a prophecy parallel to his twentieth-century discourses—both inextricably linked with God's covenants concerning karma, free will and grace:

"If ye do return unto the LORD with all your hearts, then put away the strange gods and Ashtaroth from among you, and prepare your hearts unto the LORD and serve him only: and he will deliver you out of the hand of the Philistines."[67] Later, when King Saul disobeyed God, Samuel freed the people from his tyranny by anointing David king.

True to the thread of prophecy that runs throughout his lifetimes, Saint Germain was Saint Joseph of the lineage of King David, son of Jesse, chosen vessel of the Holy Ghost, father of Jesus in fulfillment of the word of the LORD to Isaiah— "There shall come forth a rod out of the stem of Jesse, and a Branch shall grow out of his roots...."[68]

We see, then, in each of Saint Germain's embodiments that there is present the quality of alchemy—a conveyance of Godly power. So ordained the instrument of the LORD, Samuel transferred His sacred fire in the anointing of David and just as scientifically withdrew it from King Saul when the LORD rejected him from being king over Israel.[69] This unmistakable sign of the Seventh Ray adept, often in humble garb, was also present as

the Holy Spirit's power of the conversion of souls
and the control of natural forces in his life as
the third-century Saint Alban, first martyr of the
British Isles.

A Roman soldier, Alban hid a fugitive priest,
was converted by him, then sentenced to death for
disguising himself as the priest and allowing him
to escape. A great multitude gathered to witness
his execution—too many to pass over the narrow
bridge that must be crossed. Alban prayed and the
river parted—whereupon his executioner, being
converted, begged to die in Alban's place. His
request was denied and he was beheaded that day
alongside the saint.

But Saint Germain was not always to be
counted in the ranks of the Church. He fought
tyranny wherever he found it, including in false
Christian doctrine. As the Master Teacher behind
the Neoplatonists, Saint Germain was the inner
inspiration of the Greek philosopher Proclus (c.
A.D. 410–485). He revealed his pupil's previous
life as a Pythagorean philosopher,[70] also showing
Proclus the sham of Constantine's Christianity and
the worth of the path of individualism (leading to
the individualization of the God flame) which
Christians called "paganism."

As the highly honored head of Plato's Academy at Athens, Proclus based his philosophy upon
the principle that there is only one true reality—
the "One," which is God, or the Godhead, the final
goal of all life's efforts. The philosopher said,

"Beyond all bodies is the essence of soul, and beyond all souls the intellectual nature, and beyond all intellectual existences the One."[71] Throughout his incarnations Saint Germain demonstrated tremendous breadth of knowledge in the Mind of God; not surprising was the range of his pupil's awareness. His writings extended to almost every department of learning.

Proclus acknowledged that his enlightenment and philosophy came from above—indeed he believed himself to be one through whom divine revelation reached mankind. "He did not appear to be without divine inspiration," his disciple Marinus wrote, "for he produced from his wise mouth words similar to the most thick-falling snow; so that his eyes emitted a bright radiance, and the rest of his countenance participated of divine illumination."[72]

Thus Saint Germain, white-robed, jeweled slippers and belt emitting star-fire from far-off worlds, was the mystery Master smiling just beyond the veil—mirroring the imagings of his mind in the soul of the last of the great Neoplatonic philosophers.

Saint Germain was Merlin. The unforgettable, somehow irretrievable figure who haunts the mists of England, about to step forth at any moment to offer us a goblet of sparkling elixir. He the 'old man' who knows the secrets of youth and alchemy, who charted the stars at Stonehenge, and moved a stone or two, so they say, by his magical powers—who would astonish no one if he suddenly appeared on a Broadway stage or in the forests of the Yellowstone or at one's side on any highway anywhere.

For Saint Germain *is* Merlin.

Enter Merlin January 1, 1987, with his final prophecy to heroes, knights, ladies, crazies, and villains of the Aquarian Camelot.

Merlin, dear Merlin, has never left us—his spirit charms the ages, makes us feel as rare and unique as his diamond and amethyst adornments. Merlin is the irreplaceable Presence, a humming vortex about whose science and legends and fatal romance Western civilization has entwined itself.

It was the fifth century. Midst the chaos left by the slow death of the Roman Empire, a king arose to unite a land splintered by warring chieftains and riven by Saxon invaders. At his side was the old man himself—half Druid priest, half Christian saint— seer, magician, counselor, friend, who led the king through twelve battles to unite a kingdom and establish a window of peace.

At some point, the spirit of Merlin went through a catharsis. The scene was one of fierce battle, the legend says. As he witnessed the carnage, a madness came upon him—of seeing all at once past/present and future—so peculiar to the lineage of the prophets. He fled to the forest to live as a wild man, and one day as he sat under a tree, he began to utter prophecies concerning the future of Wales.

"I was taken out of my true self," he said. "I was as a spirit and knew the history of people long past and could foretell the future. I knew then the secrets of nature, bird flight, star wanderings and the way fish glide."[73] Both his prophetic utterances and his "magical" powers served one end: the making of a united kingdom of the tribes of the old Britons. His pervasiveness is recalled in an early Celtic name for Britain, "Clas Myrddin," which means "Merlin's Enclosure."[74]

By advising and assisting Arthur in establishing his kingship, Merlin sought to make of Britain a fortress against ignorance and superstition where Christ achievement could flower and devotion to the One could prosper in the quest for the Holy Grail. His efforts on this soil were to bear fruit in the nineteenth century as the British Isles became the place where individual initiative and industry could thrive as never before in twelve thousand years.

But even as Camelot, the rose of England, budded and bloomed, nightshade was twining about its roots. Witchcraft, intrigue and treachery destroyed Camelot, not the love of Launcelot and Guinevere as Tom Malory's misogynistic depiction suggests. Alas, the myth he sowed has obscured the real culprits these long centuries.

'Twas the king's bastard son Modred by his half sister Margawse[75] who, with Morgana le Fay and a circle of like sorceresses and black knights, set out to steal the crown, imprison the queen, and destroy for a time the bonds of a Love that such as these (of the left-handed path) had never known nor could—a Reality all of their willing, warring and enchantments could not touch.

Thus it was with a heavy heart and the spirit of a prophet who has seen visions of tragedy and desolation, fleeting joys and the piercing anguish of karmic retribution endlessly outplayed, that Merlin entered the scene of his own denouement, to be tied up in spells of his own telling by silly, cunning Vivien—and sleep. Aye, to err is human but to pine for the twin flame that is not there is the lot of many an errant knight or king or lonely prophet who perhaps should have disappeared into the mists rather than suffer sad ignominy for his people.

Some say he still sleeps but they grossly underestimate the resilient spirit of the wise man rebounded, this time in thirteenth-century England disguised as Roger Bacon (c. 1214–1294). Reenter Merlin—scientist, philosopher, monk, alchemist and prophet—to forward his mission of laying the scientific moorings for the age of Aquarius his soul should one day sponsor.

The atonement of this lifetime was to be the voice crying in the intellectual and scientific wilderness that was medieval Britain. In an era in which either theology or logic or both dictated the parameters of science, he promoted the experimental method, declared his belief that the world was round, and castigated the scholars and scientists of his day for their narrow-mindedness. Thus he is viewed as the forerunner of modern science.

But he was also a prophet of modern technology. Although it is unlikely he did experiments to determine the feasibility of the following inventions, he predicted the hot-air balloon, a flying machine, spectacles, the telescope, microscope, elevator, and mechanically propelled ships and carriages, and wrote of them as if he had actually seen them! Bacon was also the first Westerner to write down the exact directions for making gunpowder, but kept the formula a secret lest it be used to harm anyone. No wonder people thought he was a magician!

However, just as Saint Germain tells us today in his *Studies in Alchemy* that "miracles" are wrought by the precise application of universal laws, so Roger Bacon meant his prophecies to demonstrate that flying machines and magical apparatus were products of the employment of natural law which men would figure out in time.

From whence did Bacon believe he derived his amazing awareness? "True knowledge stems not from the authority of others, nor from a blind allegiance to antiquated dogmas," he said. Two of his biographers write that he believed knowledge "is a highly personal experience—a light that is communicated only to the innermost privacy of the individual through the impartial channels of all knowledge and of all thought."[76]

And so Bacon, who had been a lecturer at Oxford and the University of Paris, determined to separate himself and his thoughts from the posing and postulating residents of academe. He would seek and find his science in his religion. Entering the Franciscan Order of Friars Minor, he said, "I will conduct my experiments on the magnetic forces of the lodestone at the selfsame shrine where my fellow-scientist, St. Francis, performed his experiments on the magnetic forces of love."[77]

But the friar's scientific and philosophical world view, his bold attacks on the theologians of his day, and his study of alchemy, astrology and magic led to charges of "heresies and novelties," for which he was imprisoned in 1278 by his fellow Franciscans! They kept him in solitary confinement for fourteen years,[78] releasing him only shortly before his death. Although the clock of this life was run out, his body broken, he knew that his efforts would not be without impact on the future.

The following prophecy which he gave his students shows the grand and revolutionary ideals of the indomitable spirit of this living flame of freedom—the immortal spokesman for our scientific, religious and political liberties:

> I believe that humanity shall accept as an axiom for its conduct the principle for which I have laid down my life—the right to investigate. It is the credo of free men— this opportunity to try, this privilege to err, this courage to experiment anew. We scientists of the human spirit shall experiment,

experiment, ever experiment. Through centuries of trial and error, through agonies of research . . . let us experiment with laws and customs, with money systems and governments, until we chart the one true course—until we find the majesty of our proper orbit as the planets above have found theirs. . . . And then at last we shall move all together in the harmony of our spheres under the great impulse of a single creation—one unity, one system, one design.[79]

To establish this freedom upon earth, Saint Germain's lifestream took another turn—as Christopher Columbus (1451–1506). But over two centuries before Columbus sailed, Roger Bacon had set the stage for the voyage of the three ships and the discovery of the New World when he stated in his *Opus Majus* that "the sea between the end of Spain on the west and the beginning of India on the east is navigable in a very few days if the wind is favorable."[80]

Although the statement was incorrect in that the land to the west of Spain was not India, it was instrumental in Columbus' discovery. Cardinal Pierre d'Ailly copied it in his *Imago Mundi* without noting Bacon's authorship. Columbus read his work and quoted the passage in a 1498 letter to King Ferdinand and Queen Isabella, saying that his 1492 voyage had been inspired in part by this visionary statement.

Columbus believed that God had made him to be "the messenger of the new heaven and the new earth of which He spake in the Apocalypse of St. John, after having spoken of it by the mouth of Isaiah."[81]

But did the brave captain also foresee the New World as the place for the reincarnation of those same souls who had been his subjects some fifty thousand years before? Lifetime by lifetime, Saint Germain, whether his outer mind was continuously cognizant of it we know not, was re-creating that golden pathway to the Sun—a destiny come full circle to worship the God Presence and reestablish a lost golden age.

As Francis Bacon (1561–1626), the greatest mind the West has ever produced, his manifold achievements in every field catapulted the world into a stage set for the children of Aquarius. In this life he was free to carry to its conclusion the work he had begun as Roger Bacon.

Scholars have noted the similarities between the thoughts of the two philosophers and even between Roger's *Opus Majus* and Francis' *De Augmentis* and *Novum Organum*. This is made even more astounding by the fact that Roger's *Opus* was never published in his lifetime, fell into oblivion, and not until 113 years after Francis' *Novum Organum* and 110 years after his *De Augmentis* did it appear in print!

The unsurpassed wit of this immortal soul,

this philosopher/king, this priest/scientist, might easily have kept its humor with the stubborn motto drawn from tyrants, tortures and tragedy: If they beat you in one life, come back and beat them in the next!

Francis Bacon is known as the father of inductive reasoning and the scientific method which, more than any other contributions, are responsible for the age of technology in which we now live. He foreknew that only applied science could free the masses from human misery and the drudgery of sheer survival in order that they might seek a higher spirituality they once knew. Thus, science and technology were essential to Saint Germain's plan for the liberation of his Lightbearers and through them all mankind.

His next step was to be nothing less bold than universal enlightenment!

"The Great Instauration" (restoration after decay, lapse, or dilapidation) was his formula to change "the whole wide world." First conceived when Bacon was a boy of twelve or thirteen and later crystallized in 1607 in his book by the same name, it did indeed launch the English Renaissance with the help of Francis' tender, caring person. For over the years, he gathered around himself a group of illuminati who were responsible among other things for almost all of the Elizabethan literature—Ben Jonson, John Davies, George Herbert, John Selden, Edmund Spenser,

Sir Walter Raleigh, Gabriel Harvey, Robert Greene, Sir Philip Sidney, Christopher Marlowe, John Lyly, George Peele, and Lancelot Andrewes.

Some of these were part of a "secret society" that Francis had formed with his brother, Anthony, when the two were law students at Gray's Inn. This fledgling group, called "The Knights of the Helmet," had as its goal the advancement of learning by expanding the English language and by creating a new literature written not in Latin but in words which Englishmen could understand.

Francis also organized the translation of the King James Version of the Bible, determined that the common people should have the benefit of reading God's Word for themselves. Furthermore, as was discovered in the 1890s in two separate ciphers—a word-cipher and a bi-literal cipher embedded in the type of the original printings of the Shakespearean Folios[82]—Francis Bacon *was* the author of the plays attributed to the actor from the squalid village of Stratford-on-Avon. He *was* the greatest literary genius of the Western world.

So, too, was Bacon behind many of the political ideas on which Western civilization is based. Thomas Hobbes, John Locke and Jeremy Bentham took Bacon as their ideological starting point. His revolutionary principles are the engine that has driven our nation. They are the very essence of the can-do spirit. "Men are not animals erect," Bacon averred, "but immortal Gods. The Creator has given us souls equal to all the world, and yet satiable not even with a world."[83]

Francis Bacon also continued the task he had begun as Christopher Columbus, promoting the colonization of the New World, for he knew that it was there that his ideas could take deepest root and come to fullest flower. He convinced James I to charter Newfoundland and was an officer in the Virginia Company, which sponsored the settlement of Jamestown, England's first permanent colony in America. And he founded Freemasonry, dedicated to the freedom and enlightenment of mankind, whose members played a large part in founding the new nation.

Yet he could have been an even greater boon to England and the whole world had he been allowed to fulfill his destiny. The same ciphers which run throughout the Shakespearean plays also run through Francis Bacon's own works and those of many of his circle of friends. Both ciphers contain his true life story, the musings of his soul, and anything he wished to bequeath to future generations but could not publish openly for fear of the queen.[84]

Its secrets reveal that he should have been Francis I, King of England. He was the son of Queen Elizabeth I and Robert Dudley, Lord Leicester, born four months after a secret wedding ceremony. But she, wishing to retain her "Virgin Queen" status and afraid that if she acknowledged her marriage, she must give power to the ambitious

Leicester, also lest the people prefer her male heir to herself and demand the queen's premature withdrawal from the throne, refused to allow Francis, on pain of death, to assume his true identity.

The queen kept him dangling all his life, never giving him public office, never proclaiming him her son, never allowing him to fulfill his goals for England. No, she would not allow her son to bring in the golden age of Britannia that was meant to be, but never was. What cruel fate—a queen mother unbending, contemptuous before her golden age prince!

He was raised the foster son of Sir Nicholas and Lady Anne Bacon and at age fifteen heard the truth of his birth from his own mother's lips in the same breath with which she barred him forever from the succession. In one night his world was in a shambles. Like young Hamlet, he pondered over and over the question, "To be or not to be?" That was *his* question.

In the end, he determined not to rebel against his mother or later, against her ill-fitted successor, James I. This despite the great good he knew he could bring to England, despite his vision of the land "as she might be, if wisely governed."[85] He knew he had within himself the power to be a monarch such as the land had never known, a true father of the nation. He wrote of the "impulses of the godlike patriarchal care for his own people" he would exercise[86]—shades of the golden age emperor of the Sahara.

Fortunately for the world, Francis determined to pursue his goal of universal enlightenment in the avenues of literature and science, as adviser to the throne, supporter of colonization, and founder of secret societies, thereby reestablishing the thread of contact with the ancient mystery schools. The outlet of his wounded spirit was his cipher writing in which he poured out his longings to a future age.

By the time of his death in 1626, persecuted and unrecognized for his manifold talents, Francis Bacon had triumphed over circumstances which would have destroyed lesser men, but which for him proved the true making of an Ascended Master.

May 1, 1684, was Saint Germain's Ascension Day. From heights of power well earned and beyond this world's, he still stands to turn back all attempts to thwart his 'Great Instauration' here below.

Desiring above all else to liberate God's people, whether they would or no, Saint Germain sought a dispensation from the Lords of Karma to return to earth in a physical body. They granted it and he appeared as the Comte de Saint Germain, a "miraculous" gentleman who dazzled the courts of eighteenth- and nineteenth-century Europe as "The Wonderman." His goal: to prevent the French Revolution, effect a smooth transition from monarchy to a republican form of government, establish a United States of Europe, and enshrine the fleur-de-lis as threefold flame of God-identity in every heart.

Though admired throughout the courts of Europe for his adeptship—removing the flaws in diamonds, disappearing into thin air, writing the same verses of poetry simultaneously with both hands, accomplished in many languages, fluent in any subject, recounting any history as an eyewitness—he failed to secure the anticipated response. Though willing to be entertained, the royalty were not easily prodded to relinquish their power and move with the winds of democratic change. They and their jealous ministers ignored his counsel and the French Revolution ensued.

In a final attempt to unite Europe, Saint Germain backed Napoleon, who misused the Master's power to his own demise. The opportunity to set aside the retribution due an age thus passed, Saint Germain was once again forced to withdraw from a karmic situation. In this episode, though clearly visible as the mediator, Saint Germain with his miracles *en main* and his prophecies fulfilled could still be ignored! What would it take to turn people's hearts?

The Ascended Master abandoned his sponsorship of Europe, turning instead to the New World, upon which he had kept a watchful eye for several centuries. Even as Francis Bacon, he had seen America as his last hope. He wrote in cipher, "I trusteth all to the future and a land that is very far towards the sunset gate. . . . I keep the future ever in my plan, looking for my reward, not to my times and countrymen, but to a people very far off, and an age not like our own, but a second golden age of learning."[87]

Having discovered the continent and encouraged

its colonization, he must also insure a proper foundation for the new nation. Saint Germain stood by George Washington throughout the Revolution and during the winter at Valley Forge. His past efforts in initiating the society of Freemasons had enfired many of the key figures of the Revolution. General Washington, Alexander Hamilton, James Madison, John Hancock, Benjamin Franklin and as many as fifty-three out of the fifty-six signers of the Declaration of Independence were all members of the Masonic order,[88] whose principles had guided them in founding the new nation. Further, Saint Germain called for the signing of the Declaration of Independence, directed the writing of the Constitution and anointed Washington first President of the United States.

America was secured as the land of opportunity and Saint Germain devoted himself to the raising of the consciousness of her people.

In the twentieth century, the Master went before the Lords of Karma to plead the cause of freedom for and on behalf of the original 576 he had sponsored, expanding that circle to include the Lightbearers of all centuries—the original Keepers of the Flame who had come with Sanat Kumara as well as the children of God who had been evolving unto the spiritual gifts and graces through earth's numerous ages.

However, as the decades have passed, the rate of increase in the return of mankind's karma has precipitated what is known as the Dark Cycle—the era of Chaos and old Night whose signs are foretold in Revelation, even as the hoofbeats of the Four Horsemen can be heard throughout the land.

Let us listen to the prophet Samuel—dubbed Uncle Sam by his people—who has indeed begun to sound his prophecy to the chosen. He has warned that the I AM Race—those who have the seed of the name I AM THAT I AM within their hearts—"have not hearkened unto the LORD, nor have they fulfilled the wholeness of the Law."

Therefore, the Master says:

> Some among this people must be and become direct initiates of Sanat Kumara, for always there has been the requirement of the ransom. Let those who are the inner circle of the devotees, those who are the firstfruits who come and stand as the ensign of the people, raise up the banner of Christ as the one whom they serve, the one who by his very Communion promise at the Last Supper designated each and every son and daughter of God for the internalization of the Word . . .
>
> Unfortunately, and this word is mild, but it is unfortunate indeed that the laws of Christ and his Teachings, so meticulously brought forth to the close initiates, are not fully known today, having been taken even from the holy people. Therefore, to obey Christ becomes the challenge of the hour— to find the Person of that Christ, to find the Way and the Teachings.

You have received the lost Word and the lost Teachings of Jesus Christ through our effort....As a result of this, you have been strengthened and protected in that Word and Teaching. And some from among you have taken their leave at the conclusion of their embodiment and gone on in the full resurrection with Jesus Christ.... Thus, the proof of the Teaching and the Path is that it leads one successively to that higher and higher consciousness whereunto the individual is assumed into the very heart of the I AM Presence [becoming indeed the pure Person of that Christ].[89]

Today, as we see the cycles of earth's returning karma reach a mounting crescendo wherein even the four sacred freedoms are threatened, the Brotherhood has set aside a place in America's Rocky Mountains for the pursuit of the Lost Teachings of Christ to their fullest expression.

Saint Germain spoke of it in 1983 when he said that we have come "to a similar moment to that of that final hour of the golden age when I presided where the Sahara now is. My family is much larger than it was then, for I include every one of you who love me as my very own family.... In that hour, our family was taken to the golden etheric city of light. In this hour, we have summoned you to a higher place in the mountains of the north."[90]

As the outpost of the Royal Teton Retreat, it is called the Royal Teton Ranch. Beloved Jesus announced on May 31, 1984, that to this Inner Retreat in southwestern Montana, to this "Place Prepared," Lord Maitreya had come again to re-open his Mystery School, which had been withdrawn from the physical octave just prior to the sinking of Lemuria.

Let us see what we may accomplish for our beloved Terra and our brothers and sisters on earth with the renewed opportunity the Hierarchs of the Aquarian Age, our beloved Saint Germain and his twin flame, the Ascended Lady Master Portia, have given to us.

Let us study to show ourselves worthy of the gifts of prophecy and of the working of miracles which he brings. And most importantly, let us strive to the utmost to overcome personal and planetary karma through those invocations to the violet flame and Seventh Ray rituals of transmutation we once knew, that the prophecy of Saint Germain's Great Golden Age may be fulfilled.

The Keepers of the Flame have vowed to be victorious in this age. And they shall!

Lives of Great Men All Remind Us . . .

In studying the lives of the Seven Chohans of the Rays, not only those lives which culminated in their ascension but also those which went before, we come to understand in the sine wave of their accomplishments and setbacks what is that unique path of Christhood we must forge and win on the seven rays that lead us Home at last to the primordial Light of the Sun behind the sun.

Come, let us join hands as we form a solar ring here below and love and learn together from the wayshowers the most joyous calling of our Lord—how we can be victorious overcomers in earth's schoolroom and do it not for ourselves alone but for the blessing of all life!

For we should learn to use the world, not to abuse it. So the saints tell us. And these are not mere visionaries who have lived hypocritically. These are extraordinary intellects who have known the Mind of Christ, people of spiritual ingenuity from whom our age can learn.

Yes, we can learn from the activities of Saint Francis of Assisi. We can learn from the activities of Prince Mori Wong of Koko Nor and Akbar the Great as well as other luminaries and revolutionaries whose names, by device, have not landed in the forefront of world thought.

We can learn from the activities of our Brother Christ Jesus in his lifetimes which he spent in Israel preparing for the final one—when he was Elisha (ninth century B.C.) apprenticed to the alchemist, healer and prophet Elijah; or when he was Joseph (seventeenth or nineteenth century B.C.?) with his coat of many colors, favorite son of Jacob, the envy of all the rest, whose seed, reincarnated in the nations of the English-speaking peoples, are still the envy of all the other tribes reborn.

Were we also there with him? And did we help or hinder him while he yet wrestled with his soul or ours?

These things we wonder in the silent musings of our souls and well we should, for what we have done or left undone tells much about what we are doing or should be today. And ever-present karma, through the hand of Opportunity, is an interval of time and space. And these, too, are the spiritual graces, kal/desh,* given to us to set the record straight.

Whilst acquainting us with the Chohans, Jesus also told us of his endearment to Saint Germain when the Lord of the Seventh Ray was embodied as his father, Joseph. He spoke of their profound love for one another and of their service together in the sponsorship of the true seed of Abraham, the Hebrew lineage of Sanat Kumara's Lightbearers.

Moreover, he spoke tenderly of their close association when Saint Germain was the prophet Samuel and he anointed the soul of David—Jesus himself—as King of Israel (c. 1000 B.C.), and together they challenged the mad King Saul, seed of the Evil One, who fell on his sword in battle for fear of the spirit of the departed Samuel.

He said that under Saint Germain's Seventh Ray dispensation in Aquarius we could accelerate the balancing of our karma of many lifetimes by using his violet flame decrees—and that with their continued use and our reliable progress on the Path, Saint Germain and his beloved Portia would

*from the Sanskrit *kala* "time" and *desha* "space."

sponsor the reuniting of twin flames first on inner levels and then on outer levels—karmic circumstances permitting.

We can learn from the blessed Chohans because they are so real. Then and now these were and are people like ourselves. Endowed with the God spark, they creatively exploited its splendor and reflected the inner radiance to a world through the mirror of consciousness. And it shone through the mortal form. And when the form was no more, the soul—enlivened by its own star fire—stepped forth from the coil of mortality to transcend the law of rebirth, having outlived its usefulness.

Sic transit gloria mundi. Thus passes the glory of the world. Enter the glory of the next.

We can also learn from the victories and setbacks of our own past lives.

Jesus told us that he had brought Elizabeth and me together as twin flames for our mission in publishing abroad the Everlasting Gospel—to tell the world of his Word and Work as we had done again and again in previous embodiments, sometimes together and sometimes apart. The Lord told us it wouldn't be easy but he said that in the end the Light would prevail and eventually his true Teachings, lost and found again, would cover the earth[91]—but not until we had borne some hardships of personal and planetary karma. He spoke of the trials and persecutions that follow the disciple up the mountain until their ghosts, weary of the ascent, fall by the wayside—just so many fetters that cannot cling.

And in a rare moment Jesus looked into our eyes and told us that depending on the response of the Lightbearers to Saint Germain's dispensation of the violet flame and the timing of the karmic cycles, earth changes would possibly come to pass before his full glory would be (or could be) universally taught and accepted. "But," the Beloved said, "fear not, I will be with you in the place I have prepared."

The Master revealed to each of us separately through the mirror of his consciousness scenes of our association with him—myself as John Mark, the scribe and author of the second Gospel, sometime companion of both Peter and Paul. He showed me that I had learned from Peter's own lips some of the personal anecdotes—tales told on Peter by himself— which gave that Gospel details on the impetuous one drawn from the more human side of his life.

To Elizabeth he gave the recollection of herself as Martha, attentive to his needs, preparing his meals and a comfortable home at Bethany. The Master showed her scenes where he had instructed Mary, Lazarus, herself, and the inner circle in the secrets and rituals of advancing Christic initiation.

You will recall that Martha was the one who professed her belief in Jesus as the Incarnate Word: "Yea, Lord: I believe that thou art the Christ, the Son of God, which should come into the world."[92]

This statement came from direct knowledge and the inner knowing of the personal Christ which Jesus imparted to those who were able to receive it: to those he knew would not tumble headlong into the Devil's trap of the idolatry of the Master's person or their own—or both. Thus he taught us that to the carnally minded the knowledge of the mysteries without the keys of discipleship and initiation under the Cosmic Christ is *a most dangerous thing.*

And we remembered his counsel: "Give not that which is holy unto the dogs, neither cast ye your pearls before swine, lest they trample them under their feet, and turn again and rend you."[93]

By and by, each on our own, we confirmed our past lives and one another's—happily announcing to each other: "Do you know who you were at the time of Jesus?" and the reply was the same, "Yes, I do. Do you know who *you* were?"

Once in a dictation through me Jesus announced: "I spake long ago unto Martha and I said unto her, 'Mary has chosen the better part.'[94] Today your beloved Messenger Elizabeth, who is the reembodiment of Martha, is with you, now choosing the better part and to render her service in this day."[95]

The Master's comforting flame of forgiveness made her eyes burn with tears of gratitude as she remembered the chastisement of her Lord. And as I felt his love flood her heart, she seated at my side on the platform, I too knew the grace and mercy of my Saviour.

Jesus' subsequent revelation to us that Martha's sister, Mary, had reincarnated in the late nineteenth century as Mary Baker Eddy explained Elizabeth's childhood devotion to Christian Science, as she had found in Mrs. Eddy's writings "footsteps of Truth" and the thread of contact that reestablished the outer tie with Jesus' heart and message.

Such moments as these when we find ourselves caught up in the heart of Jesus are truly intervals of eternity when the world stands still and only Jesus is real, filling the earth and sea and sky of our interior castle with his loving, masterful Presence.

Later the Master revealed to us that we had kept his flame within the Church in later centuries, I as Origen of Alexandria and Saint Bonaventure, messenger of his Eternal Mind, she as Saint Clare and Saint Catherine of Siena, messenger of his Sacred Heart.

Just so, you, too, at a certain point in your spiritual awakening and chelaship under one or more of the Ascended Masters, may have revealed to you your past embodiments. This may take place in Saint Germain's retreat in the Rocky Mountains called the Cave of Symbols, at the Grand Teton or Darjeeling, as we shall soon see, or in another retreat of the Great White Brotherhood.

When you have sufficiently prepared yourself for a psychological probe of past circumstances effecting current events in your life, the Master will lead you before the Cosmic Mirror in the Royal Teton Retreat. At first glance it looks like an ordinary motion picture screen. The Master selects certain records taken from akasha which are also contained in the memory of the soul, and upon the Cosmic Mirror they come alive.

This is beyond 3-D—you are there! A portion of a past life, or more than one, passes before you, but you are a living part of this nonfiction play of light and darkness with shades of grey. It is almost too much to handle. Instantly you are aware, as in an orb of all-knowingness, of the ramifications of your karma even as you relive the emotions, the premeditated thoughts and the acts themselves.

This could be a most painful experience, you tell yourself, all the while sensing your Higher Consciousness standing guard and telling you gently but firmly not to give way to extremes of despondency or ecstasy, but to face the future with a hope based on the scientific knowledge that in your hands lies the power to change.

Thus, a few segments a session are given, and you soon see the wisdom of the Law that requires adjustment through your application of the violet flame to those scenes and memories until balance is restored. You appreciate as never before that starry Mother, beloved Astrea. And you can't wait to give her 10.14 decree that invokes the circle and sword of blue flame of the Universal Kali in, through and around the cause and core of every binding, blinding record.[96]

And you know *and* see that you've got work to do. And you know that you are going to work harder than you have ever worked before—to slay the dweller-on-the- threshold of your synthetic self that you just saw and felt strutting around on (in) that Mirror. You look forward to establishing a new equilibrium by mastering the very circumstances you've just relived.

And so the Master tells you to "go back to the scene of the crime," go back to your physical body where your physical karma was made and work things out by Divine Love and the violet flame. When the necessary clearance of the astral and mental bodies is accomplished, Saint Germain tells you, you will be ready for the next session of therapy—the Ascended Master way.

This process is accelerated, he explains, through the curriculum of the Universities of the Spirit conducted by the Seven Chohans at their etheric retreats and it is fully anchored in the physical through intensives conducted by the Messengers and their staff at Summit University.

Beloved El Morya gives his chelas a similar initiation in Darjeeling. You remember his description in his letters to the chela on the Path:

"It is time to enter the chamber designed with blue and gold motif where there is a screen and seats arranged in theater style. For to understand your path, your very personal path to salvation, you must have the perspective of your past and how you have created the present—both at personal and planetary levels. Come, then, and let us see how we shall, in the magic of the flame, discover the designs of your soul destiny.... Now scenes of life in ancient Thrace appear on the screen, and we find ourselves in the marketplace of a forgotten city in the land that is now Turkey..."[97]

Thus unfolds a most intriguing tale—a scene of the pathos of an ancient karma come full circle in the lives of the viewers, to whom the Master also revealed the efficacy of the violet flame which they observed clearing the records on the screen right before their eyes. With such a profound insight as to the outworking of cosmic law, Morya's students return to their physical body consciousness determined to "make things right"—and you do too.

For the Lord of the First Ray promises: "The lessons learned by the soul out of the body during sleep are not lost but become a part of the composite of subconscious self-awareness, surfacing just enough to prick the soul memory and prod it to decisive action."

Indeed, the quickening of the outer mind to this inner soul experience, once it has returned to waking consciousness and the five senses, is often accomplished adroitly by the Master through the associative technique, or the arrangement of uncanny circumstances that loose the soul memory, sometimes in a torrent of emotions, as major turning points in her evolution and karma are relived.

Once again you stand before the Cosmic Mirror, expectant yet not knowing what to expect! This time Saint Germain shows you the original blueprint of your divine plan that was imprinted upon your etheric body when you were conceived in the heart of God. Thus, you learn another reason for reviewing your past lives one by one: it is to determine what portion of that plan you have outpictured to date and what portion you have not.

Now you can literally see and hear and feel (yes, and taste and smell!) the conditions in your little world that you have to correct—and there's no question about it: it's got to be done!

Thank God for the Cosmic Mirror!

Thank God for the violet flame!

There they go: the good momentums you've developed over lifetimes, the hang-ups and knotty problems of the past and present. And by your pluses you cancel out your minuses. You really believe and you *are* determined to fulfill that divine plan with your twin flame, very soon—as the history of the soul is reckoned.

What's more, Saint Germain tells you that you can call forth the talents you have developed in past ages, for these are stored as treasure in your causal body. With these you can elevate and bless and heal in the name of Jesus and your own Christ Self, endowing many with your past momentums of fruitful activity.

What's most amazing is Saint Germain's assurance that the manifestation of these gifts is not dependent upon the recall of your outer memory! But, he cautions, it is subject to the law of karma and what you the individual son of God will do (in accord with the gifts of the threefold flame and free will) with your spiritual resources once they are made available to you.

Hey! It's all up to me. I can do anything I want to—with God.

And so, elated, you return from this soul journey to the fireside of familiar hearth and home to resume reading about your inner soul experiences as recorded in "The Mirror of Consciousness"...

Mysteries of the Great Creative Self

Kings and poets and prophets and ordinary people have lived upon this earth and, by the hand of God, endowed our civilization with treasures from their causal bodies. And artists have profiled our spirits' strivings:

As Leonardo da Vinci unveiled with scientific precision the intricacies of Nature, as Rembrandt, in light, painted magnificently, as Titian in glowing colors brought to our attention the things of the subtle and fiery world, as Botticelli triumphed in Love and Logos over brute instincts, as Paolo Veronese, the Venetian master, in his feasts of color was able to capture on canvas the essence of the sacred fire in his studies of religious figures— so we, too, may reach out today (if we will it so), in the Eternal Now, to outline on the canvas of our lives the images of Christ we see.

Yes, reach out to God, not with the violence of the violent ones who "from the days of John the Baptist until now" would still steal the mysteries of heaven,[98] if they could. But with a cosmic outreach, placing one's hand trustingly in the hand of the Father, let us retrieve from the dim and distant past those great spiritual treasures that are the birthright of the sons and daughters of God—still marrying and being given in marriage on planet earth, still making love and war as they wait for Messiah.

I cannot believe that great men and women who have dotted the long historical stream were without the capacity to endow the centuries with unspoken tributes. I believe that their thoughts have never died but live to enrich us today. I believe they are a part of the world forte of self-knowledge and the world treasure-house of knowing God and knowing the elements and the mysteries that comprise the Godhead.

And what a delight this is! Why, it enhances our own capacity to retrieve in this moment something of the wonders of God's love as it has flowed through other hearts of his Mystical Body in a uniquely creative way.

What an abomination it would be if all that we could be today had been lost as potential because it had not been recorded in the sacred fires of akasha. What utter uselessness to man's striving in any age if the fruit of his joyous interchange with the Infinite should not live after him but be interred with his bones. But the truth is that the essence of Self—that something of lasting worth— lives on in akasha to be assimilated again and again through the race memory that is the collective spiritual evolution of high souls.

And what is akasha but creative substance itself upon which is stamped the memory of the eternal perfection outplayed in lives that have won and lost. Eternal perfection that our souls have glimpsed and grasped and let go of again and again. Eternal perfection in the cup of the moment that, like a hummingbird of delight, yet quivers in the atmosphere of the planet as it does in every little cube of cosmic space in all eternity.

As mirrors of both the divine and the human consciousness, these noble lifestreams, heaven-sent, have been mediators of the Word and the Work of God. Come, let us run for their Coming Revolution in Higher Consciousness. Yes! Let us be runners for earth's freedom, bearers of the torch of Aquarius kindled on heavenly altars. Where they have stooped to give Christ's cup of cool water to the little ones, let us also pause in our preoccupations to be ministering servants—through the mirror of their example.

What we say is not a preachment; it is a release of the living Word, who creates the fiber of our very bones—whose creative and re-creative processes never stopped and are ongoing. Just as cellular life lives and dies and is reborn according to the etheric blueprint which governs our entrances and exits at the molecular level, so we witness our cyclic rebirth in the creative fires.

Yes, a part of us is being reborn every moment—a part of us. Billions of parts return to the white-fire core of the Great Creative Self to be repolarized and thence to return in a new form for active duty.

This is the law of energy flow at the microscopic level. It is the 'reincarnation', if you will, of the very members of our bodies. It is Paul all over again saying, "I die daily."[99] And, we would add, "Daily I am born again as new life infills my soul . . . and the cosmic tides roll in and the cosmic tides roll out."

As every good gift and every perfect gift is from Above, so the release of the Word cometh down from the Father of Lights—with whom is no variableness, neither shadow of turning.[100]

Even so, our discourse comes directly from the archives of the Great White Brotherhood, where we find recorded the cosmic momentums of the victorious overcomers. Ascended Masters are they—who have taken dominion over their own foibles and fanciful doings and the temporary turnings of mankind's activities, mastered time, space, energy veils and worldly illusions and accelerated into the fiery coil of the I AM THAT I AM.

These conquering heroes have produced in their lives a momentum of excellence. And then, by the miracle of divine intervention and their own swing toward Perfection, they have released themselves from the entangling moss that sought, as by root weeds, to bind them deep within the subterranean earth.

The dark ones sought to overtake them, ah yes, by cunning and a calculated suppression of the Law of the One, so that they could not move forward or backward, to the right or to the left, being root-bound by a treacherous tradition that allowed not for the spiritual evolution of the soul.

All of this they overcame. Like the Lamb with his chosen and faithful who overcame ten horns and ten kings,[101] from the center of their being they released that divine seed with all of its internal vibrancy of cosmic action—until all turmoil and all struggle ceased and the seed, nestled in Mother Earth, swelled in the warm soil, protected by veils of invisibility.

Deep in the heart of the earth was the penetration of the magnificent rays of the sun. And then the little stalk came up—the green shoot of the first manifestation of Nature—like unto the embryonic manifestation of man or woman born of God within the womb of Matter as a tiny babe. This tiny babe—and we were all that—was destined to produce the miracle of the ages in consciousness.

It would have been no great victory for the Father, who created worlds without end turning in space, to produce the miracle of himself in his beloved Son, Christ Jesus, only to say to the world, "This is my only begotten Son...," and then leave it go at that, denying all other Sons (for whom he had also created the opportunity of partaking of the cosmic wafer) the substance of the Universal Body of God.

No, the greater miracle is the gift of free will that allows for the calling and the free election of all Sons of God to enter in to the divine inheritance. The miracle is that there is a choice and that, given free will, to be or not to be—with all of the delusions of Death and Hell and the lies of the archdeceivers of mankind (told and retold unto the death toll of individuality)—*some do choose and choose aright, some win the crown of eternal Life.*

Yes, some make it all the way to coequality with the firstborn. This, my beloved, is the great miracle of Life that God has placed before you. You can choose today to be that miracle Christ in action. It's not too late.

"Let this Mind be in you which was also in Christ Jesus, who, being in the form of God, thought it not robbery to be equal with God."[102] Be mindful, then, to equate yourself with the image of Christ, whose mirror image ye are, for thereby ye rob not but are robed in your lawful garment.

The statement "This is my Body which is broken for you"[103] contains a true and mystical meaning: it is the breaking of the loaf of Christhood, that all might have their divine portion, or crumb of God Identity, as a fiery seed-spark anchored within their own heart chakra.

And into the earth the Light poured and

poured again and created the warmth that would produce the germinal action of the seed, that the green shoot should come up, that the stalk should unfold, that the flowers should appear upon the branches of life (in the case of child-man, as the chakras upon the spinal stalk); and that the fragrance from bud to bloom, mind you, of the tiny babe would permeate the atmosphere of a planet with the immortality of God, the celestial sweetness whereby each soul comes to recognize its own supreme purpose:

"This is my immortal Light Body which is broken for you"—to attain the consciousness of the immortal Light Body and to lay it upon the altar of the children of the Light.

What a tragedy that so much of the world, hungering and thirsting after righteousness, cannot be filled—*because of their unbelief!*[104]

We may say this, but if we view this age and the crystallization of its ill-conceived concepts as the syndrome of mankind's failures to recognize God, then we should also see that the malady of their maladjustment to the Divine Self is being overlaid and complexified by factors of control in the media:

Now from every billboard, newspaper, magazine, TV and radio station we hear pronouncements from the Seat of the Scornful by 1,001 experts, preachments from the Throne of Ignorance channeled through the self-righteous know-it-alls in every field and, alas, carried piggyback by ordinary people in their human sense of struggle — the most fertile field I know for the sowers of world condemnation!

And neither the malady nor the pseudo-cures or epicures produce a damned thing! And childman, conceived in the Central Sun, is lost in the planetary wilderness of five billion people!

When we journeyed to the remote parts of India, when we traveled in Africa, Europe and across the United States, we were intrigued by the glaring similarity between people. They all come into this world with "two eyes, a nose, and a mouth," arranged in a random but detectably similar karmic outline. They look quite a bit alike.

Some speculate there are a hundred and forty-four and others a hundred and forty-four thousand archetypes of the Christic seed of the Solar Logoi in the world. Through the generations of the root races* these types have combined and been affected by individual and group karma. Nevertheless, if you look very carefully, you'll observe that these models are repetitive. You see them in downtown Colorado Springs; you go over to Calcutta, Damascus or Accra and, apart from a little darkening of the skin, the same faces appear in an only slightly different mode or stature.

These archetypes are based upon Elohimic law — the law of the Father-Mother God as the Elohim of creation. This "Divine Us"[105] we know

---

*According to esoteric tradition there are seven primary aggregates of souls, that is, the first to the seventh root races. Each has a unique archetypal pattern, divine plan and mission to fulfill on earth, and Manu (group leader). In addition, other evolutions of light have been born among the root races.

as twin flames of the Divine Whole—seven in the outer spheres, five in the inner—represents the divisions of the Godhead in its various functions and activities.

Elohim are the instrumentalities of the Word, the Creators of form in Spirit and in Matter. The seven bodies of man* are their seven wonders of the Macrocosmic/microcosmic worlds. Wherefore the being of man, through interpenetrating sheaths of cosmic consciousness conceived by Elohim, experiences Life simultaneously in these several octaves and those above.

Man "made a little lower than the angels, yet crowned with glory and honor"![106]

We look around and we ask ourselves, "Where is the glory? Where is the honor?" Surely not in temporal things. There are ways that one can find God, even now. But these are not stereotyped.

You would find—if you knew the workings of cosmic law, as it was revealed to my soul as Origen of Alexandria, for example—that you would be able to unravel some of the scriptural mysteries for yourself. And you'd find it's a lot more fun than crocheting a bedspread. It can even be more fun than watching the World Series!

We get involved in sports and physical exercise to a degree, we keep ourselves trim and we advocate that you do, too. These things, like yoga, T'ai Chi Ch'üan or other of the martial arts, are for a purpose. They are not to be taken as an end in themselves, however, for ours is a culture of the

*See pages 328–32.

Spirit (as opposed to being a physical culture for its own vain ends).

But, fear not, one does not need to become a sissified, ossified example of the Ascended Masters. One can be, as God has made us all to be, an example of a well-rounded person who has had all of the square corners knocked off, you understand.

Sometimes life deals us a sledgehammer blow. Life seems crushing at times, and I think nowhere more so than in the sudden turn of events or misfortune which we simply cannot fathom because of our basic misunderstanding of our relationship to God. We just don't understand the rules of this game of life we've been playing for aeons — sometimes winners, sometimes losers, sometimes on the opposing team, sometimes on the Home team.

How easy it is for man to misunderstand the things of the Spirit that are so simple, when he is ignorant of karmic law or the potential for problems of past lives to replay themselves suddenly — for his growth.

Now, Origen, so they tell me, was a great lover of the Logos and a seeker of Truth. In his work *On First Principles* he explains that "the aim of the Holy Spirit, who thought it right to give us the divine Scriptures, is not that we might be able to be edified by the letter alone or in all cases, since we often discover that the letter is impossible or insufficient in itself because by it sometimes not only irrationalities but even impossibilities are described.

"But the aim of the Holy Spirit is that we

should understand that there have been woven into the visible narrative truths that, if pondered and understood inwardly, bring forth a law useful to men and worthy of God."[107] (emphasis added)

And Jesus' words also ring true: "Ye do err not knowing the scriptures nor the power of God."[108] Thus, in our ignorance we cannot possess our souls, can we? The fact is we suffer mightily from our ignorance of cosmic law.

Now, concerning God's work and our own, if we were interested in just earning a living, how happy we might be to divest ourselves of the garments of spiritual teacher. What pleasure it would be for a while—if a livelihood were our only concern—to be able to work eight hours a day and then come home and say, "Now the day is over. My period of rest is drawing nigh."

For we find that as we look up and see the Father's fields whitened to the harvest,[109] there is only work and more work. But, you see, we are not interested in the mere pleasures of a mundane routine. Actually, we'd be bored stiff. On the contrary, I find immense happiness in the words of God, which are so precious to us, that came through Christ Jesus. He said, "My Father worketh hitherto and I work"[110]—and this, too, is a scriptural mystery that needs to be decoded.

Interesting phrase, isn't it? We understand ourselves—you and me—as working hand in hand, heart to heart with the Father through the same universal Mind that was in Christ Jesus. He also said, "My meat is to do the will of him that sent me, *and to finish his Work.*"[111]

All of us have our own work to do. But it is God's Work on earth that we must truly make our own, as President Kennedy said[112]—that we may one day work his Work in heaven. And nowhere is this Work more apparent than in the spiritual field.

Truly, it is a joyous spiritual labor that engages all of our forces as we seek to remove the many veils of self-illusion and confusion behind which good people have cloistered themselves from Reality. These hang between the layers of consciousness as partitions of inner self-division and walls that keep out God and loved ones. And we must train others to do the same Work—*for it is the mighty Work of the ages.*

And we also know firsthand the meaning of spiritual liberty—and spiritual bondage. Having ourselves been bought with a price,[113] we have come with Christ to set the captives free.

I (Mark) remember so well my musings on God as a child—and I speak not from an ivory tower or attainment at the top of the stairs, but as one who swings by the grace of God upon a rope, my life being in his hands. I speak of my own childhood experiences when I scarcely knew what was behind the appearances all around me and I speculated as a child speculates (even as a baby in his crib speculates). I pondered upon the meaning of life and in my childlike way I said, "What is life all about?"

SUMMIT UNIVERSITY PRESS®

Non-Profit Publisher since 1975

Tell us how you liked this book!

Book title: _____

Comments: _____

_____

_____

What did you like the most? _____

How did you find this book? _____

☐ **YES! Send me FREE BOOK CATALOG**   ☐ **I'm interested in more information**

Name _____

Address _____

City _____

State _____ Zip Code _____

E-mail: _____

Phone no. _____

Your tax-deductible contributions make these publications
available to the world.

Please make your checks payable to:
Summit University Press, PO Box 5000, Gardiner, MT 59030.
Call us toll free at 1-800-245-5445.
Outside the U.S.A., call 406-848-9500.
E-mail: tslinfo@tsl.org
www.summituniversitypress.com

491-LTKSP #6350 5/05

BUSINESS REPLY MAIL
FIRST-CLASS MAIL   PERMIT NO. 20   GARDINER MT

POSTAGE WILL BE PAID BY ADDRESSEE

SUMMIT UNIVERSITY PRESS®

PO Box 5000

Gardiner, MT 59030-9900

And then an answer came from within myself
as I lay on my stomach on a pile of sand looking at
the blue sky, the drifting clouds, and all that I saw
before me. And as I fashioned castles out of sand,
I knew that they were temporary sand castles that
could be trampled upon by a foot or washed away.
I knew all of this. But as my mind dwelled in the
realm of the sand—my little eyes and ears being
focused on passing games—there was another part
of me that was far, far away in the blue sky.

And when I say this, I jest not. I knew that
I was there at the same time that I knew I was here!
Do you understand? I knew there was something
in me that had a point of contact with the universe,
but my child mind grasped only the simplicity of
the moment—not the complexity.

The Master said, "Unless ye become as a
little child, ye cannot enter into the kingdom
of heaven."[114]

Can we grasp this principle of being able to
descend in consciousness to the child level and at
the same instant being able to go out with the
maturity of the living God who created the cosmic
wristwatch with all of its superb intricacy and the
sublimity of our bodies and the vessels of our
minds, who arranged the wafers of creation as discs
of light thinly pressed between the substance of our
worlds—and we ourselves the chalice of Nature
and all of this?

And yet, would we be content at this moment,
would we be satisfied with our physical bodies, if

there were not also—as a sponge retains both water and air—a chalice for the deep feelings of God and the thoughts of his Mind? Try feeling without a heart or thinking without a brain! Or doing both without the chakras and central nervous system!

You hear the beating of your heart, you feel the pulse of the mind and yet you know within yourself that the heart and brain can do nothing until energized by the currents of the soul. *Something is there that is greater*, something that has a reach and a stretch beyond our physical capacity—something that can contact Infinity from the realms of time and space!

And so, from the point of this realization, we want to remind you of the importance of what we may call the simultaneous action of universal spiritual worship—that is, of right action being the culmination of our worship.

While I agree that it may be folly to worship without the totality of worship that is involved in doing "the things which I say," as the Master said[115]—to be involved only with the written word, only with the word of devotion, without actually carrying out the Word in some ultimate usefulness in our lives, would be a gross error.

Yet this very thing goes on all over the world. The Master said, "This people draweth nigh unto me with their mouth and honoreth me with their lips; but their heart is far from me."[116]

So, as we think of the activities, relatively (more or less) real and unreal, that are going on in the world that by stark contrast compel the divine answer, let us think of a little prayer meeting in Jerusalem two thousand years ago at which the Master Jesus presided with a handful of his disciples.

By the flickering light of little lamps dipped in oil, they conducted a period of intense devotion and contact with the miracle of the first love of God. They did not feel lost in time. There had been ages before them and there would be ages after them. And most likely, they had been and would be active participants in both.

They knew the Living God, and their knowingness is a tangible reality that can be conveyed— as though it hung in the air, a thing in itself, waiting to be plucked by us to make it our own as we gather today, candles lit in prayer, with the Son of God and all his immortal saints.

Messengers for Christ

One of the most profound experiences I have had in recording the Lost Teachings of beloved Jesus all these years was in my communion with the Lord and his "little brother" Saint Francis (who goes by the name of Kuthumi, "Koot Hoomi" or "K.H." among the Eastern mahatmas) as they dictated to me their series of letters on *Prayer and Meditation* to disciples of Truth in every quarter of the globe.

You see, the mantle of Messenger of the Great White Brotherhood we wear is actually an auric field—an ovoid of sacred fire—placed upon us by the Master Jesus with Saint Germain, Mother Mary, El Morya and Kuthumi, who assisted the beloved Christ in our very specific and rigorous training to serve as their amanuenses (spiritual scribes, or secretaries).

These Masters, together with others we have named and many saints who have ascended from the mystery schools of East and West, use that 'mantle'—actually a highly charged electronic energy field—to transfer not only the Lost Teachings of Jesus to his disciples on the path of individual Christhood but also the initiations of the sacred fire.

These initiations are given as a transfusion of concentrated spiritual power conveyed by the Ascended Masters to their devotees through the magnetic field of our auras and chakras. Thus, to their own chelas the immortal Gurus offer from their hearts a portion of their attainment, drawn from the glorious momentum of their service to Life and oneness in the Godhead. This takes place both through the fohat of the spoken Word and the ritual of the "laying on of hands"[117] in one-to-one physical contact or by other means, such as the use of gemstones or crystals, herbs or elixirs and the serving of Holy Communion, any of which may be charged by the Master's portion he desires to transmit to his chelas.

When an Ascended Master's delivery in dictation, discourse or sermon is attended in person or on tape, either way (for the Lord is always in the midst of his own) his Light, focused through physical sound impinging on physical matter, does indeed convey his consciousness for renewal, uplift and restoration. And this, too, is initiation.

Thus, through this anointing to a calling beyond ourselves and our humble abilities, we received the spiritual gifts of prayer and meditation—of the science of mantra, the divine decree and the invocation unto the Lord GOD—from the hearts of the World Teachers. This office of the Great White Brotherhood—the office of World Teacher, whose holders represent the Universal Christ to earth's evolutions—is jointly carried by the Masters Jesus and Kuthumi. Together they are bearing the responsibility for our preaching of the Everlasting Gospel in every nation, that the full message of Christ might be known in every heart, that the end (fulfillment) of the dispensation of Pisces might come.[118]

Toward that goal the World Teachers also dictated forty-eight *Corona Class Lessons . . . for those who would teach men the Way*, which they released to world teachers in training. These lessons are the true Christian's guide to the true mysticism of our Lord.

Jesus told Martha—and I have witnessed the akashic records of that event—that bearing the Flame of the World Mother two thousand years hence, she would be his instrument in proclaiming his Teaching. This Teaching, he said, the false priests would be sure to adulterate to their self-serving ends as ever they had done in each prior two-thousand-year dispensation of the Universal Christ. Moreover, the true healing and restoring of the Lost Word and even the Lost Arts of Healing — arts sent by Sanat Kumara and reignited by Padma Sambhava — would likewise be denied the people in the last days of Pisces.

Thus it is in the context of a two-thousand-year mission that our cup runneth over with joy in the privilege of preparing these precious Pearls of Wisdom on *Prayer and Meditation* containing the nectar of Christ in the most poetically beautiful, profoundly intimate impartations of the Son of God on his communion with the Father through the art and science of perpetual prayer.

Let me share with you — even as the Master broke the Bread of Life for us all — these lines of dear Kuthumi, who approaches the heart of each supplicant with true reverence, humility and wisdom:

The miracle of attunement is many sided. Our beloved Jesus has emphasized continual prayer. I have been asked by the brothers of Light of the Darjeeling Council to discourse on the subject of meditation. Let the words of my mouth and the meditation of my heart be acceptable in thy sight.

Jesus and I desire jointly that the words and deeds that men do should be Godlike. Prayer and meditation are like twins framing the pathway to holiness and delight. Just as prayer or entreaty makes contact with God, drawing down into the world of the seeker the rays of divine intercession, so meditation lifts up the son of man that he may be bathed in the radiance of the Eternal.

Meditation is an aerating of the mind, a flushing-out of silt and misconception. Meditation is for purification. It is the thought of man about his Creator. The dust of the world must be blown away, the threshing floor of the heart of man swept clean. In prayer man makes intercession to God for assistance; in meditation he gives assistance to God by creating the nature of God within his own thoughts and feelings.

Many pray from the standpoint of the sinner asking forgiveness for sin. But after forgiveness what? After forgiveness for the sin must come the re-creation of the Divine Man. As man was framed in the mortal image, so must he be formed now in the image of the Eternal. It has not been enough that the image of God, from its lofty position, has been vouchsafed to every man. The gift has not been received in manifestation.

Therefore, to meditate upon the gift is to draw the attunement of the soul toward the harmony of God-realization. If man has been a thief, now he becomes the giver. If he has thought evil of others, now he becomes the mediator, the intercessor, the meditator upon their perfection as well as upon his own, reaffirming by his acts the mission of the Christ.[119]

Beyond the verses recorded by us as scribes there are those "unspeakable words not lawful for a man [or woman] to utter,"[120] as the apostle Paul referred to his own communion with the Lord. More than this we cannot say.

Yes, we have journeyed with him to exalted spheres and inner retreats of the Great White Brotherhood and we have seen the hierarchies and hosts of heaven as well as the things which are coming upon the world by its own karma—the karma of spiritual neglect and nonaccountability for physical deeds, the doings of peoples and nations for which so few are willing to pay the price.

Yes, we have been given knowledge and certain powers not communicable and nontransferable—knowledge and powers that come to the disciple who reaches levels of service and responsibility where these can no longer be withheld—because the Great Law demands it and will not withhold from the Lord's servant the spiritual gifts necessary to the carrying out of his assignment and office.

For God is no respecter of persons (pure sons). What one man has done any man can do. What God will perform in and through one of his servant-Sons he will perform through any who will similarly qualify himself. Jesus said, "I go to prepare a place for you that where I AM [in consciousness and service] there may ye be also."[121] This shows the nonexclusivity of the mission of Jesus in heaven as well as on earth.

"This is my Universal Body of Light *broken for you.*" The Lord shares not only his Mission and his Teaching but his very Being—his life and breath, his essence and path of initiation. Everything he tells us and shares with us, beloved, is his way of showing his Love: "All that I AM I give to you, that you also may become who and what I AM and no less the incarnation of the Universal Christ on earth and in heaven than I AM."

Thus, our understanding is daily being exalted to the higher octaves of God's grace by the direct intercession of the Ascended Master Jesus Christ and other Lightbearers of East and West who have also mounted the coil of sacred fire to ascend out of the mortal socket. From our experience on the inner planes and the outer, we are convinced that the chela's personal and ongoing contact with this Avatar as well as with the cloud of witnesses, the saints robed in white, that heavenly company known as the Great White Brotherhood, is both necessary and preordained to the accomplishment of reunion with God.

Many among earth's evolutions have received increments of the fires of freedom and the vigil of the Lady with the Lamp: the Goddess of Liberty, who keeps the flame of the Woman clothed with the Sun in New York harbor, as she is the guardian of the gateway to the New World and the lost Atlantean continent.

This Mother figure, unifying force of a nation compelled to rediscover its identity through her heart, has dictated words of Love to a mighty people who have yet to awaken to their reason for being. May they do so before it is too late:

> We long ago won our victory and attained our ascension by this path. I became the Goddess of Liberty, having liberated personally millions of souls on a number of planetary homes prior to my ascension. And since then I have never ceased to bear that flame of Liberty to those just about to come into their own who needed a transfusion of Light from my heart.
>
> O beloved, I have rejoiced to see their faces, their hearts, and their souls aglow. I give to you that infusion that you might be myself in form....
>
> I come, then, as your blessed Mother still standing and keeping the flame at the doorway to America. It is a mighty gate through which the entire span of the evolutions of the world have passed at one time or another—even on ancient Atlantis, when the gate [as it still stands] was on the west side of that continent....
>
> I come bearing the torch of the Central Sun, a rekindling fire of illumination. I am

Liberty, mother of nations and planetary spheres and of your blessed hearts of fire.

I am come for the awakening of the ancient memory. I come for illumination and the consuming of that which burdens the mind and soul. And what is that burden, beloved? It is the burden of ignorance of the Law and the ignoring of the path of Love. Thus, I call all of those who are of the Light from one end of the earth to the other into the very heart of allegiance to the Law of the One.[122]

"Which of you," as Jesus said, "by taking thought can add one cubit to his stature?"[123] Which of you, if you wanted to, would be able to change yourself? Who among you can reverse the downward trends of a civilization and a continent? Yet this we must do if we are to survive the course of our soul's evolution on this planet.

For we are living in the "time of trouble" prophesied by Daniel when a certain people whose names are to be found written in "the book" shall be delivered.[124] It is the great prince of the archangels, Saint Michael, also prophesied by Daniel as standing "for the children of thy people," who today is calling out from among the nations those who know from within that they must take part in the great awakening and the great gathering of the elect.[125]

To assemble those who have kept the flame

of the Motherland throughout all ages and on all continents, Saint Germain, hierarch of the Aquarian age, anointed us as Christ's Messengers in this era of deliverance. He conferred upon us the office of the Two Witnesses who should prophesy in the last days[126] and he sponsored Summit University as the modern-day mystery school to bring to the remembrance of the Children of the Sun their lost and forgotten heritage.

Those who attend our quarterly conferences are electrified by this beloved Master of Freedom and his Coming Revolution in Higher Consciousness—whose entrance on the world stage Jesus' angel foretold, saying: "But in the days of the voice of the seventh angel, when he shall begin to sound, the mystery of God should be finished, as he hath declared to his servants the prophets."[127]

His name—Sanctus Germanus—means simply "holy brother." His followers he has called to be Keepers of the Flame—of Life and Liberty and the Great Awakening. Their motto: "To know, to dare, to do and to be silent." Acutely aware of the mounting problems facing the people of earth, they join forces to direct the violet flame into a diseased planet plagued by war, famine, and injustice in every quarter.

You, too, can hear and study the important messages delivered by the Ascended Masters on how to deal with the forces shaping our lives and the future of our civilization. And you can take advantage of a full course of study given in our seminars and retreats. And we welcome you to do so.

And so, if we are willing to lose our sense of sophistication, regardless of how much we know or think we know, if we are willing to apprentice ourselves in greater measure to the Godhead and to tie ourselves willingly to the Great White Brotherhood (in other words, to get on the bandwagon with the Ascended Masters in this age), if we're willing to be taught, if we're willing to allow ourselves to become involved in the great divine experiment, in the cosmic adventure—then heaven has a valuable lesson to teach us.

For example, much of the early embryonic teachings of the Great White Brotherhood are set down already in the Keepers of the Flame Lessons. Did you know that this organization has a fraternity in it? Like the Knights of Columbus, the Masons, or even the Rosicrucians or any fraternal or secret order descended from the Rose Cross, our fraternity, founded by Saint Germain, has teachings.

These teachings reveal the early experiments in spiritual alchemy whereby, through the practical application of the Law, your whole mind and being can shift from the limited mind to a mind that is open to God—like a great funnel. And when this happens, you're going to be very happy—spiritually happy and fulfilled.

Those of you who are not Keepers of the Flame still have the opportunity to read our *Pearls of Wisdom*. And what are they? They are letters to all sincere seekers of Truth from the Ascended

Masters, such as Saint Germain, Mother Mary, Paul the Venetian, and many of the great Eastern Adepts, together with El Morya, whose portrait, painted from the likeness given to H. P. Blavatsky, hangs in our chapel at headquarters and in our centers throughout the world.

Originally sent out as weekly messages from the Masters to their disciples, they contain priceless instruction for your study of the Great Law governing your soul's incarnation on earth. They are truly Pearls of great price, without price.

We don't charge anything for our teachings. Our costs only—paper, printing, postage, bindery, distribution, and basic needs of our staff—we pass along to you. But the teaching itself never has a price tag. We do send the *Pearls of Wisdom* all over the world to thousands of people, but we don't ask you to come up here to the altar and make a public display of yourself, as the Reverend Billy Graham and other preachers do.

I'm not trying to be irreverent concerning anyone or his religion and I do recognize the value of a public confession of Christ—as long as the confessors understand what is happening. For it can be the first and most important step in a man's salvation, but it can never be more than that if he doesn't go out and "work the works of him that sent me,"[128] imitate the path of the Saviour, drink all of his cup and bear the fruit of his own Christ consciousness with signs following.[129]

So we don't ask you to confess Christ, lest you

rest easy and get into that lazy belief system where Jesus did it all and paid your karmic debts in full. All we ask is that you avail yourself of what God has already placed in store for you through Jesus' Lost Teachings dictated by the Ascended Masters and published as *Pearls of Wisdom* since 1958. These are now appearing in bound volumes which have traveled around the globe.[130]

A Revolution for All Christendom

Thus, we preach that the denial of the present potential of God's children on earth today to realize their individual Christhood and to attain to divine Sonship lies at the crux of all problems personal and planetary. For we believe that the denial of this Truth of very truths in the hearts of God's children was the first 'photon' of Antichrist's philosophy that, from the foundation of this world, spawned the modus of the Liar and the Murderer of Messiah.

So far have they deluded us into their idolatrous dogma of the exclusivity of Jesus in his mission that they get us to weep and wail over Jesus' crucifixion every year on Good Friday instead of focusing our prayer power in a worldwide spiritual rebirth and revolution, engaging all of Christendom in the challenge of the crucifiers of our children and youth. This is the crucifixion that is *the happening* of today. And it's the one we're supposed to be doing something about.

We speak of the crucifixion of Christ in our

children through drugs and the death culture of marijuana, cocaine, rock music and the raping of their chakras through the squandering of the life-force in every manner of perversity and promiscuity. From abortion to child abuse, child molestation, child pornography and prostitution to teen dropouts and suicides, it is the denial of the innate potential for personal Christhood in everyone born of God that we are seeing every day everywhere as the Good Friday 'spell'.

I use this term because most of the world are spellbound before this aggression, this atrocity. And it is being celebrated as a Black Mass, a rite to Satan, not once a year but seven days a week, not by the dear followers of Christ who have become sheep led astray, but by the fallen angels in embodiment, by evil men, seed of the Devil, call them what you will—they are the crucifiers of our Lord *in* his children. These destroyers have all the help they could ever want in the milk-toast, mealy-mouthed preachers and politicians who say and do everything else but lead a fiery revolution in defense of the children of every nation.

And I hope that by my words to you, which are the living Truth, and the words of Jesus Christ to the churches today some will be sparked, some will be wrenched free from the grip and spell—some will laugh those accusers of the brethren to scorn when they tell you you are sick, disturbed, demented, brainwashed or programmed if you believe that Christ in you can save the world.

Well, Jesus believed that Christ in him could save the world and we believe that Christ in him will save the world. But Jesus also believes that Christ in each one of us can and will save the world. He has told me so. He said it plain: "Ye are the Light of the world. A city [citadel of Christ consciousness] that is set on an hill [of attainment] cannot be hid."[131]

He said, *Ye are the Light of the world....* So why shouldn't we stand firm on his belief in us and in Christ with us—affirming it and confirming it with signs following?

Why are we so easily intimidated and dissuaded by mass opinion molded by the media and the architects of a brave new world? Are we afraid to be crucified with Jesus and his little children whom he suffered to come unto him? If we are afraid to be crucified for his name's sake or theirs, we are not worthy of him, we mock his Christianity, and we are accomplices of the devils who murder the souls of the very Lightbearers Christ sends from heaven to fight side by side with us in this Armageddon.

Oh ho, you say, the Devil can't murder a soul and what does it matter if he aborts a body or a life, because the soul itself is not touched. Again ye do err, not knowing the scriptures! And those very devils who are destroying your children know the meaning of scripture better than you do, and better than the pastors who have unthinkingly handed down the premeditated tradition which has adversely affected your thoughts and acts.

Ezekiel says, "The soul that sinneth, it shall die."[132] The devils know this, so they entice the soul to sin so it will die in its sin—precisely why Jesus warned the children of the Light: "He who [under the influence of Satan] shall blaspheme against the Holy Ghost [ascribing to the Devil the Word and Work of the Son of God] hath never forgiveness [not until he stops sinning!], but is in danger of eternal damnation."[133]

Jesus also said, "Fear not them which kill the body, but are not able to kill the soul: but rather fear him which is able to destroy both soul and body in hell."[134]

So Jesus told you there are powers in hell— and he was referring to the fallen angels—who to this day are going about denying the words and works of Christ *in you* and destroying souls. And Mother Mary told you at Fátima in 1917 that many souls would be lost because of the failure of the Church to courageously challenge World Communism.[135] And Jesus showed John in his Revelation that some souls for their unredeemed evil works (karma) would pass through the second death in the Last Judgment.[136]

So now will you believe that the soul can be lost?

Now will you believe there is a war going on and that it's being waged by these wolves in sheep's clothing who, moving among the true pastors, don their white collars and feign pure motives but are nevertheless frocked in black, the color of the false hierarchy that has also duped them?

Now, before it's too late, will you believe that the war is being waged for one purpose: the death of *your* soul—its Light, its faculties, its sensitivity, its integrity, its very Life?

You just can't ignore the Cosmic Law any longer!

Because if you do, you won't make it through the labyrinth of your own human creation—much less the astral plane!

Well, I for one have given and shall continue to give my life many times over for the promulgation of this Truth. For it has been spoken to me by the Father, by his Son Jesus, and by the Archangels and their legions who battle daily in defense of the Light in these little ones and who need your prayers and dynamic decrees in order to take authoritative and decisive action on earth.

And I don't care what anyone thinks of me or says about me—not by anyone's hypocrisy or entrapments or ridicule shall I be moved. Nor will I recant Christ's doctrine which I preach and which is carefully and thoughtfully set forth in the works published by Elizabeth and me. And may my poor example encourage you to take a stand with all your heart and life for what you believe in.

Just be sure you know the source of your information and that it is the highest. Just be sure you stand on the principle of Jesus Christ, and him transfigured before you—yes, crucified, resurrected and ascended *before you*. And then be sure you know why you believe what you do, that you have objectively considered every side of the question and that you are not the victim of another man's foolhardiness.

Beware of those prowling spirits which are discarnate entities, impostors of the Holy Ghost who tell you you are possessed of the Spirit when you are demon possessed of evil forces like the sorcerer whom Paul found at Paphos—drunk with his own power, seduced by demons, whom the Lord blinded "for a season" at the word of Paul.[137]

Too many Christians today are greedy for the spiritual gifts, thus giving themselves up to seducing spirits instead of waiting for the true initiations of the Holy Spirit through the Maha Chohan and the Chohans of the Seven Rays.

This is the grave danger people open themselves up to in their spiritual ambition and spiritual pride in receiving the Holy Ghost or becoming healers or miracle workers or in their desire to speak in tongues. And in their very human passion for the gifts, they have missed the zeal of the LORD which they must have to free the little children from both embodied and disembodied devils who assault their senses, their chakras and their sweet, trusting hearts.

Men and women of faith, take to the streets and preach the Truth for your own souls' sake; for there is where the slaughter is, and too few raise a hand or a cry. The wars declared on drugs, poverty, pornography, child abuse and abortion have not been won—for want of Christed ones to lead the battle, unashamed to proclaim the Ascended Masters as the uncompromising victors capable of winning today—*if we let them.*

Atlantis Revisited

The Ascended Masters are our Elder Brothers and Teachers. It has ever been so. They, the wayshowers of our spirits' fiery destiny, have from the beginning held the vision of epochs of perfection we once knew.

For we, too, were embodied on ancient Lemuria, a civilization and a Motherland that brought forth the highest development of culture, science, and technology ever known on this planet. Her golden ages exceeded in every field of endeavor the most advanced developments of modern man.

Indelibly inscribed in the records of our own subconscious is the memory of an era when the life-span of a people was measured in centuries rather than decades, when we, too, walked and talked with the Immortals, were never separated from our twin flame, and beheld our Teachers face to face.

When life on the continent of Mu was corrupted by aliens and fallen angels with their grotesque genetic miscreations, mocking the Godhead and violating the sacred science of the Mother by engaging men in wars of the gods, the Masters withdrew from the masses and gathered their initiates in mystery schools to guard the Light of the Mother flame and her wisdom.

Just before the climactic end when the desecration of the holy shrines and the abominations of the flesh of man and beast had all but extinguished the divine spark in her people, the warning was sounded by the hierarchs of the Cosmic Council that the Great Law would return full circle and in full force the vileness of mankind's deeds. And the children of Mu, the few who heeded their prophets and got out in time, beheld from afar as their beloved Motherland went down midst smoke and fire in sudden violent cataclysm such as the world has never seen, not before or since.

In more recent ages, prior to the Egyptian civilization, we recall the land of Poseid—also known as Poseidonis, Atla, or Atlantis—portions of which were nigh the Azores. We recall the capital of Caiphul described by Phylos the Thibetan in his book *A Dweller on Two Planets*—"the Royal City, the greatest of that ancient day, within the limits of which resided a population of two million souls, unencompassed by walled fortifications." The author says its broad avenues were

shaded by great trees; its artificial hills—the largest surmounted by governmental palaces, and pierced and terraced by the avenues which radiated from the city-center like spokes in a wheel. Fifty miles these ran in one direction, while at right angles from them, traversing the breadth of the peninsula, forty miles in length, were the shortest avenues. Thus lay, like a splendid dream, this, the proudest city of that ancient world.... Though it had no walls, around the whole city extended a huge moat, three-quarters of a mile broad by an average of sixty feet in depth and supplied by the waters of the Atlantic....

A marked feature of Caiphul was the wealth and rare beauty of its trees and tropical shrubbery, lining the avenues, covering the multitudinous palace-crowned hills, many of which had been constructed to rise two or even three hundred feet above the level of the plain. Trees and shrubs and plants, vines and flowers, annuals and perennials, filled the mimic canyons, gorges, defiles and levels which it had delighted the art-loving Poseidi to create. They covered the slopes, twined the miniature cliffs, the walls of buildings, and hid even the greater part of the steps which led in wide-sweeping banks to the edges of the moat—overlaying everything like a glorious verdant garment.[138]

Some of us recall these early experiences as though it were yesterday. Twelve thousand years ago Atlantis was a part of our world. It is recorded in Genesis that before the flood which sank the mighty continent of Atla "the earth was corrupt before God, and the earth was filled with violence. And God looked upon the earth, and, behold, it was corrupt; for all flesh had corrupted his way upon the earth. And God said unto Noah, The end of all flesh is come before me; for the earth is filled with violence through them; and, behold, I will destroy them with the earth."[139]

The same cycles of vileness and wickedness that had destroyed Lemuria were now closing in on titanic Atla—the continent, they said, that "even God couldn't sink"—and would later crystallize the judgment of Sodom and Gomorrah, Pompeii, and other cultures corrupted by the love of pleasure before God.

As man's love for God and the devotional exercise *(bhakti)* of his heart to the living Word deteriorated, the flame within the temples went out and the heart flames of the people flickered and waned. Then came the day when all was buried by mud, walls of mud. So passed the glory of the gods that were made of clay and with them their mechanization man—dust to dust, mud to mud.

Lord Lanto, speaking of his recollections of the last days of Atlantis, once said:

Light is the Light of Knowledge and it was conveyed in part to the hierarchs of Atlantis. I know, for I lived and walked among them. I beheld all that they did of nobility and grandeur.

I saw their achievements in science and

invention. I beheld the minarets of Atlantis and the beautiful sailing vessels which plied the seas of the world. I saw the statues of Atlantis created by a special chemical and alchemical process which to this present day is unknown to mankind. I watched as the permanent glaze was applied to these statues which caused them to glisten in the sun with a whiteness which men of today have not seen.

I observed how decadence came into the priesthood and crept into the masses of mankind as political infidelity spread abroad throughout that land and among the priesthood as well. I saw how the powers of dissolution [disillusionment] worked no miracle except to bring despondency to the youth who were waiting and looking to the aged and mature to bring forth some form of salvation against the creeping paralysis of immorality which became prevalent throughout the land.

I saw how the beautiful white color of the glistening statues, representing the culture of that age, was blackened by the sordid despair which corroded men's sense of values and destroyed all the beauty that had been ages in accumulating. That which happened, which became reality, that which existed which is the story of Atla, queen of the sea, is a record of man's infamy—a record of man's despair.[140]

The people of that continent have continued to reembody throughout the ages, some descending to the same levels of darkness, others rising to win their ascension. And free will is the sole survivor of every (man's) cataclysm—the free will to make it right and build again in the next round. What else can you do when all of your past lies in rubble and ashes at your feet?

Thus, under the direction of the Brotherhood, mystery schools emerged here and there—in ancient China and India and more recently in the appearance of the Hebrews and their prophets, the Sangha of the Buddha, Pythagoras' Academy at Crotona, the Druids, the Essenes, Christ's community of the called-out ones, and the School of the Sangreal at King Arthur's court.

And so, we see that at Luxor and various mystery schools across the planet, the torch of the Mother and the Motherland has been passed. But it has not been seized by the majority, although many have benefited from the various flames which still burn in etheric octaves in the retreats of the Masters around the world.

And so it is in these flames that we discover we are not that far apart from each other— Christian and Jew, black man and white man, Chinese and Indian. For these too were there on Atlantis—and some that had no Life in them.[141] Nevertheless, all races and peoples upon the face of the earth in whom there burns the divine spark are made by one God for one destiny.

The destiny must be grand. It must be noble.

It must be worthy. And if we will it so, we can be a part of that destiny. Or we can deny ourselves that destiny by indulging ourselves in the enmeshing concepts of hatred (which is always "self"-hatred in one form or another) directed against ourselves and other selves and, beyond these, against the Great Creative Self, yes, the singular object of many men's contempt. For many are wed to the dweller-on-the-threshold, the seething, touchy synthetic self.

Charged feelings of hatred are incendiary, hot coals of hellfire and damnation heaped upon rivals in the schoolyard of life. These may very well destroy "thine enemies" but they will always return to the point of origin—you—to do their greatest damage. No, you will not escape your hatreds. For hatred shrivels the soul. Hatred makes small the mind. And the matrices of hatred produce the bane of unhappiness.

Therefore, learn from the Maha Chohan how you can bind the beast of self-hatred by cords of the Ruby Ray!

If we would know God, we must know the meaning of Love in all its wonders—not a love that reaches out to grasp something or someone, but a love that reaches out as the angelic hand of Charity either to receive or give, according to heavenly polarities, that we may become identified with the nature of God.

What is the nature of God? The nature of the living God is Spirit and he is spiritual. He *is* Love. And his Love is spiritual, blanketing humanity with the fulfillment of the essential needs of soul and body.

By contrast, we see the dying world of the nonreceptive in the homicides and fratricides of warring gangs and gangsters and rival ethnic groups positioned for battle in the streets of our large cities.

Mass murder in the name of peace. Terrorists terrorize in the name of freedom. Yet these, too, are the remnants and renegades of Atlantis revisited. And airplane and highway disasters take their toll—'accidents' of our karma. Not to mention physical cataclysm in the earth body, constant death by cancer and other effects of mass hatred boomeranging, in effect, as a spiritual suicide on the guilty as well as the seeming innocent in the course of just "ordinary living."

It is the dying of the world of untouchables we see. Those untouched by Love—by choice. Fists clenched, arms folded in disdain, daredevils defiant of Life. Someone once called them "mindless Atlantean masses." But if God as Love is everywhere, how can this be!

Free will, as everyone knows, or should, is the key to the God experience—and Love and Life and Happiness! This we have already explained. And in your hands we have placed the Master's key: our exegeses on the doctrine of free will—a teaching of Christ that implicitly denies predestination even as it affirms the law of karmic accountability *and* reincarnation as the logical consequence of the exercise of free will. Therefore let us press on with our search for the New Atlantis reborn through the gifts and graces of the Person (pure servant-Sons) of the Holy Ghost.

Those who have not penetrated the spiritual realms sparkling just beyond their enjoyment of this earthly existence with its everyday montages of life and death—these have not truly lived. Accept it or not, and like it or not, the reason is *they have not willed it so.* And the words were never so true, "They have never lived. They can wait to die."

They have not taken the first spiritual gift which predestines the nine, multiplier of the sacred Three-times-Three: free will. They have not used it to develop the original grace that came before the nine: the divine spark—God Identity vested in the threefold flame of Life. Nor have they anticipated the LORD's descent in the all-power of heaven and earth vested in the Holy Christ Self—bodily.

Past Lives and Present Performance

Life does not consist of bowls of jelly, and bowels of pork and beans, and world fame and the accumulation of "pieces of eight" and "pieces of four," as the pirates hoard gold then and now. Life does not consist of any of that. No, a man's life never will consist in the abundance of the things which he possesses—even if *he* thinks so.

Jesus warned us of covetousness in the human spirit—the grasping, greedy desires that smolder and simmer as envy but never come to a healthy boil to be distilled into the steam of powerful self-effort to duplicate the abundant life, fair and free and God-given by oneself unto oneself. And this, too, is karma. And the law of karma must be reconsidered by reasoning man and woman in the light of soul reincarnations revisited, lest they be denied the victory over this self that was and is not and yet lingers on.

Take heart, for he said: "If ye have faith as a grain of mustard seed, ye shall say unto this mountain, Remove hence to yonder place; and it shall remove; and *nothing shall be impossible unto you.*"[142]

Don't you see that we, of necessity, as teachers of Light, cannot afford to care what anyone thinks of what we say or what we do? We must be strictly honest before man and God; otherwise our words have no meaning. But because they stem from the criteria of divine experience, they do have meaning—as many of you know—but only by the endowment of God's grace.

And so when we speak of Atlantis, you must understand that we speak from experience. For we were also there, as many of you were and as many of mankind were, in past lives. Our lives consist not of threescore and ten but of threescore and ten in segments, repeated again and again as oft as need be, that we may learn.

For life is not a meaningless sine wave that, like the light of far-off stars, travels through light-years of space and speaks of a burned-out star that fills an empty socket.

We are speaking of the continuity of individuality—*your* individuality. *You* have lived before. And in your life before, the mirror of consciousness peeped through the windows of your being as it is doing today.

You could not put together a complete chronology of all of your lives. And those who tell you they will give you a "life reading" of your past embodiments will ofttimes fill you with a lot of bunk that might entertain your mind and fatten your ego, but it will never profit your soul, which would do better by far to dwell in the realm of mastering cosmic law so that you may be able to live today in a victorious way and not rehearse your experiences of twelve thousand years ago as though they have any specific import to your fellow men.

They are only important to you insofar as you learn the lessons of your past performances, applying them to your current situation. The evaluation thereof is not made by the outer mind but by the soul with the beloved Christ Self, who examines the fruits of each episode on the stage of life and thrusts back upon your evolving self the present cosmic opportunity to learn life's lessons and to conquer the anti-self.

Yes, you are here to learn. You are here to grasp cosmic law in order that you may be able to live in a masterful way—not as a dominant person over others but as a person who takes dominion over himself.

I like to remind my students and myself of the proverb attributed to Solomon: "He that is slow to anger is better than the mighty, and he that ruleth his spirit than he that taketh a city."[143] So don't you mind hearing me repeat it, because you will hear it until you fulfill it. Not because of me but because of cosmic law.

But what is the meaning of mastering yourself? Why, I'll tell you. You're just three people rolled into one, in a manner of speaking. You have a physical body and that physical body really doesn't mean any more than a mustard seed unless it grow and become the greatest of herbs.[144]

Then, you see, the physical body will be like the mustard tree that shoots out great branches where the birds come and lodge. It will be the spinal support where the vessels of thought and feeling and memory are draped and the expansiveness of the Universal Mind interpenetrating all through elemental life will be a haven of meditation for souls in flight to find their Maker.

Your physical body is where it all comes together—without it you can't meet the challenges and the loves of your destiny in the physical plane. But what is even more important than your body, which is very important indeed as long as you need it, is the manifestation of you as a person.

You are not your body. Your body is the house in which you live. Your body is a sponge. And what does a sponge soak up? The sponge soaks up the water of your emotional body, the body of feeling. It also absorbs the air of your mental body—the air of thought awareness ('aw*air*ness') whereby you gain the mastery of the mental plane.

So what is it that gets hurt when someone you meet doesn't speak to you on the street? Is it your body? I don't think so. Is it the other three coats you hang on it? Hardly. Is it God? Can you imagine that God is going to be hurt because someone didn't recognize you? Of course not. What is hurt is the human ego. And why is it hurt? It is hurt because of the feelings, the crushed feelings. "Why, he didn't even recognize me!" we say.

This is a folly of an energy drain, if I ever saw one! It pulls the plug of equanimity and lets your energy go right down the drain in a vortex of offense. And if you get angry with this person, the sewer of the mass consciousness splashes back in your face—because you're disturbed with people. So you trouble their 'waters' and then you have more than a tempest in a teacup to deal with.

You have to learn to be absolutely calm, absolutely undisturbed, no matter what anybody says or thinks about you. I said *anybody*—your best friend or your worst enemy.

And that's a very hard thing to do until after a while you come to a certain place where you suddenly decide, "Why, I have so much energy— God gave me just so much, but even what I have can be measured as my allotment for everything that I have to do in this life. So if I squander it on self-indulgent sympathies, idle chatter, and the frittering away of time and space (which are also a part of my energy allotment), then just when I need it for my mission, I won't have it!"

Well, God doesn't send you down here without some money in the bank. Can you imagine the Father sending the son into a strange land without provision? But each one must learn to value the Father's trust and the trust account he has set up in one's name. For there are no two alike.

When you discover your divine resources and how to use them to harness your human potential, you will appreciate the fact that a wise and loving Father gave you just what your personality requires to succeed on earth and in heaven. But if you spend it on riotous living, like the prodigal son who wasted his substance, then you'll be on your knees praying for another opportunity.

And I pray you'll get it, too. But we must never take for granted the Father's love. We must love him enough to conserve his Light so that we will have it to comfort his own in their extremities.

Reminds me of my little girl Moira. She stood up in the bathtub one night recently while taking a bath. She looked down at her body and she said, "Why, I've got a new body! I just came down from heaven." She had just begun to realize that she wasn't in the same body she had been accustomed to being in.

Why, of course she had got a new body! — and another opportunity, like the prodigal son. Our loving Father has dealt with us in the same way the earthly father of the prodigal son dealt with him on his return from the 'far country' where he had spent all he had. He so rejoiced to see him alive and well that he gave him a 'new robe', 'new shoes' and a 'new ring', plus a feast—the fatted calf was killed for the occasion.[145]

This parable teaches the lessons learned by a soul who went forth into physical embodiment ("a far country"), a place far removed in vibration from the heaven-world where she had been dwelling. In her journey through the lower octaves she lost the vision and the memory of her commitment to the purity of Life. Now she is called Home where she once more basks in the Sun of Love that endowed her mission in the beginning and receives her still to prepare for another round, this time to be God-victorious.

The robe is the new body, the shoes are a new understanding, and the ring is a new protection and authority, signifying that the Father will not reduce the son to servant as punishment for his sins but instead will give him the opportunity to go forth again, hopefully the lesson learned, to wisely govern himself and his energy. The new life of the Spirit bestowed on him is symbolized in the fatted calf.[146]

The judgment of the Father upon the prodigal soul is clear: Let us celebrate your soul's safe return to the etheric plane—"My son was *dead* [died in matter] and is alive again [in Spirit]; he was lost in the astral plane and is found in his Father's country. Now, therefore, let him rest with me awhile and then go forth again, this time to conquer time and space by bearing my Light to liberate all life on earth."

And so, we all got new bodies when we were little. In fact, if you want to know the truth, we're all more or less prodigal sons. And our work and the Father's work that we must finish before we're free from the karmic rounds of reincarnation on earth is to undo the work of the sons of Belial.

Most of us had the realization of our new bodies sometime between birth and age seven. But we don't all remember the moment when it dawned upon our outer minds that the soul had actually reembodied. This is because such an idea does not have acceptability in our culture. To speak in such terms before our families would be as though we were speaking in a foreign language not understandable to those who are the most powerful molders of our personalities.

At an early age we learn to conform to these influences that come through people and their subtle subconscious pressures. We are anxious to please and to avoid the displeasure of our elders. Thus, most children repress their early memories of past lives and inner-level experience prior to birth — or they entertain them only as part of their make-believe world.

But while he was on earth Jesus taught reembodiment. The assertion of this fact evokes a furor in otherwise rational circles. Therefore, we need to examine more closely his words and the record, not only of the events but of the attitudes of John and Jesus midst the tumultuous confrontations their Persons and Teachings aroused.

Reincarnation: The Prophecy of Elijah Come Again

You will remember that when Jesus and the disciples were coming down from the mount of transfiguration, they asked the Master, "Why say the scribes that Elias must first come?"[147]

They were talking about the prophecy of God given through Malachi: "Behold, I will send you Elijah the prophet before the coming of the great and dreadful day of the LORD; and he shall turn the heart of the fathers to the children and the heart of the children to their fathers, lest I come and smite the earth with a curse."[148]

What did God mean when he said he was going to send us Elijah the prophet before Messias? Just that! Elijah was going to be reborn in the flesh in a new body before the birth of Jesus Christ!

Then Jesus told his disciples, "Elias must truly come first and restore all things." And he told them how it is written of the Son of man that he must suffer many things and be set at naught. "But I say unto you that Elias is come already, and they knew him not but hated him for the Word's sake, and they have done unto him whatever they would, as it is written of him. Likewise shall the Son of man suffer of them."[149] "Then," Matthew writes, "the disciples understood that he spake unto them of John the Baptist."[150]

Don't you remember how Salome danced before King Herod? And how he sware to her that whatever she asked of him he would give it to her, up to half of his kingdom? And she went out and asked her mother, Herodias, "What shall I ask him for?" And her mother (whose illicit relationship with Herod—she was his brother Philip's wife— had been publicly denounced by the fearless forerunner of Christ) said with utter despite, "The head of John the Baptist."

And so Salome, in one of the most infamous acts of all Nephilim history, demanded the head of the Lord's Baptizer. And Herod was too proud a god to break his oath before the other gods—even for fear of the Word. And so at the king's command they cut off the head of the reincarnated prophet Elijah. And it says they brought John's head to her in a charger,[151] which means they brought it in on a meat platter for everyone to see.

But John had his final word to the Children of the One—from the platter itself his Spirit cries out to this day: See what they have done to me! So will they do to you. Repent and be saved by the putting on of thy full Christhood, the robe of immortal Life I now wear.

Jesus foreknew John's death as well as his own. John had foreknowledge of these events also. He knew his Life must decrease, in order that the

Light (the Universal Christ consciousness) in Jesus might increase.[152]

It says John the Baptist came eating "locusts and wild honey."[153] Some say the term *locusts* refers to the pods of the carob tree. It's called St.-John's-bread. Others take it literally because locusts are part of the Middle Eastern diet to this day.

I think the message of John the Baptist's life, whether he was a vegetarian or not, is one of self-effacement for a holy purpose that we might well follow. As the desert was devoid of encumbrances, so his diet was sparse. The vastness of his internal space, reflected in his environment and habits, was his preparation for the Lord's descent and himself as his Messenger.

We have to understand that these mysteries are plain. "Elijah come again." Do you know what was so wonderful about Elijah the prophet? He went up "by a whirlwind" into heaven. Most people think he went up "in a chariot of fire" drawn by "horses of fire." I never knew what that meant when I was a boy. But when I became a man Jesus taught me about every man's ascension in the Light as he is caught up unto God by the Holy Spirit's cloven tongues of sacred fire.

But he taught me about other ascents too.

UFOs, Space People, and Sons of Belial

No, I am not a disbeliever in UFOs and space people. The evidence is there. I'm more concerned with the question, Who are they? and what kind of evolution are they? Because most people I know just naïvely take it for granted that they're benign benefactors or the scientist saviours of the world. Because they've been taught it's superstitious to believe in evil—or evil forces or evil empires or evil invaders from outer space!

But if you really want to know the truth, they don't want to know. The people just don't want to know about evil in any form—least of all what's lodged in their own psyche—nor about omnipotent beings from the beyond, neither of which they feel capable of tackling. They don't want to know about it so they deny it. It's the old head-in-the-sand scenario.

Oh, I used to talk to people about such things, but not anymore. Nowadays I can't tell all I know or what I've seen or who I've met and where.

Question: Does God need spacecraft to move his sons and daughters through time and space? From time and space to infinity? And if he doesn't *need* them, do his sons and daughters sometimes use spacecraft, like we use cars and planes, because it's convenient?

Answer: No and Yes. Maybe. Jesus said, "No man hath ascended up to heaven, but he that came down from heaven, even the Son of man which is in heaven."[154]

This teaching establishes the premise that in order to ascend, one must have descended in the first place. It is clear that the soul who would mount the golden spiral staircase, where by and by, with the turning of the spiral, eternity displaces time and space, must have decclerated down the staircase — must have come from starry heights or other suns we no longer call home.

Well, the definition about the "Son of man" and the qualifications for the ascent do give us pause. For if the law governing the ascent applied to everyone, it would have been superfluous to mention it at all. And our Lord was anything but superfluous, wouldn't you say? Evidently, there are some evolutions on earth who descended from heaven and some who did not. And just where these others came from and who they are is entirely another question.

Perhaps we may glean something of the world that was Elijah's point of original embarkation in Jesus' rebuke to the Pharisees who challenged his authority to act in the name of God as his Son: *"Ye are from beneath, I AM from above. Ye are of this world, I AM not of this world."* [155]

The question that this raises is: If Jesus was not "of this world," was he from another? Another planet in this system or another system of worlds? And did he and John the Baptist, therefore, come from the same place?

Many people who believe in reincarnation also believe that we have lived on other planets. And if you point out that scientists consider Venus, Mars, or Mercury and the rest of the planets uninhabitable, they'll tell you that life could exist there in other dimensions where other kinds of bodies are similarly adapted to other environments than ours. And that you, therefore, can't see the life-waves of these other worlds because they're out of our spectrum.

Some people also believe that spacecraft sighted hovering over planet earth, that seem to disappear in and out of our frequency, actually have the technology to do just that—to turn a frequency dial that enables them to go in and out of our range very quickly. This explains, they say, why "now you see them and now you don't!"

One more question: If when Jesus said, "I am not of this world," he meant only that he was from heaven and not from earth, then why didn't he just say so?

By the way, most people who believe they came to earth after having lived on other planets believe they got here through the process of rein-carnation. However, through regression* back to the days of Atlantis, some remember crash-land-ing their spacecraft and being marooned on planet earth, reincarnating among its evolutions to the present with still no expectancy in the foreseeable future of returning by spaceship to their home stars!

Now, as if the "ye are from beneath" quip were not enough of an outrage, Jesus also told them that they were neither children of Abraham nor sons of God the Father. On the contrary, he pointed them out as the seed of the Devil, the fallen archangel Lucifer, saying, "and the lusts of your father ye will do."

---

*For a spiritual perspective on regression and hypnosis, see note on page 285.

Was he suggesting they were the descendants of the Watchers (Gen. 6:1–4)—fallen angels who lusted after the daughters of men and had come down to earth to cohabitate with them? He tore off their masks and exposed them as the sons of rebellious angels (perhaps those of Rev. 12) who had been cast out of heaven into the earth (i.e., into earth bodies) and accused them of being fully and presently engaged in lustful, murderous, and lying practices against the children of Light.[156]

For this he incurred their unmitigated and undying wrath. They sought to stone him because *he was a Son of God*—a Christed one—and they were not.[157] And they crucified him to get even with Father and Son—because the Light of the Logos was not in them.

This Satanic rite performed on Golgotha was a bloodletting ceremony to steal the Light-essence of the Son of God. For this he pointed the finger not at the Jews. Of them he said, "Father, forgive them; for they know not what they do."[158] By his very submission to the public crucifixion, he indicted the fallen angels, the bastard race who had embodied among Jew and Gentile alike (the Sanhedrin as well as the gods of Rome) to destroy the doctrine of Moses and the prophets, just as they would one day attempt to destroy Christ's doctrine.

"Why did Jesus tell it the way he did?" you ask, "and complicate our life for two thousand years? Did he have to get into this whole mess of the fallen-angel controversy that has plagued

theologians for many centuries down the pages of
the Old and New Testaments?"

Indeed he did. He told it the way he told it,
beloved, because he foreknew the drama of his
own final act on the stage of life *and* because he
foresaw *your* own path of initiation parallel to his.

Your Saviour knew you would be confronted
by the seed of that 'reptilian' evolution that ascends
out of the pits of this world but cannot scale the
heavens—No way! Though they build their towers
of Babel to the skies and attempt to mount the
stairway of the degrees of Christic initiation in
their spacecraft, they cannot cross the barrier to the
plane of Spirit.

They once descended in a funnel of their own
blasphemy of the Word—this seed of the anti-
Light. Having spent their coil of sacred-fire allotment on the condemnation of Messias and on
accusations made against his brethren "day and
night,"[159] having misused the Word in execrations
and incantations, and the building of sex cones as
their counterweight to the ascension flame—they
could no more ascend.

They had both squandered and imprisoned by
black magic the light of the base-of-the-spine
chakra, the Mother light which is for the building
not only of the ascension coil but also of the
deathless solar body (one the "stairway" and the
other the "vehicle" needed to transcend the dimensions of time and space).

This is the cornerstone of the ascent—the base chakra—and no other can be laid than this which has been laid by your Christ: the white stone of the ascent.[160] Citizens of this world had this race of serpents become and so they would remain until "death and hell" (their byword and their by-product) should be cast into the all-consuming 'lake' of sacred fire "prepared for the Devil and his angels."[161]

Jesus Christ—the One Sent[162] to save the Children of the Sun from the sons of Belial, the seed whose generation is from beneath—chose the day after the feast of the tabernacles to expose his killers, the Pharisees and the chief priests, as the embodied fallen angels (both Watchers and Nephilim). He did this not privately in deference to his accusers, but publicly in the temple so that the people could bear witness—"Indeed this is the very Christ!"[163]—and be saved forevermore by their belief-tie to that Christ.

He told it the way he told it when and where he told it, beloved, so that you also would know what is the nature of this planetary beast that must be confronted by your soul in Christ ere you yourself get the victory the same way the saints before you have gotten the victory: "And they [the Children of the One] overcame him by the blood of the Lamb and by the word of their testimony."[164]

For the same reason, Jesus allowed himself to be seized, bound, tried, condemned to death, scourged, stripped, mocked, spat upon, humiliated, crucified, and jeered as he hung on the cross. Neither did John, imprisoned by Herod, seek to circumvent his fate by divine intervention.

The Saviour and his Messenger who went before him wanted you, beloved, to understand the psychology of the fallen ones (the people of the original lie,[165] the offspring of the Liar) and know them by their fruits[166]—even through their cunning imitation of his Word, their clever disguises, smiles, glad-handing, and quoting of scripture— and underneath it all their murderous intent to "destroy your soul in hell."

Once you know their formula, once you've got the number of the beast and the image out of which he was made (not Christ's but the Devil's) and his mark[167]—the stamp of his genetic code so unlike the seed of the Ancient of Days, who were and are the true Hebrews through Abraham and his Christ—then you can clean escape all that is from beneath.

Then *you will* ascend to "my Father" and "your Father"[168] (my Mighty I AM Presence and your Mighty I AM Presence), whence we descended together as the sons of man (the sons of His *man*ifestation) in order to rescue the children of the Light—the very ones who had forgotten their God Source and their fiery destiny by the genetic 'brainwashing' of the fallen ones on Atlantis.

Yes, we came for the selfsame mission Jesus did. As he said, "For [the] Judgment [of the seed of the Wicked One] I AM come into this world" and "to go after the lost sheep of the House of Israel" — the seed of the Ancient of Days (Sanat Kumara).[169] As the Master on occasion answered the plea of those not of the seed of Sanat Kumara, so he assigned both Jew and Gentile into the care of his apostles.

Today the spirit of the "beast of blasphemy"[170] operates through the Atlantean cultists and certain of the laggard UFO people reborn, with their mechanized Martian and monkey races in tow. These comprise, among others, the religious and political fanatics (cult-watchers, deprogrammers, mind kidnappers, et al.) and many sophisticated anti-freedom forces in the economies of East and West who parade and beat their pots and pans and pan-theisms in the name of freedom.

At inner levels these have vowed to tear by any means the children of the Light from their emergent Christhood. Christ is the judge of the oppressors of my people and he will bind the sons of Belial through the indomitable Word spoken out of the mouth of the little child: "They shall not pass!"

Now, in the matter of the ascent and the descent again of John the Baptist—this is a very extraordinary phenomenon, as we mentioned in our last chapter. For he also came for the judgment of the race of serpents. And his fire is upon them to this day! He came by God's grace to clear the way for the Avatar's coming—to clear his path of serpents, even as the bodhisattvas clear the path of the Coming Buddha, and the angels clear the highway of our God.

God sent John the Baptist because none other could perform the task He wanted accomplished: the fiery trial of the forces of Antichrist. And it was done. And the LORD released through this emissary of heaven whom Jesus called "a burning and a shining light" a judgment of "unquenchable fire" that is not yet spent but shall fulfill its purpose in this age—and none shall escape this "prophet of the Most High," this "horn of salvation" who set in motion the deliverance of the seed of Christ out of the hand of the fallen angels.

You see, he had an extraordinary commission that only an Ascended Master could perform. His rebirth on earth was a special dispensation.

By contrast, some quite ordinary people I've known go around telling other people that they're Ascended Masters reborn. Or they say that Maitreya's taken a physical body. This they'll do to impress you and to gather a circle of devotees around themselves.

So I want you to know that better than ninety-nine times out of a hundred it's simply not true. And whoever is telling you this may be a member of the false hierarchy or somebody who's been duped by it. For very seldom in cosmic history (and I know cosmic law as you may know jurisprudence) does anyone who ascends back to God— that is, who actually goes through the ritual of the ascension, experiencing the acceleration of his molecules into the white-fire core of Being—return via reincarnation to this stinking world.

That's what it is on the outside. You know that. I think it's pretty nice, but it's still stinking—compared to heaven. If you don't believe it, go over to India! When we flew over Bombay, as we approached the landing strip, the stench of India rose up through the bottom of the airplane. And when we got out, we knew it!

Poor old George Lancaster and John Anderson—they stood there in Bombay, India, early in the morning. They had been up for probably fifteen or twenty hours and they were hungry. So they ordered a nice big breakfast. And lo and behold, they brought us bird's eggs on a platter! And the men who served them—first they wiped our chairs and the floor underneath the chairs with a dirty rag, and then they used the same rag to polish the plates on which they served us our food!

But after we came back to Bombay, on our return trip to the United States, we thought it looked like heaven because the rest of India was even worse!

Yes, we have a stinking world here, whether we know it or not. But we don't have to get messed up with it. We can keep our consciousness above the fly line of human despair and UFO interference with our ascent to the holy mountain of God. We can raise up our consciousness toward God, thank heaven. And we can envision for this world a new heaven and a new earth[171] where that which is beneath mirrors in Truth that which is above.

Masters and Disciples Mirror God's Word and Work

In his vision of heaven today, man does not have the correct interpretation of Reality. Heaven can be an amplification of all the good things that we see in this world. And most people don't know it. "Eye has not seen, nor has ear heard, neither have entered into the heart of man the things which God has prepared for them that love him."[172]

Now, in this concept of the love of God we may say, "Well, how can we love God more?" I want to tell you that if you do not love your fellow man whom you have seen, you can never correctly love God whom you have not seen.[173] And therefore, we start right here, loving humanity free from all the degradation and stench of mortality, carnality, and the frustrations of this energy whirl which we've all got ourselves into to some degree or other.

What a magnificent place this is if you view it as a schoolroom from which you can graduate and ascend the stairs, step by step, through the initiatory process to where you discover and take hold of your dominion over yourself! And you keep hold of it, now, and don't you let go of it!

"Well," you say, "that doesn't matter." That matters completely! Because this sponge we're talking about—saturated with the water element (the feelings), saturated with air (referring to the thought undulations of the mind) — must be under the control of the Christ as the animating principle of the sponge; or the soul itself, as prisoner of the mortal matrix, will toss and turn and roll like a man in a barrel going over the proverbial Niagara Falls.

It matters, you see, because if you don't control the vessel, it will control you. It's one or the other and there's no in-between. Through the mastery of thought and feeling, man is able to attain immortality, because he attains Godlikeness.

You never saw the Master Jesus when he was not the master of the situation in the total picture of his life! He walked on the water. He commanded the elements. He healed the sick. He raised the dead. He was conscious of his Father in heaven. You can be that.

He doesn't say to you: "Get away from me! I'm holier than you are. I don't care anything about you because you have such a puny mind and your soul is basically ignorant."

No, no, nothing like that from Jesus. He says, "Come unto me, all ye that labor and are heavy laden, and I will give you rest. Take my yoke, *yoga*, upon you and learn of me [take my consciousness of my sacred labor, my Christhood bearing the burden of world karma, my God awareness bearing the glory of the LORD's Dharma — take it upon your chakras and learn of my Guru, the Ancient of Days]; for I am meek and lowly in heart, and ye shall find rest unto your souls. For my yoke, *yoga*, is easy and my burden in heaven and on earth is truly Light."[174]

So the world today tries to make a bromide out of it. You know what a bromide is? It's a headache powder. What they want to do with what they think are the true teachings of Jesus is keep repeating them over and over to relieve stress or to neutralize pain. And in the euphoria of gospel songs and Elysian fields, they lose the thread of contact with Christ the burden-bearer, who teaches us that every man must bear his own burden of karma and balance it (i.e., make it Light), as the Master of masters did through the sacred fire of his own Christ Self.[175] By this path alone did his soul attain self-mastery in a number of incarnations prior to the final one.

This step cannot be skipped simply because "Jesus did it for us." Yes, the Saviour did it *before* you so that you could walk in the footsteps of your Teacher. He taught by example, because you must do the things he did—drink his cup, all of it, and ascend with him to the plane of the Universal Christ.

"I must work the works of him that sent me ..."[176] It's time you figured out (1) who sent you, (2) what are his works, and (3) how *you* are going to accomplish them. For now you see Light, but the night of personal and planetary karma cometh and then you may not be able to complete the work of your fiery destiny.

"Work while ye have the Light"[177] of your I AM Presence shining through your heart to lighten the way of your soul's overcoming *in the physical octave.* This is where you made your karma; this is where you must balance it.

Your karma is *your work.* You want to get *it* out of the way so you can do *the LORD's Work.* His Work is bearing world karma, but it's Light Work. Because through the mighty threefold flame of his most Sacred Heart, he has mastered the art and science of balance—holding the balance of personal/impersonal forces. His work is the 'mighty Work of the ages'.

Our Buddhist brothers and sisters call it the Dharma. Implicit in this concept, also reflected in Jesus' message, is the fact that the Work *is* the Teaching, and the Teaching becomes the Work. The two together define our divine duty to be who we are in God *right here on earth.* And this is the Dharma.

Be who you are! That's the fiat of Gautama Buddha, our dear brother who, far from pagan, occupies his place in the spiritual hierarchy of the planet, fully supportive of and complementary to Jesus' mission. And you would be amazed at how sweet he is, how wise, how tender and jocular he can be; yet the profoundness of his powerful presence is beyond telling. Only the vibration apprises you of the worlds of his dominion and his supreme bliss in upper spheres.

In his office as Lord of the World, Gautama maintains the thread of contact with the heart chakra of every lifestream on earth from Shamballa—and now from the Western Shamballa over the Heart of the Inner Retreat. It is the communication of his consciousness to our hearts through this our recourse to his magnificent abiding threefold flame that gives us the ever-present sense that God loves us. Such is the beautiful vigil of the one of whom John spoke as "the God of the earth" (Rev. 11:4), before whom the Two Witnesses stand.

Thus, our sacred labor must also be, like that of our mentors, to love the LORD our God with all of our heart and soul and mind[178] through loving and serving his children. And this we do best through magnifying the Divine Design.

Now, the real purpose of the motion picture industry is to capture the Divine Design in everyday life and to mirror it on screen; to show the negative imagings of men only to exemplify right choice by contrast with the wrong choice and its consequences. We and our children should go home from the movies with a clear and compelling reason to work the Works of our Father on earth simply because the work of the Devil doesn't pay—moreover, it robs us of our birthright.

But, for the most part producers and directors today have turned it all around. In the movies they are making these days, it seems they try to create a division in your consciousness by showing you a wicked scene and then having a statue of the

Blessed Virgin standing nearby. Or they'll take a holy temple somewhere and they'll show a picture of desecration. This is to create a dichotomy in the mind, a split in the feelings, and a division of the four lower bodies whereby they drive through their wedges to mold mores and public opinion.

People are not smart enough to catch the trends of the dark powers of the world that dwell in high places.[179] (I'm not speaking of altitude!) They try to create a division in our minds by "riding piggyback" on something that either has value or has none. They try to associate objects and scenes that are incongruous or highly offensive, assaulting the senses in order to disorient us and brainwash us, thereby disrupting (1) the natural order and beauty of our internal cosmos and (2) our values and most cherished beliefs. Well, they're tricksters—that's what they are!

By the way, have you ever seen the Indian rope trick? How many here have ever seen the Indian rope trick? Well, that makes it very good, 'cause I haven't seen it either! But I've heard about it, and sometimes hearing about it from a reliable source is just as good as seeing it. Of course, I'd still like to see it sometime—I did see fakirs and snake charmers and some genuinely holy men and women in India. But I'll tell you about the Indian rope trick.

A small boy, eleven or twelve years old, stands there with this supposed master of the occult legerdemain. So he takes a rope and he throws it up into the sky. It probably goes fifty or seventy-five feet into the air, straight up, and it becomes stiff as a board. Then the little boy takes hold of it and, hand over hand, he climbs until he gets to the top of the rope. Then the master down below snaps his fingers and the boy disappears from the top of the rope and the rope falls to the ground.

You know, I think you could buy the heart of the world with that trick. I've often wondered why they don't come over here to America and perform it in Madison Square Garden or something—put it on television. Enough people have seen it; God knows that it is not an illusion—it really happens, as many other miraculous things happen.

So we live in a time of miracles. There're quite a few people who can also perform miracles but who won't. And the question is, Why?

It becomes a matter of cosmic ethic. Because a miracle is most often a setting aside of karmic law or natural law in order to allow the original covenant of grace betwixt God and man to function blissfully and harmoniously without the interference of man's sin and sinful sense.

If the law of karma, then, be set aside so that the individual is suddenly freed from karmic debt, someone must pay the price and someone must guarantee that the soul for whom the karmic law is set aside will learn the intended lesson, repent, and ultimately repay Life for the gift of forgiveness.

Since many people learn only by 'working through' their problems and their psychology, to interfere with this process by the interruption of the precise outworking of karmic law becomes an immoral act against the soul and the cosmos of souls of which he is an integral part.

In this light, may you understand that miracles are just not always the best substitute for working out your salvation "with fear and trembling," as the scriptures say,[180] signifying the requirement of respect for karmic law and that creative tension necessary for the forming and re-forming of Christ in the heart of the individual.[181]

And I kind of think it's obvious that this is what God thinks, because he does not squander his miracles on infidels but often he will lavish the believer with untold grace. But when he does, you can bet there is good reason and good karma meriting blessing upon blessing returning in kind to the beloved what he has given others.

It just so happens that the miracle I deem the highest is a changed life! This is a life that is free from its chains. *Chains* and *change*. Those are key words to remember. (Little boys manage to keep some of each in their pockets 'cause they're smart!)

Unless you have a knowledge of your God Presence, unless you understand the mysteries of your being in a more complete way—as the Masters have taught us those mysteries and made them plain—there is little doubt in my mind that you have some chains forged around you.

But, by a like token, there is little doubt in my mind that those chains can be shattered through the process of cosmic change—that you can evolve,

that you are evolving, that you will evolve, and that
when you evolve, you will find that many of the
things which I say to you which may seem strange
to you at first are very natural.

You know, one of the strangest things — one
of the weirdest ideas I ever heard in my life — is the
concept that people think the Ascended Masters
are dead. That's like saying the saints are all dead.
Well, we might be dead here, but they're not
dead — it's a cinch! And they don't have a great deal
of trouble in communicating with us. And what
they say is extremely valuable, because you're not
hearing from a human being at all. You are hearing
from a divine being. Yes, indeed.

The Christ was here on earth. Remember
that. He was here in the flesh. Great avatars have
been engaged in human activities. Do you think
that Saint Joseph was not the father of quite a few
children? Do you think that Mary the Mother
of Jesus had only one son? She had several other
children later. Did you know that? Jesus had
brothers and sisters.[182]

They don't want you to know that because it
brings Mother Mary much closer to your own
circumstance, and they want to keep her on a
pedestal — aloof. So they tell you Joseph had children by a previous marriage. Anything but the
Truth that will make you free to walk and talk with
the Ascended Masters, including Mary and Jesus,
as your closest companions on the road of life.

When the Truth is really known, you will see

that the whole generative and regenerative process comes under divine direction. And it is God's experiment of joy to the world. God is giving us the opportunity of finding ourselves right here in the veil of time—and in the substance of space.

I was just reading the other day about the late Bishop Pike and Arthur Ford, the great spiritualist medium. And the writer said that right now these two souls are very popular in the astral realm and of great interest to its inhabitants. I can see that they would be.

I remember the time I was speaking out against some of the things Bishop Pike was saying—as you know, he set out for the Holy Land to relive the experiences of Jesus and the prophets, got lost on the desert, and perished. He told a reporter I knew that he went there because that was the place where he felt closest to his son who had committed suicide.

So, some woman in the audience got up. She defended Bishop Pike to the nth degree, and she said, "How dare you say anything about that great and good man?"

So I said to Morya, "I'm really on the spot. I'm on a bed of spikes right now and please get me off of it." And Morya said, "You just tell that woman that Pike's peak is not the Summit!" He's really quick with the rapier thrust of his First Ray mind.

It's like the time I was up in San Francisco and near Berkeley, and there was a young man there who was a draft dodger. And, of course, we have some of them here, too, you know, and we're all good friends. The point is, this was a draft dodger who didn't like me. And he'd heard how many good things had been done through me, the great work that God had done—and I can assure you God did it and not I! And he turned to me and he said, "Well," he said, "if you're so good," he said, "how come you're left here on earth?"

I said, "Morya, *help!*"

Again the Master Morya told me what to say. "Just tell him," he said, "that God doesn't skim off all the cream!" Tongue in cheek, that was what Morya wanted me to do. The young man had quite an unusual experience afterward. I won't even go into that.

But what we are concerned with is bringing the Truth to people—the Truth that'll free people and liberate them so they can find God.

If you could scratch the air and pull apart the air and see what's behind the air, why, it would look just like a backdrop on a stage. And by getting behind it, or to the bottom of it, as they say, you would see "it's only a paper moon, sailing over a cardboard sea . . . It's only a canvas sky, hanging over a muslin tree," as the song goes. You know what I mean? "But it wouldn't be make-believe, if you believed in me."[183]

What makes life real are not the props but the real people we know and love. When we believe in God and we believe in people because God is in them, then we have the thread of contact with the real world.

Take a stone wall. It looks pretty real and pretty solid. And if you bump your head against a stone wall, it hurts. But if you really understand that it's all an illusion of the mind and that behind the illusion there is God, you will not only be able to drive your car through that wall but you will perform the even greater feat of understanding yourself and keeping the ups and downs of this life in perspective.

As my wife said this morning—which I thought was very interesting—she said, "Do you know the meaning of the word *atom?*"

I said, "No, what's atom exactly?" She said, "Well, atom is 'Alpha-to-Omega!'"

And I thought that was very good: A—Alpha, *t*—to, *o-m*—Omega. That's the way it goes! The energy of God in motion in the heart of the atom oscillates in the polarity of cosmic principle. It's real interesting, isn't it? And God taught her that and she wanted to share it with me. And so I give it to you and together we rejoice that in little things, simple things, there are great lessons to be learned.

One time I asked God, "What does the word *government* mean?" He said, "That's rather simple." He said, "The *g* stands for God and the *o-v-e-r* stands for over, the *m-e-n* for men, and the *t*, as the sign of the cross, means 'in Christ'— God-over-men-through Christ."

And he said that those to whom authority is

given in the world, like the great politicians—you know, Richard, "poor Richard," and other public figures famous and infamous—are supposed to be God's overmen. And so they are when they let the government be upon the shoulders of Christ: Christ in them, Christ in you and me—the hope of glory[184]—in our government. And so they're not truly God's overmen when they rule by the human ego instead.

This screen—just the idea that we can paw it open, you see, and poke a little hole in it and peep through and see what's behind it—makes you realize that you really can be in control if you want to be.

You know how you go by one of these construction sites in the city where they have all the boards built up, and then the kibitzers come along. They finally succeed in putting knotholes in them and then they call it "kibitzer's korner." And you'll come along and you'll see a whole bunch of people peeping through these different knotholes, offering free and mostly unwanted advice on the project.

Well, don't get the idea that right now God isn't constructing a new world just because this one's falling apart—because he is! And he's constructing a new you, too. Only it helps a great deal if you know it. See, he can do it without you knowing it. But he prefers that you know it, because when you work with him, you swim with the current. When you work against him, you're swimming upstream. That's what a lot of people are doing. So don't you do it.

Move with the currents of eternal Life and be the mirror of God's consciousness on earth. Let everybody you meet see a little bit o' heaven in your smile.

And your life will truly be worthwhile.

Note on regression and hypnosis:

Some of the evidence for reincarnation comes from those who have recalled past lives through regression under hypnosis or autohypnosis. Although these findings are interesting and often confirm the teachings on reincarnation and the afterlife that have come down to us through various spiritual traditions, I do not recommend hypnosis as a tool in therapy or in delving into past lives.

Hypnosis, even when done with the best of intentions, can make us spiritually vulnerable. It can open us to elements of the subconscious and unconscious of the practitioner. Through hypnosis we may also prematurely uncover records of events from past lives that we are not ready to deal with.

Notes

For an alphabetical listing of many of the philosophical and hierarchical terms used in *Lost Teachings on Keys to Spiritual Progress*, see the comprehensive glossary, "The Alchemy of the Word: Stones for the Wise Masterbuilders," in *Saint Germain On Alchemy.**

For more information about the Ascended Masters, Elohim and angels mentioned in this book, see Mark L. Prophet and Elizabeth Clare Prophet, *The Masters and Their Retreats* and *Lords of the Seven Rays*.

Epigraph facing page 1

1. I Cor. 2:10–13, Jerusalem Bible. **The Jerusalem Bible** is a Roman Catholic translation of the Bible originally done in French at the Dominican Biblical School in Jerusalem (1956). The English equivalent (1966) was translated directly from ancient Hebrew and Greek texts and compared with the French translation, using recent research in archaeology, history, and literary criticism. The Jerusalem Bible uses more colloquial language than older translations of the Bible and is considered an accurate and scholarly work.

---

*Books and audio recordings listed in these notes are published by Summit University Press unless otherwise noted.

Chapter One THE LADDER OF LIFE

1. Matt. 11:7, 9; Luke 7:24, 26.*
2. II Cor. 3:6.
3. John 14:16, 26; 15:26; 16:7.
4. Acts 7:54–60; 8:1.
5. Acts 9:1–25.
6. John 15:20.
7. See Elizabeth Clare Prophet, *The Lost Years of Jesus.*
8. Matt. 3:13–15.
9. Hos. 11:1; Matt. 2:15.
10. Matt. 24:27.
11. Jude 4.
12. Luke 8:30.
13. Acts 2.
14. Acts 10.
15. Acts 16:26.
16. Rev. 14:6.
17. Matt. 24:35.
18. Matt. 16:19.
19. Matt. 16:18.
20. See *The Living Flame of Love* in *The Collected Works of St. John of the Cross,* trans. Kieran Kavanaugh and Otilio Rodriguez (Washington, D.C.: ICS Publications, 1973), pp. 569–649; *Saint John of the Cross on the Living Flame of Love,* 8-audiocassette album, Summit University Lecture Series for Ministering Servants taught by Mark L. Prophet and Elizabeth Clare Prophet.
21. John 8:12; 9:5.
22. **Jesus' progressive revelation delivered by the heavenly hierarchy:** The opening and closing chapters of the Book of Revelation tell us that Jesus Christ himself personally instructed John through his angel: "The Revelation of Jesus Christ, which God gave unto him, to shew unto his servants things which must shortly come to pass; and he sent and signified it by his angel unto his servant John.... I Jesus have sent mine angel to testify unto you these things in the churches" (Rev. 1:1; 22:16). In addition, there are

---

*Bible references are to the King James Version unless otherwise noted.

revealed throughout the Book of Revelation a number of
heavenly beings, members of the cosmic hierarchy of the
Great White Brotherhood, who communicated to John.
Among them are: one of the four and twenty elders, who
told John to "weep not: behold, the Lion of the tribe of
Juda, the Root of David, hath prevailed to open the book"
which "no man in heaven, nor in earth, neither under the
earth, was able to open..., neither to look thereon" (Rev.
5:3, 5); the angel who bade John take the little book and
"eat it up, and it shall make thy belly bitter, but it shall be
in thy mouth sweet as honey" (Rev. 10:9); "one of the seven
angels which had the seven vials," who showed John "the
judgment of the great whore that sitteth upon many waters"
and revealed to him "the mystery of the woman, and of the
beast that carrieth her, which hath the seven heads and ten
horns" (Rev. 17:1, 7); "he that sat upon the throne" and
commanded John to "write: for these words are true and
faithful," and proclaimed, "I am Alpha and Omega, the
beginning and the end. I will give unto him that is athirst
of the fountain of the water of life freely" (Rev. 21:5, 6);
and "one of the seven angels," who showed John the City
Foursquare and "a pure river of water of life, clear as
crystal, proceeding out of the throne of God and of the
Lamb" (Rev. 21:9–27; 22:1). Apart from these direct
encounters, John heard the voices of other angelic messengers whom he does not say he saw, and he had visions of
divine beings and multitudes whom he saw or heard who
did not speak to him directly.

23. John 5:39, 40; 6:27–29.
24. Luke 24:45, 51.
25. Luke 24:37, 38; Mark 16:14.
26. I Cor. 15:50.
27. Phil. 2:11.
28. Luke 17:21.
29. Morton Smith, *The Secret Gospel: The Discovery and
    Interpretation of the Secret Gospel According to Mark*
    (Clearlake, Calif.: Dawn Horse Press, 1982), p. 15.
30. Ibid., pp. 16–17.
31. Mark 14:51, 52.

32. Smith, *The Secret Gospel*, pp. 80–81. Some scholars disagree with Smith's interpretation of the young man. They suggest that the man in the linen cloth was a literary device created by the author to enable the reader to identify more deeply with the spiritual life of the early followers of Jesus. See explanatory note on the existence of secret teachings and initiatic rites in *The Lost Teachings of Jesus: Missing Texts • Karma and Reincarnation*, p. 257 n. 102.
33. Mark 10:46.
34. Smith, *The Secret Gospel*, pp. 69–70.
35. Ibid., pp. 41–42.
36. James M. Robinson, gen. ed., *The Nag Hammadi Library in English* (New York: Harper & Row, 1977), p. 118.
37. Irenaeus, *Against Heresies* 3.11.9, in Alexander Roberts and James Donaldson, eds., *The Ante-Nicene Fathers*, American reprint of the Edinburgh ed., 9 vols. (Grand Rapids, Mich.: Wm. B. Eerdmans Publishing Co., 1981), 1:429.
38. Ibid., 1.20.1; 3.11.8, 9, in Roberts and Donaldson, *Ante-Nicene Fathers*, 1:344, 428–29.
39. Ibid., 2.22.5, in Roberts and Donaldson, *Ante-Nicene Fathers*, 1:391–92.
40. G. R. S. Mead, trans., *Pistis Sophia*, rev. ed. (London: John M. Watkins, 1921), p. 1.
41. John 8:28, 29; 12:44, 45; 14:7–11, 24.
42. John 14:6; 1:9.
43. John 18:38.
44. Acts 8:39, 40.
45. **Bilocation:** the state of being or ability to be in two places at the same time.
46. Paramahansa Yogananda, *Autobiography of a Yogi* (1946; reprint, Los Angeles: Self-Realization Fellowship, 1975), pp. 216–17.
47. Charles Mortimer Carty, *Padre Pio: The Stigmatist* (Rockford, Ill.: Tan Books & Publishers, 1973), p. 69.
48. Ibid., pp. 72–73.
49. Ibid., pp. 63–64.
50. Ibid., p. 63.
51. John 3:17; 10:10.

52. John 8:58.
53. Matt. 19:16, 17; Mark 10:17, 18; Luke 18:18, 19.
54. The authors of this book have verified that **Saint Francis taught reembodiment** from their own reading of the akashic records (see p. 292, n. 60). [old 291 n. 59] Manley Palmer Hall also makes note of this fact in *Reincarnation: The Cycle of Necessity* (Los Angeles: The Philosophical Research Society, 1946), p. 82, as does Dr. Leslie D. Weatherhead (see Lytle Robinson, *Edgar Cayce's Story of the Origin and Destiny of Man* [New York: Berkley Publishing Corporation, 1976], p. 192).
55. **Origen and his teachings anathematized at the instigation of Justinian and Theodora:** In his zeal to restore the Roman Empire (now called the Byzantine Empire) to its former estate and bring unity to its Church, Justinian I (483–565) desired to rid his realm of any belief or teaching that was not orthodox. For some "heretics" and pagans this resulted in the death penalty, for others persecution and confiscation of property or the closing of schools of philosophy. One unorthodox movement, which was becoming popular in the monasteries of Palestine, was a pantheistic mysticism that based itself on a form of Origenism. After receiving complaints about these Origenists, Justinian issued a long edict denouncing Origen as a heretic and convened a local synod in Constantinople in 543 to anathematize ("curse") certain of his teachings. Especially troublesome were Origen's teachings on the preexistence of souls and the preexistence of the soul of Jesus, which did not support the current trend in the still formulative Christian doctrine.

　　One of the major doctrinal problems that had caused a growing breach between the Eastern and Western Church was the centuries-long controversy over the relationship of the human and divine natures in Christ. (See *Lost Teachings on Your Higher Self* [in The Lost Teachings of Jesus series], pp. 257–62.) During Justinian's reign, this controversy centered around Monophysitism, a doctrine with strong support in the eastern provinces which contended that Jesus' nature was wholly divine even though he had taken on a human body. In this as in all matters concerning the Church, Justinian took the leading role. The emperor himself was a supporter of the orthodox view accepted at the Council of Chalcedon in 451 that the divine and human natures coexisted in Christ. But his empress, Theodora, was a champion of the Monophysites. Some claim it was under her influence that Justinian tried to bring about an agreement between the two factions.

In an effort to appease the more moderate Monophysites, Justinian decided to follow a policy that affirmed the two natures of Christ but subordinated the human element to the divine. To this end, he issued his own edict in 544 condemning three groups of writings that he charged were tainted with Nestorianism—a doctrine which held that the human and divine persons were separate in the incarnate Christ and which had been declared heretical by the Church. His measure provoked an outcry from bishops in the West, who viewed the emperor's action as a repudiation of Chalcedon and an endorsement of the Monophysites. The ensuing conflict, known as the Three Chapters controversy, eventually caused Justinian to summon the entire Church to the Fifth Ecumenical Council (also called the Second Council of Constantinople) in 553. The council confirmed the imperial edict of 544 as well as Justinian's anathemas against Origen and his writings.

Almost all the bishops in attendance represented the Eastern Church, however, and Pope Vigilius refused to attend. In fact, the legitimacy of the anathemas against Origen is still debated by scholars today because there are no records documenting papal approval of the condemnations. Furthermore, the council was not successful in meeting Justinian's goal of uniting the Church, which remained bitterly divided for more than a century. For further reading, see Elizabeth Clare Prophet, "The Origen Conspiracy," in *Fallen Angels and the Origins of Evil*, pp. 365–74; and Joseph Head and S. L. Cranston, comp. and ed., *Reincarnation: The Phoenix Fire Mystery* (New York: Crown Publishers, Julian Press, 1977), pp. 144–48, 156–60.

56. Gal. 6:7.
57. Matt. 5:48; II Cor. 13:11; II Tim. 3:17; James 1:4; Gal. 4:19.
58. For further teaching, see *Karma and Reincarnation: Transcending Your Past, Transforming Your Future,* by Elizabeth Clare Prophet and Patricia R. Spadaro; and *Reincarnation: The Missing Link in Christianity,* by Elizabeth Clare Prophet with Erin L. Prophet.
59. John 3:17.
60. **Akashic records** consist of the vibrational imprint, upon etheric substance known as akasha, of all events which have ever transpired anywhere and everywhere in the physical universe—layer upon layer. These can be read by a qualified spiritual seer; and they are always read by the Ascended Masters to calculate the impact of past cause-effect sequences on persons, places, and projects in the present. The records of individuals are similarly recorded on scrolls (a vast computation of the Mind of God which computer technology is beginning to apprehend). Imagine stored microfilm of millions of years of personal and planetary history containing, thought pulsation by thought pulsation, the total experience pattern of every soul who has come forth from the Central Sun into the Matter spheres since the Great Outbreath of this cosmic cycle! In the final tally when "the leaves of the Judgment Book unfold," the records not of the Light which are judged unworthy of permanence are consigned to the sacred fire. Only that which vibrates with the ultimate God-Good is retained forever, and souls purified and made white also become permanent atoms in the Universal Body of God.
61. Hamlet in Shakespeare, *Hamlet,* act 3, sc. 1, line 67.
62. Thomas Hughes, *Tom Brown's School Days* (New York: A. L. Burt Company, n. d.), pp. 212–13.
63. Gen. 28:12.
64. Rev. 2:11; 20:6, 14; 21:8.
65. The **dweller-on-the-threshold** is a term sometimes used to designate the not-self, the synthetic self, the dark side, the conglomerate of the self-created ego. The dweller appears to the soul on the threshold of conscious awareness,

where it knocks to gain entrance and become the master of the "house." See Mark L. Prophet and Elizabeth Clare Prophet, *The Enemy Within: Encountering and Conquering the Dark Side.*

66. Matt. 17:10–13.
67. John 9:1–3.
68. Exod. 33:20.
69. I Cor. 15:31.
70. Rev. 12:7–9.
71. **Pagan sacrifice noted in Old Testament:** Lev. 18:21, 27; Deut. 12:31; I Kings 11:7–8; II Kings 3:27; 17:31; **engaged in by Israelites:** II Kings 16:3, 4; 17:16, 17; 21:3, 4, 6, 7; 23:4–15; Isa. 57:5–8; Jer. 7:30–32; 19:4–6; 32:34, 35; Ezek. 16:18–20, 21, 36; 20:28, 31; 23:37; Hos. 4:13.
72. Ezek. 18:4, 20.
73. Matt. 25:41.
74. Matt. 28:18.
75. Matt. 25:1–13; 22:1–14. For further teaching on the **deathless solar body,** see Serapis Bey, *Dossier on the Ascension: The Story of the Soul's Acceleration into Higher Consciousness on the Path of Initiation,* pp. 154–59.
76. Isa. 61:2.
77. Rom. 8:6.
78. See *Hilarion the Healer: The Apostle Paul Reborn,* teachings of Mark L. Prophet and Elizabeth Clare Prophet, compiled by the editors of The Summit Lighthouse Library, from Meet the Master series.
79. II Kings 2:9–15.
80. John 3:30.
81. Matt. 19:30; 20:16; Mark 9:35; 10:31; Luke 13:30.
82. Phil. 2:5–7.
83. John 13:4, 5; Matt. 20:26, 27; 23:11; Mark 9:35; Luke 22:26, 27.
84. I Cor. 3:16, 17; 6:19; II Cor. 6:16.
85. Luke 23:34.
86. Matt. 5:44, 45.
87. Mohandas Gandhi wrote in his autobiography that the precept "Return good for evil" was his guiding principle. "It became such a passion with me that I began numerous

experiments in it," he says. In 1897, for instance, when Gandhi returned with his family to South Africa, he was beaten in Natal by an angry crowd of whites who accused him of bringing an unwanted flood of Indians to settle in their province. Gandhi, however, refused to prosecute his attackers. He claimed they had been misled by the untruths spoken about him and placed the responsibility instead on the local leaders, who "could have guided the people properly." In 1907, on his way to register under the Asiatic Registration Act adopted by the Transvaal government in South Africa, Gandhi was assaulted and severely beaten by fellow Indians. Most of the Indian community was strongly opposed to the registration act, but Gandhi agreed to comply to the measure on the condition that the act be repealed if the Indians registered voluntarily. When the battered Gandhi regained consciousness, he found out that his attackers had been arrested and immediately asked that they be released. "They thought they were doing right," he said, "and I have no desire to prosecute them."

Gandhi displayed the same spirit of forgiveness when he discovered that one of his close associates was a government informer. The man later opposed Gandhi openly, yet when he became ill Gandhi not only visited him but assisted him financially. "In time, the backslider repented," biographer Louis Fischer records. "Hostile critics are doing me a service," Gandhi once wrote. "They teach me to examine myself. They afford me an opportunity to see if I am free from the reaction of anger." And on another occasion he remarked, "To be truly non-violent, I must love [my adversary] and pray for him even when he hits me." See Mohandas K. Gandhi, *An Autobiography: The Story of My Experiments with Truth* (1927, 1929; reprint, Boston: Beacon Press, 1957), pp. 35, 189, 195; Louis Fischer, *The Life of Mahatma Gandhi* (New York: Harper & Row, 1950), pp. 81–82, 101, 238, 347.

88. John 1:3.
89. The quoted passages from Saint Jerome's biography of Saint Hilarion are taken from Rev. S. Baring-Gould, *The Lives of the Saints*, rev. ed. (Edinburgh: John Grant, 1914),

12:515, 516, 517.
90. Mark 4:41.
91. Ps. 139:14.
92. **Play-Doh** modeling compound is a claylike substance that can be molded into different shapes. Play-Doh is made in a variety of colors and is sold as a toy for children.
93. I Cor. 15:41.
94. Matt. 2:2.
95. James Churchward, *The Lost Continent of Mu* (London: Neville Spearman, 1959), following p. 160.
96. Eph. 3:16; I Pet. 3:4

Chapter Two THE MIRROR OF CONSCIOUSNESS

1. Matt. 5:6.
2. John 21:15–17.
3. I Cor. 12:12, 13, 26–31.
4. I Cor. 13.
5. I Cor. 13:12.
6. **Embody:** *Ensoul, enspirit,* and *enliven* are words which better in'corp'rate the sense of the noncorporeal 'embodiment' of attributes and profiles of God's divine personality—without a flesh-and-blood form, but with a spiritual Light body. "Bodies celestial," as opposed to "bodies terrestrial" (I Cor. 15:40) do have outline and form whereby the ascended servant-Son does focus the integrated consciousness of his individuality in God. Sons of God occupying certain planes of the Spirit-Matter cosmos are centered in the crystallization, or individualization, of the God flame and they use their Ascended Master Light bodies, or the bodies of the Archangelic and Elohimic planes in the case of these evolutions, to concentrate their God-identity for definition in time and space or to extend their auric fields to include planetary systems and life-waves, galaxies, or the entire universe (e.g., a pine deva—an angel who overshadows members of the elemental kingdom—extends his aura to overshadow, or protect, a pine tree or a pine forest as well as the elementals who maintain the pines under his jurisdiction). In truth God

is everywhere! And since He IS, His 'embodiment' of Himself is formed without limit, and formless if He will it so. The formed and the unformed are also yin and yang stages of the creation as thought passes from the mist to the crystal and back again. Thus we see that God is forever in a state of Self-transformation and that the alchemical process whereby the Spirit changes garments from molecule to man to Macrocosm is at the very heart of the nature of Life in its grand procession.

7. **The seven rays** are rays of spiritual light that emanate from the Godhead through the prism of the Christ consciousness. Each ray has a unique color frequency and quality, and each one represents a different path to self-mastery. The seven rays and their qualities are as follows: First Ray: blue; protection, perfection, power, will of God, faith. Second Ray: yellow; illumination, wisdom, knowledge, understanding. Third Ray: pink; love, devotion, creativity, beauty. Fourth Ray: white; purity, discipline, wholeness, joy. Fifth Ray: green; truth, healing, precipitation, abundance, science, vision. Sixth Ray: purple and gold; service, ministration, peace, brotherhood, resurrection. Seventh Ray: violet; freedom, transmutation, mercy, forgiveness, justice, alchemy. **The seven chakras** are the seven major chakras, or centers of light, anchored in the etheric body and governing the flow of light through the four lower bodies (etheric, mental, emotional, and physical) of man. They are the crown, third-eye, throat, heart, solar-plexus, seat-of-the-soul, and base-of-the-spine chakras.

8. Ps. 23:3.

9. Rom. 8:17.

10. Heb. 11:6.

11. Matt. 28:18–20.

12. Isa. 40:4.

13. I Cor. 12:1–11.

14. II Cor. 12:9.

15. Percival Spear, *India: A Modern History* (Ann Arbor, Mich.: University of Michigan Press, 1961), p. 129.

16. **"Abraham, great 'prince' of the Chaldees"**: There are a number of competing theories about the life and times of

Abraham. It was once widely assumed by scholars that the patriarchal narratives in the Bible were of questionable historical value and that patriarchs were mythical beings. Those who accepted that Abraham was a historical figure believed he was a simple nomadic or semi-nomadic Semite. Remarkable archaeological finds of the last century convinced scholars that Abraham did indeed exist; this, combined with the biblical accounts of the Hebrew patriarch, paint an entirely different picture of Abraham. Rather than a nomad leading a pastoral life, the Bible depicts him as a man of great wealth with a large household and a private army who makes military alliances, deals with kings, negotiates land purchases with important civic figures; he loves peace, is skilled in war and magnanimous in victory.

Ur of the Chaldees, the starting point of the epic of Abraham, was the capital of the Third Dynasty of Ur (c. 2112–c. 2004 B.C.), a flourishing cultural, political, and economic center vigorously engaged in international trade. The Sumerian civilization, of which it was the center, was literate and technologically advanced. "We must radically alter," wrote Sir Charles Leonard Woolley, head of a British-American team of archaeologists that excavated Ur shortly after World War I, "our view of the Hebrew patriarch when we see that his earlier years were passed in such sophisticated surroundings. He was the citizen of a great city and inherited the traditions of an old and highly organized civilization." Woolley's evidence did not go unchallenged and there are still conflicting views about Abraham which fall roughly into three schools of thought: he came from Sumer sometime during the second millennium B.C., the Kingdom of Mitanni in the middle of the second millennium B.C., or the Kingdom of Ebla during the third millennium B.C.

Developing the theme that Abraham was a Sumerian and a man of high social standing, Zecharia Sitchin contends that Abraham was of a royal, priestly family. He notes that the name of Abraham's wife Sarai (later Sarah) means "princess." Since she is Abraham's half-sister

("Indeed she is my sister, she is the daughter of my father but not the daughter of my mother," Gen. 20:12), either his father or mother was of royal descent. Since Abraham's brother Harran has a daughter who also has a royal name (*Milkha* 'queenly'), he concludes that Abraham's royal ancestry flowed through his father. Through linguistic analysis, Sitchin determined that Abraham was born not in Ur, where his biblical epic begins, but in the city of Nippur, Sumer's "religious center." Sitchin concludes that "in the ancestral family of Abraham we thus find a priestly family of royal blood."

Sitchin, recognizing the discrepancy between his theory and commonly held views, writes: "The emerging image of Abraham not as a sheepherding nomad but as an innovative military commander of royal descent may not fit the customary image of this Hebrew patriarch, but it is in accord with ancient recollections of Abraham. Thus, quoting earlier sources concerning Abraham, Josephus (A.D. first century) wrote of him: 'Abraham reigned at Damascus, where he was a foreigner, having come with an army out of the land above Babylon' from which, 'after a long time, the Lord got him up and removed from that country together with his men and he went to the land then called the land of Canaan but now the land of Judaea.'" Zecharia Sitchin, *The Wars of Gods and Men* (New York: Avon Books, 1985), pp. 281–309.

17. Gen. 17:1–2, 4.
18. Alfred Tennyson, "The Passing of Arthur," in *Idylls of the King* (New York: New American Library, 1961), pp. 251–52.
19. Heb. 11:8–12.
20. II Chron. 20:7; Isa. 41:8; James 2:23.
21. El Morya, *The Chela and the Path: Keys to Soul Mastery in the Aquarian Age*, pp. 36–37.
22. El Morya, April 10, 1977.
23. El Morya, *The Chela and the Path*, p. 23.
24. Ibid., p. 13.
25. Ibid., p. 67.
26. El Morya, *Morya I*, p. 93.
27. "Maitreya, the Coming Buddha": According to Buddhist

tradition, Maitreya, in the words of W. Y. Evans-Wentz, is "the Buddhist Messiah, who will regenerate the world by the power of divine love, and inaugurate a New Age of Universal Peace and Brotherhood." Also according to tradition, Maitreya is a bodhisattva—an aspirant for Buddhahood who pursues enlightenment for altruistic reasons—and the coming Buddha or future Buddha, who will succeed Gautama Buddha as the Buddha of the Age. As such, he resides in the abode where a bodhisattva awaits his last birth, the fourth of six heavens in the world of desire, a place called Tushita heaven. There he waits until the destined hour of his coming—an epoch whose arrival varies considerably depending on the source, one being as long as 5.67 billion years in the future. Despite the discrepancies about the number of years, in general, when the teachings of his predecessor have completely decayed, Maitreya will descend and restore the law. As noted in the *Encyclopedia of Religion and Ethics*, "the time of Metteyya [Maitreya] is described as a Golden Age in which kings, ministers, and people will vie one with another in maintaining the reign of righteousness and the victory of truth."

Maitreya's advent is well established in all schools of Buddhism—from the canonical texts of the Theravada tradition and the Mahayana school which followed to vernacular texts of popular religious sects which represent a radical departure from the mainstream of Buddhist thought. In a dictation delivered through Elizabeth Clare Prophet November 21, 1976, Lord Maitreya announced his coming as an Ascended Master: "All these thousands of years they have called me the Coming Buddha, and I have been coming and coming and coming and at last I am here! I am come! I am the Buddha of the Aquarian cycle. And therefore if you hear of 'The Coming Buddha,' you may say, 'I will relieve you, for Maitreya is relieved, for he has come into the center of the mission of the age.'" See W. Y. Evans-Wentz, ed., *The Tibetan Book of the Great Liberation* (London: Oxford University Press, 1954), p. xxvii; *Encyclopedia of Religion and Ethics*, ed. James Hastings (Edinburgh: T. & T. Clark, 1908), 1:414.

28. Isa. 55:1.
29. Lanto, in *The Opening of the Temple Doors*, by Elizabeth Clare Prophet, p. 115 (also published in 1973 *Pearls of Wisdom*, vol. 16, no. 18, p. 79).
30. Lanto, "The Science of the Heart Must Be Known by Those Who Would Accelerate Consciousness," in 1977 *Pearls of Wisdom*, vol. 20, no. 10, p. 42.
31. Lord Lanto, "Certainty in the Cup," in 1982 *Pearls of Wisdom*, vol. 25, no. 58, pp. 524–25; "Illumination for Transition: The Intensification of the Fires of Wisdom," in 1973 *Pearls of Wisdom*, vol. 16, no. 41, p. 175.
32. Gautama Buddha, "'The Teaching Is for the Many,'" in 1986 *Pearls of Wisdom*, vol. 29, no. 21, p. 178.
33. I John 4:1.
34. "The LORD's Ritual of Exorcism," in *Invocations to the Hierarchy of the Ruby Ray through the Messenger Elizabeth Clare Prophet*, looseleaf.
35. Paul the Venetian, "The Development of the Spiritual Senses," in 1968 *Pearls of Wisdom*, vol. 11, no. 3, p. 12.
36. Paul the Venetian, October 14, 1974.
37. El Morya, *The Chela and the Path*, p. 56.
38. Serapis Bey, December 30, 1977.
39. Serapis Bey, in *Opening of the Temple Doors*, by Elizabeth Clare Prophet, p. 47 (or 1973 *Pearls of Wisdom*, vol. 16, no. 13, p. 51.
40. El Morya, *The Chela and the Path*, p. 53.
41. R. A. Schwaller de Lubicz, *The Temple in Man: Sacred Architecture and the Perfect Man*, trans. Robert and Deborah Lawlor (New York: Inner Traditions International, 1977), p. 24.
42. Rev. 8:10, 11.
43. Serapis Bey, *Dossier on the Ascension: The Story of the Soul's Acceleration into Higher Consciousness on the Path of Initiation*, p. 175.
44. Ps. 46:10.
45. Serapis Bey, December 28, 1979.
46. Phil. 2:5, 6.
47. Rev. 14:6; 21:1.
48. John 14:12.

49. Gal. 1:11–24, Jerusalem Bible.
50. Ps. 19:1, 2, 7–9.
51. Hilarion, December 29, 1977.
52. Hilarion, July 9, 1967.
53. Hilarion, "Accumulations of Age-old Errors Challenged," in 1968 *Pearls of Wisdom*, vol. 11, no. 5, p. 20.
54. The eight-member **Karmic Board** dispenses justice to this system of worlds, adjudicating karma, mercy and judgment on behalf of every lifestream. The members of the board, known as the **Lords of Karma**, and the rays they represent are as follows: First Ray: the Great Divine Director; Second Ray: the Goddess of Liberty; Third Ray: the Ascended Lady Master Nada; Fourth Ray: the Elohim Cyclopea; Fifth Ray: Pallas Athena, Goddess of Truth; Sixth Ray: Portia, Goddess of Justice; Seventh Ray: Kuan Yin, Goddess of Mercy. The Buddha Vairochana is the eighth member of the Karmic Board.
55. Rom. 13:10.
56. **Spoilers:** Judges 2:14; I Sam. 13:17; 14:15; II Kings 17:20; Isa. 16:4; 21:2; Jer. 6:26; 12:12; 48:8, 18, 32; 51:48, 53, 55, 56.
57. Nada, November 7, 1976.
58. Nada, "A Path of Love," in 1982 *Pearls of Wisdom*, vol. 25, no. 62, pp. 564, 567, 568.
59. Prov. 15:1.
60. James 1:26; 3:2–10.
61. John 7:38.
62. Rev. 12:1.
63. Nada, "A Path of Love," p. 560.
64. Rev. 1:6; 5:10.
65. Nada, "Initiation Two by Two on the Path of the Ruby Ray: The Thousand-Petaled Rose of the Heart," in 1985 *Pearls of Wisdom*, vol. 28, no. 36, p. 447.
66. See Godfré Ray King, *Unveiled Mysteries*, 3d ed. (Chicago: Saint Germain Press, 1939), pp. 39–61.
67. I Sam. 7:3.
68. Isa. 11:1.
69. I Sam. 15:22, 23.
70. See John M'Clintock and James Strong, eds., *Cyclopaedia*

of Biblical, Theological and Ecclesiastical Literature [New York: Harper & Brothers, 1879], s.v. "Proclus," p. 617.

71. Thomas Whittaker, *The Neo-Platonists: A Study in the History of Hellenism,* 2d ed. (Cambridge: Cambridge University Press, 1928), p. 165.

72. Victor Cousin and Thomas Taylor, trans., *Two Treatises of Proclus, The Platonic Successor* (London: n.p., 1833), p. vi.

73. Geoffrey of Monmouth, *Vita Merlini,* in Nikolai Tolstoy, *The Quest for Merlin* (Boston: Little, Brown & Co., 1985), p. 217.

74. Brendan LeHane et al., *The Enchanted World: Wizards and Witches* (Chicago: Time-Life Books, 1984), p. 34.

75. "Sir Thomas Malory understood that King Arthur had at least two sisters. One was named Margawse, and she married King Loth and bore him four sons, the oldest of whom was Gawain. She, or another sister, alleges Malory, bore Modred to King Arthur" (Norma Lorre Goodrich, *King Arthur* [New York: Franklin Watts, 1986], p. 221).

76. Henry Thomas and Dana Lee Thomas, *Living Biographies of Great Scientists* (Garden City, N.Y.: Nelson Doubleday, 1941), p. 15.

77. Ibid., p. 16.

78. Ibid., p. 17; David Wallechinsky, Amy Wallace, and Irving Wallace, *The Book of Predictions* (New York: William Morrow and Co., 1980), p. 346.

79. Thomas, *Living Biographies,* p. 20.

80. Wallechinsky and Wallace, *Book of Predictions,* p. 346.

81. Clements R. Markham, *Life of Christopher Columbus* (London: George Philip & Son, 1892), pp. 207–8.

82. Bacon's ciphers: Francis Bacon's word-cipher was discovered by cryptographer Dr. Orville W. Owen, who published five volumes of *Sir Francis Bacon's Cipher Story* between 1893 and 1895. The story hidden in his word-cipher can be constructed by stringing together words, lines, and passages from the works of various Elizabethan writers. In contrast, deciphering the bi-literal cipher is an exact, scientific process of grouping together the italic letters (printed in two different fonts of type) that appear with peculiar frequency in original editions of the Shakespearean

plays and other of Bacon's works. This cipher was discovered by an assistant of Dr. Owen, Mrs. Elizabeth Wells Gallup, who first published the stories Bacon had concealed in his bi-literal cipher in 1899. To insure that his ciphers would eventually be discovered and his true life story revealed, Bacon had described in detail the bi-literal method of cipher writing in his Latin version of *De Augmentis* (1624), which some 270 years later Mrs. Gallup studied and applied. Ironically, Mrs. Gallup found that Bacon's bi-literal cipher contained complete directions on how to construct the word-cipher, which was actually discovered first by Dr. Owen.

83. Will Durant, *The Story of Philosophy: The Lives and Opinions of the Greater Philosophers* (Garden City, N.Y.: Garden City Publishing Co., 1927), p. 157.

84. The information detailed in the following paragraphs is taken from Margaret Barsi-Greene, comp., *I, Prince Tudor, Wrote Shakespeare* (Boston: Branden Press, 1973), pp. 56–75, and Alfred Dodd, *The Martyrdom of Francis Bacon* (New York: Rider & Co., n.d.), p. 25. See also Virginia Fellows, *The Shakespeare Code* (Authorhouse, 2000).

85. Barsi-Greene, *I, Prince Tudor*, p. 217.

86. Ibid., pp. 219–20.

87. Ibid., pp. 239, 243.

88. Grace A. Fendler, *New Truths About Columbus* (London: L. N. Fowler & Co., 1934), p. 26.

89. Saint Germain, "The Great Gathering of the LORD's Chosen People: For the Initiation of the Ruby Ray," in 1985 *Pearls of Wisdom*, vol. 28, no. 34, pp. 432, 434–35.

90. Saint Germain, February 5, 1983.

91. Isa. 11:9; Hab. 2:14.

92. John 11:27.

93. Matt. 7:6.

94. Luke 10:42, see Jerusalem Bible.

95. Jesus, April 10, 1966.

96. See decree 10.14 in *Prayers, Meditations, and Dynamic Decrees for the Coming Revolution in Higher Consciousness.*

97. El Morya, *The Chela and the Path*, pp. 38–39.

98. Matt. 11:12.
99. I Cor. 15:31.
100. James 1:17.
101. Rev. 17.
102. Phil. 2:5, 6.
103. I Cor. 11:24.
104. **Unbelief:** Matt. 13:58; 17:19, 20; Mark 9:23, 24; Rom. 11:20, 23; Heb. 3:12.
105. **Divine Us:** "And God said, Let *us* make man in our image, after our likeness . . ." (Gen. 1:26). See Mark L. Prophet and Elizabeth Clare Prophet, "The Alchemy of the Word," s.v. "Elohim," in *Saint Germain On Alchemy: Formulas for Self-Transformation*, pp. 399–401.
106. Ps. 8:5; Heb. 2:7.
107. Rowan A. Greer, trans., *Origen* (New York: Paulist Press, 1979), p. 192.
108. Matt. 22:29.
109. John 4:35.
110. John 5:17.
111. John 4:34.
112. In his inaugural address delivered January 20, 1961, President John F. Kennedy closed with these words: "With a good conscience our only sure reward, with history the final judge of our deeds, let us go forth to lead the land we love, asking His blessing and His help, but knowing that here on earth God's work must truly be our own."
113. I Cor. 6:20; 7:23.
114. Matt. 18:3; Mark 10:15; Luke 18:17.
115. Matt. 7:24; Luke 6:46.
116. Isa. 29:13; Ezek. 33:31; Matt. 15:8; Mark 7:6.
117. "Then laid they their hands on them, and they received the Holy Ghost." Acts 8:17.
118. Rev. 14:6; Matt. 24:14.
119. Kuthumi, "Meditation upon the Rainbow of Light's Perfection," in *Prayer and Meditation*, pp. 64–65.
120. II Cor. 12:4.
121. John 14:2, 3.
122. The Goddess of Liberty, "A Good Report," in 1986 *Pearls of Wisdom*, vol. 29, no. 3, p. 16; "Our Origin in

the Heart of Liberty: To Balance the Threefold Flame by True Heart Contact with Lord Maitreya," in 1985 *Pearls of Wisdom*, vol. 28, no. 45, p. 537; and "Allegiance to the Law of the One," in 1986 *Pearls of Wisdom*, vol. 29, no. 5, p. 31.

123. Matt. 6:27.

124. Dan. 12:1.

125. Matt. 24:31; Mark 13:27.

126. Rev. 11:3.

127. Rev. 10:7.

128. John 9:4.

129. Mark 16:20.

130. *Pearls of Wisdom*, teachings from the Ascended Masters dictated to their Messengers Mark L. Prophet and Elizabeth Clare Prophet, are weekly letters. They contain both fundamental and advanced teaching to guide us on our spiritual path and help us meet the challenges of our time. They are an unparalleled source of insight, inspiration and renewal. Mailed monthly. Also available on CD-ROM as *Pearls of Wisdom from 1958 to 1998*. For information or to place an order, please call 1-800-245-5445 or 406-848-9500.

131. Matt. 5:14.

132. Ezek. 18:4, 20.

133. Mark 3:29.

134. Matt. 10:28.

135. **Mary's warning at Fátima:** Between May 13 and October 13, 1917, during World War I and the fomenting of the Bolshevik revolution, the Blessed Mother appeared six times to three shepherd children—Lucia, Francisco, and Jacinta—near Fátima, Portugal. She delivered her warning of the spread of Communism and outlined her plan to "bring peace to the world and an end to war" through daily recitation of the rosary, worldwide devotion to her Immaculate Heart and penance. During her third apparition (July 13), she told the children: "When you shall see a night illumined by an unknown light, know that this is the great sign from God that the chastisement of the world for its many transgressions is

at hand through war, famine, persecution of the Church and of the Holy Father. To prevent this, I shall come to ask for the consecration of Russia to my Immaculate Heart and the Communion of reparation on the First Saturdays. If my requests are heard, Russia will be converted and there will be peace. If not, she will spread her errors throughout the entire world, provoking wars and persecution of the Church. The good will suffer martyrdom; the Holy Father will suffer much; different nations will be annihilated."

A secret part of the Fátima message, known as the "third secret," was written, sealed, and stored in the archives of the Bishop of Leiria-Fátima, not to be opened until 1960 or after Lucia's death. Pope John XXIII read it in 1960, but the Church did not officially release the message at that time. In 1963, a German newspaper, *Neues Europa*, published what it described as an "extract" from this message, as it was then "being circulated in diplomatic circles." It included a severe warning that the Church and mankind must challenge entrenched evil wherever it appears: "... Even in the highest places Satan reigns and directs the course of things. Satan will succeed in infiltering into the highest positions in the Church. Satan will succeed in sowing confusion in the minds of scientists who design weapons that can destroy great portions of mankind in short periods. Satan will gain hold of heads of nations and will cause these destructive weapons to be mass produced. If mankind will not oppose these evils, I will be obliged to let the Arm of my Son drop in vengeance. If the chief rulers of the world and of the Church will not actively oppose these evils, I will ask God my Father to bring His Justice to bear on mankind.... The age of ages is coming, the end of all ends if mankind will not repent and be converted and if this conversion does not come from rulers of the world and of the Church."

Frère Michel de la Sainte Trinité, who has conducted an in-depth, four-year study of the Fátima prophecies, contends that the version that appeared in the *Neues Europa* article is "at least four times too long" to fit on the small sheet of paper on which Lucia wrote it. He believes, with many other authorities, that the principal message of the secret involves a crisis of faith within the Church. Bishop Cosme do Amaral, bishop of Leiria-Fátima, commented in 1984: "The Secret of Fátima speaks neither of atomic bombs nor of nuclear warheads, nor of SS20 missiles. Its content concerns our faith. To identify the Secret with catastrophic announcements or with a nuclear holocaust is to distort the meaning of the Message. The loss of faith of a continent is worse than the annihilation of a nation." See Frère Michel de la Sainte Trinité, "The Third Secret Revealed...," *The Fátima Crusader,* June–July 1986.

It should be noted that in 1929 Mother Mary appeared to Lucia with the message that the moment had come in which God was asking the Holy Father, "in union with all the bishops of the world," to make the consecration of Russia to her Immaculate Heart, "promising to save it by this means." Over the years, various popes have made various blessings, but never exactly according to her direction. As a result of this gross negligence, on March 22, 1978, Mother Mary delivered a dictation through the Messenger Elizabeth Clare Prophet in which she placed the spiritual mantle of bishop on all present, thereby elevating them for that service to the appropriate level of hierarchy, whereupon the Blessed Mother formally consecrated Russia to her Immaculate Heart. True to her Magnificat, she "put down the mighty from their seats and exalted them of low degree." And Jesus' rebuke to the Pharisees was not far from our ears: "If these should hold their peace the stones would immediately cry out."

The "third secret" was subsequently published by the Church, on June 26, 2000. The document, "The Message of Fatima," included a photostat of Lucia's original letter, written in 1944, a translation, and commentary by Archbishop Tarcisio Bertone and Cardinal Joseph Ratzinger. In the vision, Lucia (now Sister Lucia, a Carmelite nun) first saw an angel who cried aloud for penance, whose flaming sword "died out" from the radiance of the Blessed Mother. Next she described a Bishop (who the children felt was the Holy Father) and others in the Church climbing a mountain that had a cross at the summit. As he was climbing, the Holy Father, "afflicted with pain and sorrow," encountered many corpses as well as a large city "half in ruins." At the top of the mountain, as he was kneeling at the cross, the Holy Father was shot and killed by a number of soldiers. The other Church members, one by one, were also killed. At the cross, two angels "gathered up the blood of the Martyrs and with it sprinkled the souls that were making their way to God."

In his commentary, Cardinal Ratzinger said that in the vision "we can recognize the last century as a century... of suffering and persecution for the Church,... of World Wars and the many local wars... which have inflicted unprecedented forms of cruelty.... So distressing at first, [the vision] concludes with an image of hope: no suffering was in vain.... From the suffering of the witnesses there comes a purifying and renewing power." Archbishop Bertone said that the release of this message by Pope John Paul II "brings to an end a period of history marked by tragic human lust for power and evil, yet pervaded by the merciful love of God and the watchful care of the Mother of Jesus and of the Church." See "The Message of Fatima," from Congregation for the Doctrine of the Faith, available on the Web (use the search words: third secret). On February 13, 2005, Sister Lucia died at age 97 at her convent in Coimbra, Portugal.

136. Rev. 2:11; 20:6, 12–15; 21:8.
137. Acts 13:6–12.
138. Phylos the Thibetan, *A Dweller On Two Planets* (Los Angeles: Borden Publishing Co., 1952), pp. 46, 47, 50.
139. Gen. 6:11–13.
140. Lord Lanto, October 30, 1966.
141. John 6:53; I John 5:12.

142. Matt. 17:20.
143. Prov. 16:32.
144. Matt. 13:31, 32; Mark 4:31, 32; Luke 13:19.
145. Luke 15:11–32.
146. **The killing of the fatted calf:** Here we see that elemental life is sacrificed that the Son of man might live again. The elementals of planet earth (long ago imprisoned in dense bodies, often grotesque, by the sons of Belial on Atlantis) now willingly take upon themselves the sins of our souls. Crucified again and again in the name of Christ, they go to the slaughter with hope, innocence, and full faith that one day we, as prodigal sons now become the sons of God incarnate, will return to them in grace their self-sacrificing love by being instruments of their resurrection from the dead form of their ages-long incarceration.

      The elementals and Nature spirits truly long for that liberation which will restore to them the higher consciousness they once knew and full participation as servants in the Lord's household. Until that day dawns when the Children of the One attain universal awareness of the Christ consciousness, they await patiently and trustingly the coming of age of their deliverers. Now look into the absent eyes of the calf, the sheep, the horse or the goat and see the pleading expression of the group animal soul whose helplessness, O man, was genetically engineered by the black magicians of Atlantis — that priest/scientist class who made themselves false gods over embodied angels, elementals, and men by genetically dwarfing their divine plan.

147. Mark 9:11.
148. Mal. 4:5, 6.
149. Matt. 17:11, 12.
150. Matt. 17:13.
151. Matt. 14:3–11; Mark 6:17–28.
152. John 3:30.
153. Matt. 3:4; Mark 1:6.
154. John 3:13.
155. John 8:23. "What you are comes from a lower evolution

that is beneath the planes of the sons of God. The I AM (or Christ) in me is from above in the realms of accelerated Light and the Mind of God. What you are is of this world that you have made a world of Death and Hell. The I AM who I am does not originate in the spirals of Death and Hell."

156. John 8:37–55.
157. John 8:59.
158. Luke 23:34.
159. Rev. 12:10.
160. I Cor. 3:11; Rev. 2:17.
161. Matt. 25:41; Rev. 19:20; 20:10, 12–15; 21:8.
162. John 6:29.
163. John 7:26.
164. Rev. 12:11.
165. See M. Scott Peck, *People of the Lie: The Hope for Healing Human Evil* (New York: Simon & Schuster, 1983), and review, "Uprooting Seeds of Evil in Human Relationships," in *The Coming Revolution: The Magazine for Higher Consciousness* (Summer 1986), pp. 100–101.
166. Matt. 7:15–20; 12:33; Luke 6:43–45.
167. Rev. 13:15–18; 14:9–11; 15:2; 16:2; 19:20; 20:4.
168. John 20:17.
169. John 9:39; Matt. 10:6; 15:24.
170. Rev. 13:1–8.
171. Rev. 21:1.
172. I Cor. 2:9.
173. I John 4:20.
174. Matt. 11:28–30.
175. Gal. 6:5.
176. John 9:4.
177. John 9:4; 12:35.
178. Deut. 6:5; Matt. 22:37; Mark 12:30; Luke 10:27.
179. Eph. 6:12.
180. Phil. 2:12.
181. Gal. 4:19.
182. **Jesus' brothers and sisters** are referred to several times in the New Testament. When Jesus came into his own country and taught in the synagogues, Matthew records

that the people "were astonished, and said, Whence hath this man this wisdom, and these mighty works? Is not this the carpenter's son? Is not his mother called Mary? and his brethren James, and Joses, and Simon, and Judas? And his sisters, are they not all with us?" (Matt. 13:54–56) On another occasion we are told that while Jesus "yet talked to the people, behold, his mother and his brethren stood without, desiring to speak with him" (Matt. 12:46). And John 7:3–5 tells of his family's disapproval of his behavior: "His brethren therefore said unto him, Depart hence, and go into Judaea, that thy disciples also may see the works that thou doest.... If thou do these things, shew thyself to the world. For neither did his brethren believe in him." (See also Mark 3:31; 6:3; Luke 8:19–20; John 2:12; Acts 1:14; I Cor. 9:5; Gal. 1:19.) Among Jesus' brothers, who are named in the Bible while his sisters remain anonymous, are James, the future head of the Church at Jerusalem and author of the Epistle of James, and Judas, or Jude, thought to be the writer of the Epistle of Jude.

The biblical allusions to Jesus' "brethren" have been the subject of great controversy over the centuries, with three major views emerging: (1) they were brothers and sisters by blood, as propounded by Helvidius (c. 380), who believed that this view was historically accurate; (2) they were the children of Joseph by a previous marriage, as suggested by Epiphanius (c. 315–403); or (3) they were cousins of Jesus—a theory put forth by the Church Father Jerome (340?–420), who strongly extolled the state of virginity over marriage. Jerome not only maintained that Mary had remained a lifelong virgin, but added a totally new concept—that Joseph had as well (a belief which has since come to be accepted by the Roman Catholic Church).

The account in Matthew 1:24, 25 that Joseph "took unto him his wife: and knew her not till she had brought forth her firstborn son" seems to infer that Mary and Joseph did consummate their marriage subsequently. Luke's choice of the term *firstborn* ("and she brought forth her firstborn son," Luke 2:7) has also been cited to show that Jesus was not the sole child of Mary. This claim has been dismissed by some on the grounds that *firstborn* could have been used to refer to the child's rights and status under the Law of Moses even if he were Mary's only son. Scholars have also pointed out that the Jewish words for relationships were not precise, and although the Greek word referring to Jesus' brothers *(adelphos)* normally means a full brother by blood, the same word is used several times in the Greek translation of the Old Testament where the relationship was that of a nephew or cousin. However, it is clear that there is no comment anywhere in scripture about Mary's perpetual virginity, about a previous marriage of Joseph, or about Mary's marital relations after Jesus' birth. And nothing is heard from the Christians of the first century on this topic. "Such an interest is the hallmark of a later Christianity," says biblical scholar Raymond Brown (*The Birth of the Messiah: A Commentary on the Infancy Narratives in Matthew and Luke* [Garden City, N.Y.: Image Books, 1979], pp. 305–6). For a more detailed discussion, see Elizabeth Clare Prophet, *The Lost Years of Jesus* (Livingston, Mont.: Summit University Press, 1984), pp. 421–29.

183. "It's Only a Paper Moon," words by Billy Rose and E. Y. Harburg, music by Harold Arlen (1933).

184. Isa. 9:6; Col. 1:27.

Index of Scripture

---

*References to the book of Enoch are from the translation by Richard Laurence. This translation along with all the Enoch texts can be found in *Fallen Angels and the Origins of Evil*, by Elizabeth Clare Prophet (Corwin Springs, Mont.: Summit University Press, 2000).

Index

The Chart of Your Divine Self

The reason we can call to God and he will answer is because we are connected to him. We are his sons and daughters. We have a direct relationship to God and he has placed a portion of himself in us. In order to better understand this relationship, the ascended masters have designed the Chart of Your Divine Self.

The Chart of Your Divine Self is a portrait of you and of the God within you. It is a diagram of yourself and your potential to become who you really are. It is an outline of your spiritual anatomy.

The upper figure is your "I AM Presence," the Presence of God that is individualized in each one of us. It is your personalized "I AM THAT I AM." Your I AM Presence is surrounded by seven concentric spheres of spiritual energy that make up what is called your "causal body." The spheres of pulsating energy contain the record of the good works you have performed since your very first incarnation on Earth. They are like your cosmic bank account.

The middle figure in the Chart represents the "Holy Christ Self," who is also called the Higher Self. You can think of your Holy Christ Self as your chief guardian angel and dearest friend, your inner teacher and voice of conscience. Just as the I AM Presence is the presence of God that is individualized for each of us, so the Holy Christ Self is the presence of the universal Christ that is individualized for each of us.

THE CHART OF YOUR DIVINE SELF

"The Christ" is actually a title given to those who have attained oneness with their Higher Self, or Christ Self. That's why Jesus was called "Jesus, the Christ." Christ comes from the Greek word christos, meaning "anointed"—anointed with the light of God.

What the Chart shows is that each of us has a Higher Self, or "inner Christ," and that each of us is destined to become one with that Higher Self—whether we call it the Christ, the Buddha, the Tao or the Atman. This "inner Christ" is what the Christian mystics sometimes refer to as the "inner man of the heart," and what the Upanishads mysteriously describe as a being the "size of a thumb" who "dwells deep within the heart."

We all have moments when we feel that connection with our Higher Self—when we are creative, loving, joyful. But there are other moments when we feel out of sync with our Higher Self—moments when we become angry, depressed, lost. What the spiritual path is all about is learning to sustain the connection to the higher part of ourselves so that we can make our greatest contribution to humanity.

The ribbon of white light descending from the I AM Presence through the Holy Christ Self to the lower figure in the Chart is the crystal cord (sometimes called the silver cord). It is the "umbilical cord," the lifeline, that ties you to Spirit.

Your crystal cord also nourishes that special, radiant flame of God that is ensconced in the secret chamber of your heart. It is called the three-fold flame, or divine spark, because it is literally a spark of sacred fire that God has transmitted from his heart to yours. This flame is called "threefold" because it engenders the primary attributes of Spirit—power, wisdom and love.

The mystics of the world's religions have contacted the divine spark, describing it as the seed of divinity within. Buddhists, for instance, speak of the "germ of Buddhahood" that exists in every living being. In the Hindu tradition, the Katha Upanishad speaks of the "light of the Spirit" that is concealed in the "secret high place of the heart" of all beings.

Likewise, the fourteenth-century Christian theologian and mystic Meister Eckhart teaches of the divine spark when he says, "God's seed is within us." There is a part of us, says Eckhart, that "remains eternally in the Spirit and is divine.... Here God glows and flames without ceasing."

When we decree, we meditate on the flame in the secret chamber of our heart. This secret chamber is your own private meditation room, your interior castle, as Teresa of Avila called it. In Hindu tradition, the devotee visualizes a jeweled island in his heart. There he sees himself before a beautiful altar, where he worships his teacher in deep meditation.

Jesus spoke of entering the secret chamber of the heart when he said: "When thou prayest, enter into thy closet, and when thou hast shut thy door, pray to thy Father which is in secret; and thy Father which seeth in secret shall reward thee openly."

The lower figure in the Chart of Your Divine Self represents you as a soul on the spiritual path, surrounded by the violet flame and the protective white light of God, the "tube of light." Your soul is the living potential of God—the part of you that is mortal but can become immortal. The high-frequency energy of the violet flame can help you reach that goal more quickly.

The purpose of your soul's evolution on earth is to grow in self-mastery, balance your karma and fulfill your mission on Earth so that you can return to the spiritual dimensions that are your real home. When your soul at last takes flight and ascends back to God and the heaven-world, you will become an "ascended" master, free from the rounds of karma and rebirth.

Further information on the Chart of Your Divine Self is given in Lost Teachings on Your Higher Self (in The Lost Teachings of Jesus series), The Path of the Higher Self (in Climb the Highest Mountain® series) and The Astrology of the Four Horsemen, by Mark L. Prophet and Elizabeth Clare Prophet.

The Lost Years of Jesus

Documentary Evidence of Jesus' 17-Year Journey to the East
by Elizabeth Clare Prophet

The Gospels record Jesus age 12 in the temple, then age 30 at the river Jordan. Where was he in the interim? Ancient Buddhist manuscripts say Jesus left Palestine and traveled to India, Nepal, Ladakh and Tibet as both student and teacher.

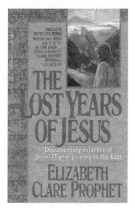

Pocketbook $7.99
ISBN 0-916766-87-X

For the first time, Elizabeth Clare Prophet brings together the testimony of four eyewitnesses of these remarkable manuscripts plus three different translations of the texts. Illustrated with maps, drawings and 79 photos.

> **"Reads like a detective thriller!** It picks you up and never lets go of you.... Elizabeth Clare Prophet puts together the missing pieces in the life of the Master that have baffled biblical scholars for centuries."
>
> —Jess Stearn, bestselling author of *Edgar Cayce, The Sleeping Prophet*

SUMMIT UNIVERSITY  PRESS
To order call 1-800-245-5445